OFFICE OF THE GOVERNOR
STATE OF MONTANA

BRIAN SCHWEITZER
GOVERNOR

JOHN BOHLINGER
LT. GOVERNOR

May 1, 2006

Greetings,

The Yellowstone Boys and Girls Ranch has been serving the youth of Montana for fifty years, and I am excited to share my praise of this organization.

Without organizations like the Yellowstone Boys and Girls Ranch, the future of our youth would be far less certain. All our children deserve the best we can offer them, especially those who experience difficulty along the way. The Ranch responds to the needs of these young Montanans by providing them with the support, education, and community they need to grow into strong adults.

This program takes an innovative approach to youth wellness. By combining their services and efforts they have become a leader in human services. Programs like this cannot be credited enough for the service they provide to our communities.

I thank the Ranch for investing in our youth and their families. The Yellowstone Boys and Girls Ranch offers these children a chance to live the lives they deserve, and we all should be proud of that success. Thank you for all your hard work, dedication, and commitment to making a difference in the lives of so many.

Sincerely,

BRIAN SCHWEITZER
Governor

STATE CAPITOL • P.O. BOX 200801 • HELENA, MONTANA 59620-0801
TELEPHONE: 406-444-3111 • FAX: 406-444-5529 • WEBSITE: WWW.MT.GOV

"*A Legacy of Caring* is a powerful story of courage, love, and understanding. Filled with hope and moving stories about caring for troubled youth and testaments from the youth themselves, this history of Yellowstone Boys and Girls Ranch demonstrates how one unique program can change hundreds of lives. A compelling read, *A Legacy of Caring* paints not only a stark picture of the state of America's youth, but also gives an encouraging glimpse of who they can become with Montanans' nurturing and guidance."

- Max Baucus, United States Senator

"On behalf of the people of Montana and our administration, I wish to convey my congratulations and sincere thanks to you for 50 years of loyal service to the children and families of Montana. I take great pleasure in recognizing Yellowstone Boys and Girls Ranch which is devoted to serving and helping the youth of our state. I wish you the best as you begin your next 50 years of service. Thank you for what you have done for Montana."

- John Bohlinger, Montana Lieutenant Governor and former Ranch board member

"As a proud member of the board of directors for Yellowstone Boys and Girls Ranch, I have witnessed some of the tremendous successes it has helped thousands of children and families achieve. I am especially inspired by the strength of its chapel program. Yellowstone's chapel has always been in the center of the campus, both physically and psychologically. Because of it, hearts have changed and lives became filled with hope and purpose – I believe if you change a heart, you can change a life. I pray for the Lord's blessing upon Yellowstone Boys and Girls Ranch as it begins a second half century of service to children and families."

- Judy Martz, Montana Governor and Ranch board member

"There is no better investment we can make than in the lives of our children. Yellowstone Boys and Girls Ranch provides a hope filled alternative to troubled children by investing in their future. Theresa and I commend Yellowstone and all its staff and supporters for 50 years of faithful service to Montana families and communities."

- Montana Governor Marc Racicot & Theresa Racicot

"In the decades since it was established, Yellowstone Boys and Girls Ranch has been a crucial provider of, and strong advocate for, mental health services and programs for emotionally disturbed youth and their families. We commend you for embracing the 'system of care' philosophy, which recognizes that a successful treatment plan must address all domains of a child's life. We also applaud your consistent support of the role of parents and other family members in treating emotionally disturbed children. We appreciate the opportunity to work with you as we strive to fulfill our mission of protecting the health and well being of Montana children. We look forward to many more decades as partners in this critical endeavor."

- Joan Miles, Director, Montana Department
of Public Health & Human Services

"I have had the privilege of serving on the Board of Directors for Yellowstone Boys and Girls Ranch in previous years as well as referring appropriate young people from our clinics to Yellowstone. The Yellowstone staff and leadership are exceptional in their dedication to the well being of each child in their programs and it's impossible to miss the compassion of the staff and commitment to their mission. There is indeed a "Legacy of Caring" at Yellowstone Boys and Girls Ranch that is unmatched by any other program that I have known."

- Nancy Meier Brown, President, Meier Clinics,
and former Ranch board member

"Yellowstone Boys and Girls Ranch hasn't just brought healing and hope to the thousands of children it served in these first 50 years…The Ranch has touched every part of Montana with the conviction that with a little extra effort and a little more heart, every boy and girl can have a bright future. Life fails some young people not at the end, not at the middle, but at the very beginning. It is these youth who have found for 50 years at Yellowstone Boys and Girls Ranch a new beginning, a place of hope, and a place of future success."

- Father Val J. Peters, JCD, STD
Executive Director Emeritus, Girls and Boys Town

"I have been working with Yellowstone Boys and Girls Ranch for nearly a decade. It is rare to find a program that more than lives up to its stated mission. In my contact with the youth who have been placed there, in my visits to Yellowstone, and in my work with the families of youth, both present and former residents of Yellowstone, the message is the same – every youth and family has value and the staff and everyone at Yellowstone will do whatever it takes to assist the youth and the family to heal."

- Micki Moran, Attorney
The Child and Family Law Center of the North Shore, LTD.

"In my capacity as a Board member and President of the former National Association of Homes and Services for Children, I often heard the name of Yellowstone Boys and Girls Ranch as one of our premier members. In time I became acquainted with the Ranch's founder and leadership and was able to confirm the high compliments through my own personal experience. Yellowstone Boys and Girls Ranch is a value driven organization which provides excellent services which celebrate the importance of young people and their families."

- Arlin Ness, President Emeritus, Starr Commonwealth

"As the President and CEO of KidsPeace National Centers, I have had the opportunity to visit a great number of child caring organizations across the country and around the world. Yellowstone Boys and Girls Ranch enjoys a long history of caring for children and of providing the highest quality care for troubled young people, and has had a tremendously positive impact on those children and the citizens of Montana. It is a privilege to be counted among the friends of Yellowstone Boys and Girls Ranch."

- **C.T. O'Donnell II, President and CEO,**
KidsPeace National Centers ORG

A Legacy of Caring

Yellowstone Boys and Girls Ranch: The First Fifty Years

by Franklin Robbie

Franklin Robbie

A Legacy of Caring
Yellowstone Boys and Girls Ranch: The First Fifty Years

Copyright © 2006 by Yellowstone Boys and Girls Ranch Foundation
PO Box 80807, Billings, MT 59108

All scripture quotations are taken from Holy Bible: New International Version. Copyright © 1973, 1978, 1984 by International Bible Society.

Editorial services by Steve Rabey. Design and layout by Jerry Jones of J. David Jones Productions. Cover design by Heins Creative of Billings, Montana. Proofing and indexing by Clive Pyne of Book Indexing Services. Printing and binding by Artcraft Printers of Billings, Montana.

Dedication

With gratitude to the thousands of youth who have inspired me with their spirit and determination to overcome great personal challenges in Yellowstone's first 50 years.

To those who willingly shared their stories, I thank them. This book, truly a love story, could not have been written without their participation. To my daughter, Kathy Robbie Hickle, who spent countless hours interviewing and capturing their stories, I am in awe of her many gifts.

To the donors who have provided the means to positive change, I thank them on behalf of the children they have served.

- **Franklin Robbie**

Contents

Preface by Sheldon Kelly............................1

Introduction: Telling the Story......................6

Section I: The Early Years

1 The Birth of a Dream..............................14

2 From Dream to Reality............................30
   Transformed Lives Jim McCombs: A Second Chance......46

3 Growing Pains....................................50
   Transformed Lives Russ White: The Place I Call Home....66

4 An Evolving Program..............................70
   Transformed Lives Rubin Ackerman: A "Love" Story.....80

5 Adventures in Fundraising........................84
   Transformed Lives Vince Wagner: Kick-Starting a Life....97

6 School Days......................................102
   Transformed Lives
   Tyler Stephens: Too Smart for His Own Good.........114

7 The Soul of Yellowstone..........................118
   Transformed Lives
   Jeanette Shannon: Careening Toward Destruction......130

8 Girls at the "Boys" Ranch........................136
   Transformed Lives Nicki Jenkins: A Place of Refuge.....150

9 "The Great Escape" and Stories of Ranch Life.........156

Section II: The Vision Matures

10 A New Day, with New Challenges 170
   Transformed Lives
   Jenna Kirwan Bertels: A New Way of Life. 184

11 From "Ranch" to "Treatment Center" 190
   Transformed Lives Jim Reed: Learning to Say Goodbye . . 203

12 A Guided Tour of Our Campus
   (And Some of the People Who Made It Possible) 210
   Transformed Lives
   Debbie Champion: "I Want to Give Back". 234

13 Changes at the Top 238
   Transformed Lives
   Tony Torres: Healing Body, Heart and Family 256

14 No More Kid Stuff. 260
   Transformed Lives
   Ella Brower: "I'd Like to Be the Face of Yellowstone
   Boys And Girls Ranch" 275

15 Giving Back to the Community 280
   Transformed Lives
   Fred Wittman: "If I Can Make It, You Can!" 293

16 A Legacy of Caring 298

Appendices 310

Index 340

Preface

by Sheldon Kelly

Ranch Alumnus and Former Staff Writer
for *Reader's Digest*

Franklin Robbie learned as a young pastor that each new church assignment--even if it meant a Montana bunkhouse for a parsonage--brought him one step closer to his dream of one day doing something larger than himself. He was not sure then what that would entail, only that its very idea drove him on to the next step.

Along the way he discovered he had a talent for getting things done while convincing others to help. One time, desperate for church funds, he challenged his farmer congregants to give only if their harvest was good. A bumper crop followed and the coffers overflowed. One is tempted to conclude other things were at play. Luck? Providence? Franklin will say only that he was blessed, and that such blessings became the single recurring theme of his long, rich life.

Step by providential step, he drew closer to something. While still a rural pastor, and calling upon the friendship of a man who had worked with Billy Graham when Graham was still unknown, Franklin found himself organizing Christian youth rallies held throughout Montana. It was probably then he realized he possessed other important talents as well: that of logistics, of organizing, and of getting the bills paid on time so that the whole enterprise could continue.

This led him to attend a 1950 national convention of top religious leaders, which, in turn, drew him to an international gathering in Brussels, Belgium. It was there, among some of the world's most assured Christian leaders, that the rural Montana pastor decided he would devote the rest of his life to helping young people.

In this manner, Franklin writes of the early steps, the minor and major preludes, which led to the founding of Yellowstone Boys Ranch. The Ranch story is told in his voice, by his hand, an account which is surely of a piece with Montana history.

This story fascinates me for several reasons.

As a Staff Writer for the *Reader's Digest* I wrote just such stories, traveling all over the nation and parts of the world to find them. They always rated near the top in our reader surveys.

Although I am now retired and living in Virginia with my wife of over three decades, I meet regularly with old Digest colleagues. I recently told them Franklin's story, and before luncheon had ended my one-time boss, the former Executive Editor and Washington Bureau Chief, had it formed in his mind for a lead piece. It is that good.

My other reason for being fascinated is more personal. In the mid-1950s, as Franklin's dream and vision coalesced, my own young life was falling apart. My adoptive parents had been struggling with a kind of severe illness no one understood, which led eventually to their tragic deaths.

I was fifteen years old and orphaned. According to

Franklin's book, that was about the time he, with his intuitive sense for talent and decency, had selected the board of directors and then recruited Bob McFarlane and Carl Orth–two men who would later figure so importantly in my life. In early 1957, while I was drifting from place to place, the board signed a contract for what today is the ranch.

There is certainty in Franklin's words. What he was attempt-

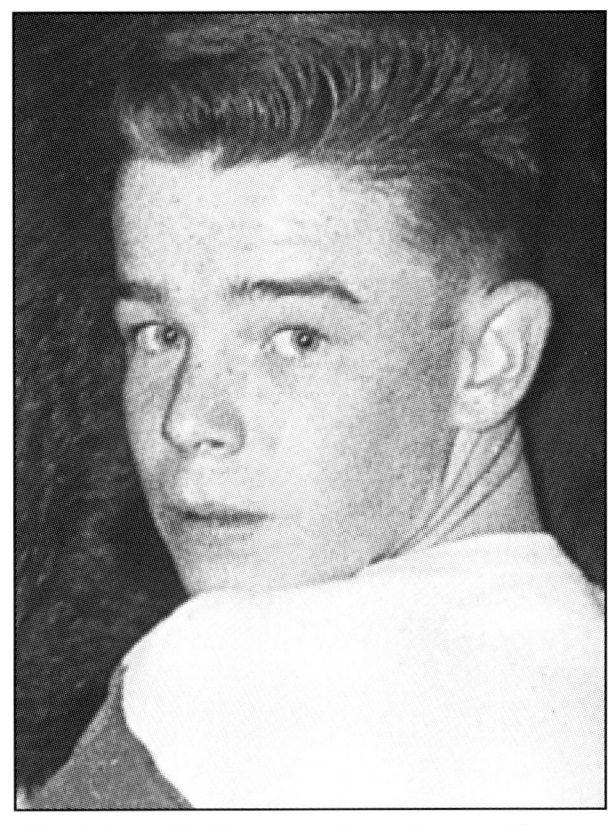

Sheldon Kelly as a Ranch youth

ing to do was neither simple nor easy, and he admits the near misses. After signing the ranch contract, a promised donor reneged, and the deal was about to fall through.

Franklin re-stated his plea to help kids, and two of the board members, Ted Keating and Bill MacKay, co-signed loans, and a third, Les Shryock, put up $5,000 of his own money. That was in April. I was then working in Washington state as a sixteen-year-old farmhand with itinerant adult friends who drank hard. By late summer I had returned to Montana, was taken control of, and per the request of my legal guardian, had been accepted at Yellowstone Boys Ranch.

This is what struck me while reading this fascinating book: what if Franklin had not organized the youth rallies? Or had not gone to Brussels? What if he had selected a different board? And what if Keating, MacKay, and Shryock had not stepped in with their names and money? What if Franklin had never self-trained as a young pastor in journalism, thereby giving him the much-needed know-how to solicit direct mail donations?

How different would my life have been without the ranch being there when I needed it, a place of refuge and healing?

How different would thousands of lives have been? Of course, I must believe it was intended to be there; I must believe Franklin Robbie, that first brave board of directors, Mac, Carl and all of the others, were all intended. Just as I was intended to come to the Ranch as one of the first of "Macs Lads," and become the first ever to graduate.

I hope I speak for all of us: Franklin's blessings have been our blessings.

Writer Sheldon Kelly (right) with Ranch founder Franklin Robbie during a 2005 visit.

INTRODUCTION

Telling the Story

On a recent Sunday morning I paid one of my frequent visits to the chapel at Yellowstone Boys and Girls Ranch. This chapel is a beautiful building that opens its doors to people of all faiths, and no faith. Each time I visit the chapel I am reminded by a simple redwood sign near the door that Ranch leaders and staff decided many years ago to name it the Franklin and Merle Robbie Chapel in honor of my late wife and me.

I got there a little early this Sunday morning, and since it was a beautiful spring day I waited outside as young people from the Ranch, our staff workers, out-of-town guests, and some of our neighbors from the surrounding area entered the chapel for our weekly service.

As I looked around, I was struck once again by the impressive campus that surrounded me on all sides. Then my mind wandered back to a beautiful spring day half a century ago when this property was little more than a simple cattle ranch with only a few humble buildings.

Today, more than two dozen buildings house the work of Yellowstone Boys and Girls Ranch, and each has its own name, its own purpose in the Ranch's work with kids, and its own history that I know so very well because God had used me and my coworkers as the "persuaders" to find the money and materials needed for each of them.

Across from the chapel is our on-campus school, the Yellowstone Academy, where 114 young people who live at the Ranch, along with other kids who face unique challenges at their home schools, attend classes under the watchful care of teachers, staff workers, and counselors. Next door to the Academy is our dining hall, where young people and staff gather for meals and special events.

All around me are the various lodges where small groups of young people live in family-style settings according to their age, their situation, and their ability to deal with the world. And located throughout the campus is housing for Ranch staff, whose around-the-clock presence provides a unique kind of supervision and care.

Through the trees to the west is a major recreation facility that houses a gymnasium, a pool, a bowling alley, exercise facilities, and plenty of equipment for keeping young people active and healthy. And to the north are a number of educational and vocational buildings that provide training in arts and crafts, auto repair, and agriculture.

Across 72nd Street to the east is a state-of-the-art clinic that provides medical and psychiatric services to Ranch residents. And further away on Hesper Road is our new equestrian center, where troubled kids have fun and gain emotional maturity by working with horses.

Leaving our campus and driving into the city of Billings one can find our community services office, which delivers the Ranch's healing care to hundreds of young people in small communities throughout Montana.

And throughout the United States there are thousands of people whose time at the Ranch helped them transform their lives, making good and productive situations out of bad and destructive ones.

In 1957, I first began describing the work of the Ranch with this simple but meaningful motto: IT SURE MAKES A DIFFERENCE WHEN YOU KNOW SOMEBODY CARES.

Outwardly, a lot has changed around here since that time. Today the Ranch has nearly four hundred employees and works with over six hundred kids and families every day. But there's been no change in the motivation of the people who work here. Caring for troubled kids is what we were about fifty years ago, and it's what we're still about today.

Over the past half century, the Ranch has grown from a few employees and a handful of farm buildings to a beautiful campus where hundreds of employees serve children and families from around the nation.

The book you are holding in your hands is my effort to tell the story of Yellowstone Boys and Girls Ranch, from its humble beginnings to its current status as a nationally recognized multi-service mental health facility preparing to celebrate its fiftieth anniversary.

My goal in writing this book is to record the history of the Ranch so readers—whether they be friends, supporters, youth we have served, or employees—understand the concern for kids that has motivated our work from the beginning as well as the efforts required to translate that concern into action.

Along the way you will meet some of the hundreds of other people who pitched in and helped us out over the years. Without them, there would not be any Ranch to write about.

When I first came to Montana, I didn't have any idea I would help start an institution like the Ranch. Even after it was founded, I couldn't imagine the complexity it would take on as it grew and evolved over the years to become the kind of diverse and dynamic organization it is now.

Unfortunately, I won't be able to share all my Ranch stories in this book, but I will do my best to tell the high points of our history and to pass on some of the lessons we have learned along the way.

12

SECTION I

The Early Years

CHAPTER ONE

The Birth of a Dream

It has been my experience that people don't arrive at their purpose in life or their sense of personal calling overnight. A game plan for life is never something that arrives pre-packaged, fully formed, and ready to implement.

Instead, calling seems to be something each one of us must work out over the period of many years as we grow in our successes, learn from our failures, and continually strive to determine what it is we are supposed to accomplish with our lives.

Looking back, I can now see how the dream that would become Yellowstone Boys and Girls Ranch slowly began to form and evolve. Dreams, like callings, are mysterious, fragile things we must strain to see, wrestle with over many years, and be willing to follow, no matter what kinds of long and winding roads or seeming dead ends they open up before us.

The dream of Yellowstone Boys and Girls Ranch began to present itself to me after I graduated from a small Bible college, answered a call to "Go west, young man, go west," and began to work with young people throughout the state of Montana.

But I am getting ahead of myself. Let's go back to the beginning.

Son of a Preacher Man

I was born in 1918 in Minneapolis, where my father Rudolph was a young pastor-candidate awaiting a new appointment to a church in the Holiness Methodist denomination. When that appointment came my parents were dispatched to establish a frontier congregation among the homesteaders of north central Montana. Their temporary residence was a vacant homesteader's claim shack on the wind-swept prairie a few miles south of Opheim, Montana.

It was pioneer living at its most rustic. The area was beautiful and conditions were quite comfortable during the mild summer weather, but life was extremely unpleasant during the long, cold winter months. That's why my parents returned to Minneapolis for the birth of their first child in December 1918.

I was the first of Rudolph and Leona's nine children born during the next two decades in Minnesota, Iowa, South Dakota, and Montana as my father accepted new appointments and moved from one church to another.

We were back in Minnesota when I was a teenager, and I graduated from high school in Clarkfield in 1937. It was time for me to decide what I wanted to do with my life. But I was growing up during the Great Depression, and our large family survived on the voluntary offerings of hard-pressed congregations. Therefore, my plans would need to be conservative.

I decided to attend the Holiness Methodist School of Theology in Minneapolis. My father had attended the school. It was affordable. I wanted to follow my father's footsteps into the ministry. And there was a pretty girl named Merle Middleton who was also planning on going to school there.

By the time Merle and I graduated in 1941, we were engaged. We got married right after graduation and I quickly received my first appointment—to pastor a tiny church outside of Ardock, North Dakota, a small, rural community sixty miles north of Grand Forks.

Franklin Robbie and Merle Middleton met as teenagers and became engaged while studying theology in Minnesota.

After two years in North Dakota, I was called to pastor the mother congregation of the Holiness Methodist denomination in Minneapolis. I was also asked to take on the added responsibility of becoming editor and publisher of the church-wide news magazine, The Advocate. This journalism experience would come in handy later on.

But after several years of this double load, I needed a break and again felt the urge to continue my search for something yet to be defined. My next assignment was to serve at a Hospitality House for U.S. servicemen operated by the Minneapolis chapter of the Christian Business Men's Committee of the USA.

I enjoyed each of these assignments, and the churches and organizations I worked with prospered during my time with them. Still, there was a sense that I had not yet found my true purpose and calling in life. I couldn't put my finger on what I felt, but it seemed there was something inside me, gnawing at me and urging me onward.

One other important thing happened during my years in Minneapolis that would have a major impact on my later life. During the 1930s and 1940s, a movement called Youth for Christ was born. I call it a movement because it started as a simultaneous response by many leaders in many cities to the problems churches were having in reaching young people.

Today many churches use contemporary music and "listener-friendly" sermons, but back then church was largely an older person's world featuring traditions, hymns, and rituals that had been virtually unchanged for decades.

The Youth for Christ leaders developed a radical new approach to reaching young people, and at the same time they helped invent something called "youth ministry." Their plan was to hold large youth rallies in major auditoriums featuring contemporary music, exciting speakers, and plenty of activity.

Torrey Johnson was a Youth for Christ leader in Chicago in the mid-40s. And by the time I was back in Minneapolis, a dynamic young Christian businessman and friend of mine named George Wilson was leading youth rallies in the city's 12,000-seat Municipal Auditorium. Wilson worked with an unknown young man named Billy Graham who served as a traveling evangelist for YFC. Later when Graham founded the Billy Graham Evangelistic Association, Wilson worked as his right-hand man, accepting the duties of treasurer and manager of everything related to funding support.

I enjoyed attending the Minneapolis Youth for Christ rallies when I could, and was fascinated by the dynamic new ways this movement was finding to reach out to young people, some of whom were struggling to find their way in the world.

What I didn't know at the time was that these rallies would play a major role in my starting Yellowstone Boys and Girls Ranch, and George Wilson was destined to coach me in ways yet to be revealed.

But in 1948, I was still trying to find and follow my dream. And at this point, my dream was leading me to Montana.

A Bumper Crop

In 1948, I heard from a wheat farmer named Guy Killion whom I had met during my Bible college days. He lived in the Knees community, which is located in the vast wheat fields east of Brady and north of Great Falls, Montana. He challenged me to move with my family so I could pastor the small community church there. I had fallen in love with the beauty of Montana and the independent spirit of its people during earlier visits to the state, so I readily accepted this new challenge.

The Knees Community Church (pictured at the beginning of this chapter) was really more like a chapel than anything most of us think of when we hear the word "church." And as for the parsonage? There wasn't one. Merle and I with our two little preschoolers, Barbara and Wesley, spent that first spring and summer in the bunkhouse on Guy's ranch.

I knew that arrangement would be fine during the warm weather, but worried about Montana's harsh winters. So I asked members of the congregation to think about building a parsonage. Perhaps understandably, these rugged farmers who depended on the mercy of Mother Nature for their very survival were not immediately persuaded to make a financial commitment to the parsonage.

So I made them an appealing offer. It was early spring, and the winter wheat standing in the fields was only six inches tall. I proposed to each of them that they commit five or ten acres of their wheat crops to the parsonage fund. That way, if there were no crops they would not be out any money. But if there was a successful harvest, they could easily come up with the money needed to move my family out of the bunkhouse.

It turned out that 1948 was one of the wettest years the Knees community had seen in a decade. Every farmer in the area had a bumper crop of wheat. In the fall we held a Harvest Home Sunday at the church, and all the farmers brought in the money they had earned from the acres they had committed to the parsonage fund months before. The proceeds were enough to build a comfortable three-bedroom house right next door to the church. My father and I, with the help of parishioners, spent that fall and winter building the parsonage. We moved in the following spring and Kathy, our youngest, completed our family the next year.

This story from my time with the Knees congregation illustrates a dynamic that has been a recurring part of my life for more than half a century. I can't take credit for making the wheat grow that year. But for as long as I can remember, I have always had a "can-do" attitude and an ability to enlist other people in whatever it was I set out to do.

In other words, I would simply say I was blessed, and this blessing continues today.

I would soon have the opportunity to test these gifts in a new location.

Great Times in Great Falls

As Merle and the children and I were getting established in the Knees community, I felt it was important to network with other pastors in the area. That's what led me to join the ministerial association in Great Falls. As I got to know local pastors and they got to know me, we occasionally talked about the needs of young people in Montana. When I mentioned having attended some of the Youth for Christ rallies in Minneapolis, they were excited to hear how these successful rallies were organized and conducted.

Before long, they agreed that it would be a good idea to hold a Youth for Christ rally in Great Falls. Because of my background in Minneapolis, I was the group's unanimous choice to lead our youth outreach efforts.

One of the first things I decided was that if we were going to organize a rally in Great Falls, I wanted to shoot high and go for the best. There were local speakers and pastors we could have used, but I contacted the Youth for Christ leaders in Minneapolis and requested that my friend George Wilson persuade Stuart Hamblin to come to Great Falls. Stuart Hamblin was a cowboy songwriter/singer and disk jockey in Los Angeles who was converted in the Billy Graham tent crusade in L.A. in 1949. George Wilson had featured him in one of his Minneapolis rallies, and I felt his testimony would challenge the ranchers of Montana.

Some of the members of the ministerial association thought I was being overly ambitious. After all, the Municipal Auditorium in Great Falls held only twelve hundred people, not twelve thousand like the arena in Minneapolis. But I gave it a try anyway. And sure enough, in June 1950, Wilson and Hamblin came to Great Falls for two nights of youth rallies.

Some of the local pastors were worried nobody would come, but we filled that 1,200-seat auditorium to capacity both nights. Now the only challenge was to pay our expenses. The first night's offering was a disaster. We received only a few hundred dollars.

Stuart Hamblin saw our plight and said, "I know I'm just the singer and the preacher, but let me take the offering tomorrow night. This is cowboy country and I understand these folks. Let me do the persuading." When we counted the offering the second night we received just over $1,200. That was roughly one dollar per person—an amazing amount for Great Falls in 1950!

After all expenses were covered, we had a small amount of money left over. George Wilson had an immediate proposal for what to do with our "profits."

"There's a national Youth for Christ convention in Winona Lake, Indiana, in two weeks," said George, "and if Franklin

Robbie is going to be your future YFC leader, you should send him to Winona Lake to meet other youth speakers and musical talent."

Everyone agreed this was a good idea, so Merle and I, along with another couple from Great Falls, drove the 1,700 miles to Indiana. The drive was exhausting, but the energy of the convention more than made up for it.

The event was an ingathering of many of the best-known up-and-coming religious leaders of my generation. Attending the convention left me feeling more inspired than ever. But it also revived my old feelings of restlessness about what I would do next.

On the Road

By the time I returned to Montana, word had spread throughout the state about the successful rally in Great Falls. Soon, people from other communities were asking me to help them organize rallies in their areas.

During my time at the convention in Indiana I had become acquainted with many of the speakers and musicians who were involved in the Youth for Christ rallies throughout the country. I began contacting these people, asking them if they could spend three or four days in Montana. If they said yes, we would try to book them for numerous rallies. During this time we organized a number of successful rallies in places like Helena, Conrad, Shelby, and Cut Bank.

I felt my vision for reaching out to youth and organizing events that would interest them was expanding. I received more inspiration and guidance the next year at the 1951 Winona Lake convention. And while there, I heard about an upcoming international gathering that seemed even more exciting. It was called the World Congress on Evangelism in Brussels, Belgium. And surprisingly, when I proposed to my congregation that I attend, they gave me their approval and took up an offering for my expenses. Other churches and

Youth for Christ Bible Clubs like the one in Helena attracted many young people throughout Montana.

friends contributed, too.

I wasn't exactly sure what it was I was going to get out of the Brussels convention, but once I got there my whole view of things was transformed.

I had been raised in a strict fundamentalist environment. Some of the Christians I had grown up around seemed much more comfortable inside the four walls of a church than they did with outsiders. But the people I met in Brussels were confident world-changers who were doing amazing things around the globe. They were deeply committed to their faith, and they believed their faith compelled them to step out into the world and make a difference there.

The things I learned in Brussels would stay with me for the rest of my life, and they would soon cause some changes to my own career and sense of calling.

During the remainder of 1951 and into 1952, I became increasingly involved in organizing Youth for Christ rallies throughout Montana. Soon, I felt I was being pulled so strongly in the direction of the rallies that I resigned my pastorate after finding another "shepherd" for my flock. I moved my family into Great Falls and, on the basis of sheer faith, became the director of Youth for Christ rallies in Montana, and, later, Wyoming. In a few short years we had thirty communities throughout these two states holding regular Youth for Christ rallies.

I would sign up a speaker and a musician, and we would hit the road. We often started in the eastern part of Montana, worked our way all across the state, then made our way into Wyoming. After three or four weeks of a rally every night in a new location, our exhausted team staggered out of Wyoming, and a new team would start all over again in eastern Montana. In addition to handling logistics for the teams, I took the responsibility in every rally of persuading the people to be generous at offering time. This was where I learned my first important lessons in fund-raising.

Before long the work was too much for me to keep up with, so I challenged a young man named Louie Kramp to join me. Louie was a Moody Bible Institute graduate who had spent a year in Billings as a church youth leader. He was on his way to Gordon College in Massachusetts to continue his theological education. In fact, he had left for college before I contacted him.

Surprisingly, he turned around and came back to Montana to work with me. Next, Louie and I brought on two other leaders to work with us: Tedd Bryson in eastern Montana and Wendy Collins in Wyoming.

Setting up a new organization and hiring people to help me run it was a new experience for me, but it seemed to come naturally enough. Once again, I felt like I was being blessed.

A "Delinquent" Named Denver

Not all our youth rallies and meetings were in municipal auditoriums. We would go anywhere we were welcomed. On Sundays we sometimes made as many as three presentations in churches. During the weekdays we would help organize extracurricular Bible clubs in public schools. And in the evenings we would hold rallies in auditoriums, churches, or other venues.

It was after we started doing evening rallies in Miles City, Montana, that I would take a few more steps toward the dream that would eventually become Yellowstone Boys and Girls Ranch.

There was a man in Miles City by the name of Casper Walhowe. This kind-hearted man was the superintendent of the State Boys Industrial School there. At that time, there wasn't really anything like modern-day childcare. Industrial schools were places that locked up boys of all ages who had gotten into some kind of trouble with the law, their schools, or their communities. I remember meeting boys there who were as young as ten.

Back then, people called these boys delinquents. But Mr. Walhowe didn't look at his boys as mere delinquents. He saw them as boys who had gone off track but who could get back on track with a little love and help. When we began organizing evening rallies in Miles City, Mr. Walhowe invited us to do afternoon programs in the Industrial School auditorium for his boys.

After the programs at the Industrial School we would stay around afterwards to talk with some of the boys. It was during one of these informal chats that I first met a boy named Denver.

Denver was a cute young kid who had four brothers. Three of them were there with him in the Boys Industrial School, and the fourth, who was actually a half-brother, was in prison at the time. If I remember correctly, the boys' father was a hard-working coal miner with little time left for the family, and their mother had been unable to control them. One by one, they got into trouble. I don't think Denver had done anything very bad, yet here he was, locked up with all the other troublemakers and "delinquents" in the Industrial School.

The more I thought about Denver being kept there with boys who were older and more devious than he was, the more it tugged at my heart. That summer I asked Mr. Walhowe if he would allow me to drive Denver to a beautiful mountain camp called Clydehurst Christian Ranch that was located on the Boulder River outside Big Timber, Montana. Permission was granted. As soon as Denver and I got to the camp, he ran from my car and joined a group of boys playing ball. For the rest of the week, Denver immersed himself in games and activities with all the other "normal" children. But then it was time for me to take him back to Miles City.

The drive back to the Industrial School was one of the longest car rides of my life. The closer we got to Miles City, the more uncomfortable Denver became. Finally, when I dropped him off with Mr. Walhowe, Denver gave me a look that seemed to say: "How can you leave me here?"

At that moment, I was struck with the idea of finding another place without locks and bars where boys like Denver could go. My sense of calling was beginning to crystallize.

Front Page News

I spoke to Denver recently. He told me that after a number of wasted years he and his brothers had eventually straightened out their lives. That conversation made me wonder: How different might things have been for Denver and his brothers if our Boys Ranch dream had materialized ten years earlier?

But back in the 1950s, kids like Denver were at the center of a national debate. I remember when a national news magazine published a major story about juvenile delinquency in

As a ten-year-old in trouble Denver Alton inspired Franklin Robbie to help "delinquent" children. Denver and Franklin recently met and discussed their lives over the last 50 years.

America. The article described gangs, violence, and various forms of mischief in the most dramatic forms. Alongside the article was a list of some of the American cities with the worst juvenile delinquency. And right there on the list was Billings, Montana!

I can still remember the effect that article had on me, on my associates in Youth for Christ, and in the Billings community. Louie Kramp also remembers the shock waves that article created:

"Franklin, the best way to describe the impact of that article was to compare it with the youth drug abuse of the past two decades," he told me. "It was that big of a deal."

Before I knew it, some of Billings' civic and business leaders had gotten together to discuss the article. Then they asked me to work with them.

Meeting Held On Delinquency In Billings, March 15

When the national media said Billings had a delinquency problem, local people decided to do something about it!

"Franklin, we've gotta do something about this juvenile delinquency problem in Billings," one of them told me. "What can you do to help us?"

This simple question would become a call to action that would change the direction of my life for the next half-century.

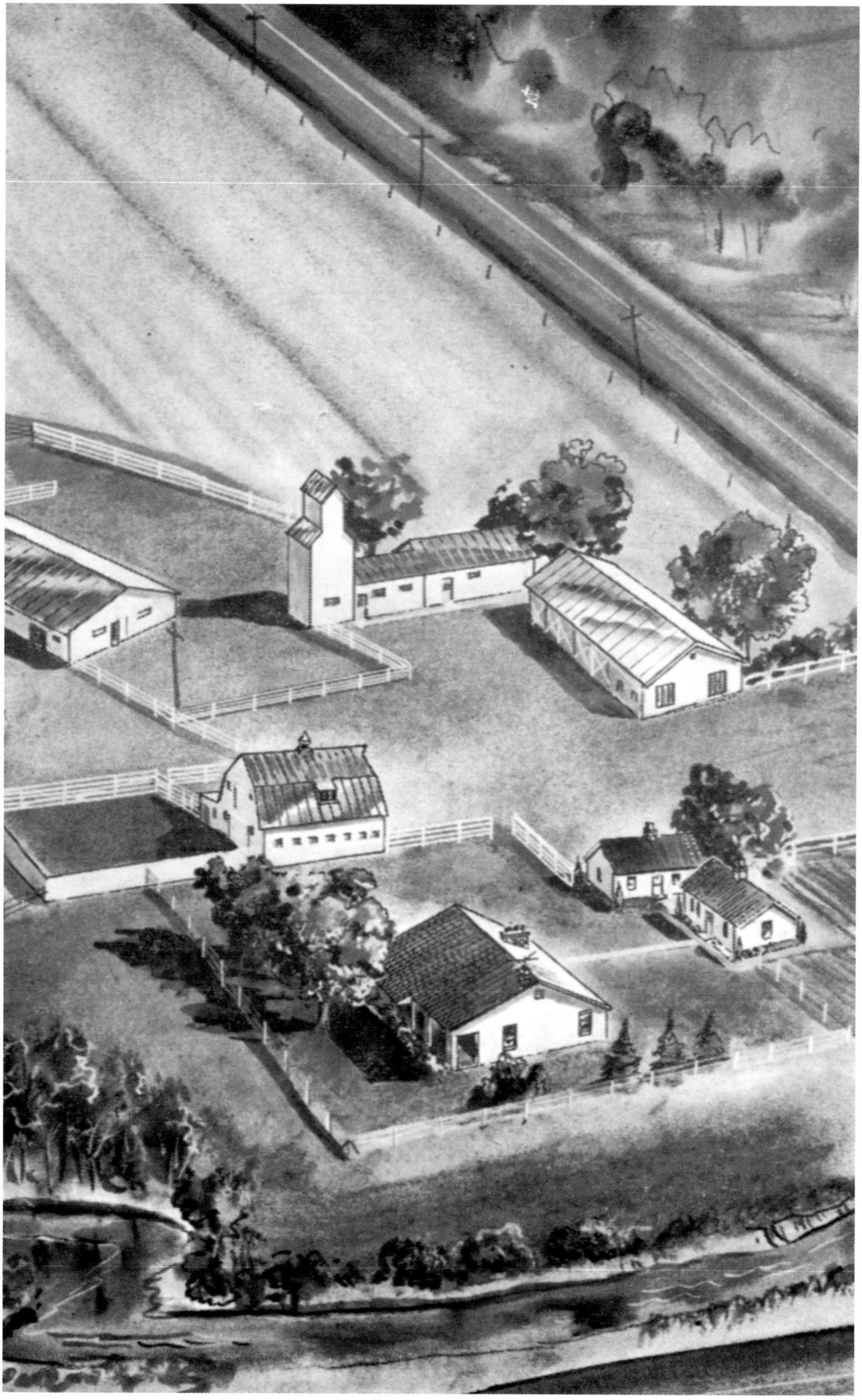

CHAPTER TWO

From Dream to Reality

After meeting troubled kids like Denver and reading about problems with teen delinquency in Billings, a passion began growing within me to provide a place where youngsters could receive the kind of caring, personal attention they didn't receive in the big, state-run industrial schools.

Now I felt it was time to put this passion into action. I didn't know it way back then, but the decisions I would make and the steps I would take in 1955 and 1956 would lead to the eventual birth of Yellowstone Boys and Girls Ranch.

Looking back now at the way things developed, I must confess that the early years of the Ranch are a testimony to the power of providence. For some reason, I had a vision for a boys ranch, the optimism to believe that such a vision could take place, the energy to pursue this vision, and the ability to share the vision with others who would support it.

Part of my confidence came from the years I had spent traveling throughout Montana and Wyoming with Youth for Christ. Along the way I had met many men and women—from pastors to farmers to parents and grandparents—who were concerned about kids in trouble and wanted to do something to help them.

Now, as I explained my vision for the Ranch to them, many of these good people became persuaded that what we were doing was worthy of their support.

Climbing a Mountain or a Hill?

Louie Kramp had resigned his position with Youth for Christ to help organize the Billings Youth Guidance Council, which worked with troubled youth. Louie told me that many of the kids he worked with came from broken homes and divided families. He believed such destructive family environments contributed to kids hanging out on the streets and joining gangs, and he felt a more positive family environment might play a powerful role in turning troubled kids' lives around.

Foster homes seemed like a logical answer to our local delinquency problems. And since there was little government funding for foster parents, Louie and I focused on recruiting families who had one important qualification: an overflow of compassion and caring.

One of the first foster families we recruited was Ted and Eleanor Keating, wheat ranchers who lived thirty miles west of Billings and were anxious to do anything they could to help. Ted was one of the original members of the Billings Youth Guidance Council, and would become one of the founding board members of Yellowstone Boys Ranch. Half a century later, Ted remains deeply committed to caring for children of all kinds.

There was only one problem with the foster home approach. A number of the families who had agreed to help quickly realized how complicated things could get when they actually had a difficult boy in their home. A number of those early foster parents soon discovered they had underestimated the complexity of these boys' problems and were in over their heads.

Such challenges only deepened my conviction that we needed a ranch focused on helping disturbed kids. And as the members of the Youth Guidance Council talked about our dreams to everyone who would listen, one of their members made contact with a wealthy businessman who said he might help us out.

"You know, I was raised as an orphan," said the businessman one day in the fall of 1955. "There ought to be a Boys Town like Father Flanagan's place right here in Montana. In fact, if somebody started a Boys Town here, I would commit to donating $50,000 to make it happen."

After years of dreaming, working with youth, and planning, this was the first real indication I had that the dream of creating a boys ranch might actually turn into reality. So I began throwing myself into all the tasks that needed to be completed if a ranch was to be created.

A Plan, a Place, a Board, and a Name

From the fall of 1955 to the summer of 1956, I traveled thousands of miles visiting other homes for boys. I knew how industrial schools worked, but I needed to do more research on how ranches for children were organized, funded, and managed. I even asked for copies of their Articles of Incorporation, their newsletters, and whatever details they were willing to share on financing.

There were so many complicated issues involved in starting a ranch that Louie and I put together a questionnaire, and I headed out on the road again to visit institutions like Father Flanagan's Boy's Town in Nebraska and Cal Farley's Boy's Ranch near Amarillo, Texas.

Cal Farley's ranch appealed to me the most, in part because it had a western setting and a rugged, outdoorsy program style that seemed like it would fit nicely in Montana. I made a return visit to Amarillo, taking Bob McFarlane and Jack Dabner who had expertise which could help me evaluate the ranch's programs and activities.

I learned a lot during these research trips, and I could see that each facility had its unique strengths that reflected the vision and personality of its founder. Along the way I also met some dedicated and talented people, including a man named Carl Orth who served as superintendent at Cal Farley's Boy's Ranch.

I also learned about a group called the National Association of Homes for Boys. I attended their second annual meeting in Dallas. Attending this convention was an eye-opening experience for me as I had the privilege of meeting and talking with other people who were moved by a passion that was similar to mine.

That meeting in Dallas was like a crash course in ranch administration, and I picked up many good ideas on fundraising. One of the most fruitful ideas concerned memorial gifts, which could honor the death of a friend or loved one by supporting a worthwhile charity.

The slogan I remembered from the convention and copied into my notebook was, *Renew the life that is ended through the life of a little boy*. Memorial gifts would be a lifesaver for the Ranch in our early years.

Meanwhile, Ted Keating and I traveled many miles examining every ranch property for sale anywhere within a hundred miles of Billings. There were a number of places, and, while several looked interesting, none seemed perfect for our Ranch.

Finally, a ranch west of Billings owned by the O'Rourke family came on the market. I knew as soon as I drove on to the O'Rourke place that it had everything we needed.

It was distant enough from Billings to provide the seclusion we wanted, but close enough to get supplies or take boys to the doctor. It had plenty of land as well as a number of solid buildings that, with a little work, would suit us during the Ranch's initial years of operation. It also had a creek we knew would provide hours of summer fun for energetic boys. Plus our location near Wyoming meant we could fulfill our goal of serving boys from both states.

Our First Board Members

Things were beginning to progress nicely now, so Ted and I formalized the group of advisors and friends with whom we had been consulting. Out of it, we handpicked a Board of Directors for our Ranch.

We didn't just draw names out of a hat. Knowing how important these leaders would be in the life of the Ranch, we carefully selected the original five members for their wisdom, their individual strengths, and their contacts with important groups in the Billings area and beyond.

I insisted that Ted Keating be one of the five, not only because of his ranching experience, but also because Ted was very active in the Billings Junior Chamber of Commerce. We knew local businessmen needed to hear details on our Boys Ranch dream.

Forrest Crum was an ex-policeman who understood troubled kids. He was also a successful land developer and house builder who was well acquainted with the building materials suppliers and several construction contractors in Billings.

Bill MacKay was a wealthy central Montana cattle rancher and State Senator who was highly thought of as a legislator. He was very close to Montana's Governor at the time, J. Hugo Aronson, and other "movers and shakers" in Helena's political and business communities, including Ken Todd, who would soon do us a tremendous favor.

Les Shryock from western Montana had been a generous

supporter of my earlier YFC efforts and was owner of the First National Bank of Whitefish. Les lived in an area that had several lumber mills, and he and I hoped they would soon become significant lumber donors to our boys ranch projects.

Frank Flynn, our Wyoming member, was superintendent of the Wyoming Boys Industrial School and an influential friend of Wyoming's Governor Milward Simpson. Flynn was also the employer of a certain gifted young man named Bob McFarlane. I was impressed with Bob's skills and attitude, and I hoped he would work for us some day.

When these five Ranch board members met for the first time, their first act was to add two more capable and keenly interested members from the Billings area.

Grace Leuthold of Molt, Montana was a rancher's wife and neighbor to Ted Keating. She was also well known in Montana and had been appointed to the Montana Child Welfare Advisory Committee by Governor Aronson. Especially concerned about problems of delinquency, Grace brought mature judgment and a woman's point of view to the conference table of the Ranch board.

Norm Warsinske of Billings was the owner and publisher of the *Western Livestock Reporter,* which covered seven Western states. Norm was personally acquainted with hundreds of cattle ranchers, and he enthusiastically "sold" Yellowstone Boys Ranch to everybody who would listen. Once the Ranch was up and running, he even wrote personal letters to many ranchers encouraging them to become donors to the Ranch! Norm clearly understood the need to eventually recruit thousands of friends as donors.

Finding the Right Name

We also agreed on a name for the Ranch. Naming institutions is always difficult, but I knew one thing: I was dead-set against calling our Ranch "Franklin Robbie's Boys Home" or anything else having such a strong personal connection to me. Instead, I thought we needed a name that would clearly explain to people who heard it who and where we were and what we did.

A good Wyoming friend named Roy Bliss spoke to me about this one day and said, "I'll tell you what to call it: Yellowstone Boys Ranch. After all, the O'Rourke ranch is in Yellowstone County. And you have set out to provide help for boys from Montana and Wyoming, and Yellowstone National Park is between these two states."

I knew as soon as I heard it that Roy had given us the perfect name. The only people who didn't like it were some of my Christian friends who were disappointed that we weren't going to call it Yellowstone *Christian* Boys Ranch. I tried to explain my reasoning to these friends.

"Here's how I see it," I said. "There are all kinds of people who care about troubled kids, and I want this Ranch to be run in such a way that any of these people will feel comfortable supporting us, even if they don't go to church."

Certainly, Christian faith convictions were a major motivation for those of us who were starting the Ranch. And, clearly, we were motivated by the example of Jesus, who cared for both the physical and the spiritual needs of the many people he came in contact with.

Still, when it came to our name, I preferred that we demonstrate our faith through the quality of our service and the dedication of our people rather than plastering it all over a billboard. While some saw this as a compromise, I saw it as a commitment to express our faith in action and other tangible ways people could see and feel.

Later on I came across a quote that expressed this point of

view. It was from St. Francis of Assisi, who instructed his brothers, *Preach the Gospel at all times, and if necessary use words.*

Tested by an Unexpected Crisis

The Board of Yellowstone Boys Ranch held its first meeting in August 1956, and the following month our incorporation papers were approved by the Montana Secretary of State.

All we needed now was property. The purchase price for the O'Rourke ranch's 160 acres of irrigated land and an excellent set of farm buildings was $85,000, with a down payment of $25,000 and the $60,000 balance on a contract spread over ten years.

Remembering the $50,000 promise from the wealthy businessman, we felt things were beginning to progress nicely. In early 1957, this businessman was away on an extended trip, and in his absence we confidently borrowed the $5,000 earnest money required by the O'Rourkes. Our ninety-day option for the $20,000 balance on the down payment would expire in April. When the man returned from his trip, we revisited him and asked about his pledge to help us get started.

To our shock, he abruptly withdrew his offer. "Sorry," he said. "I've changed my mind."

This sudden reversal sent our Board into emergency mode. We met at a hastily called meeting and plotted our strategy now that the money we had planned on had evaporated thirty days before it was needed.

We reviewed our situation and tried to estimate how much money we thought could be raised through other sources. After looking at the numbers, we were nowhere close to our goal.

The board members looked at me and asked, "So, Franklin, what do you want to do?"

I looked at them and said: "My position hasn't changed at all. I still believe there is a desperate need for our Ranch. And I believe others who share our conviction of this need will step up to the plate and help make it happen."

I suggested we do everything we could individually to raise the needed $20,000 before our April 1 deadline. When the month was up we were still nearly $10,000 short. At that point, Ted Keating and Bill MacKay volunteered to co-sign bank loans enabling us to borrow enough money to make our initial payment, and Les Shryock donated $5,000 to cover the earnest money loan we had borrowed earlier. We met the deadline and delivered the down payment needed to secure the property.

First Forays in Direct Mail

Today there are hundreds of books available on how to use mail to raise funding for charitable projects. There are even scores of books on using e-mail for fund-raising. But in 1957, I was finding out on my own how to raise the money needed to get the Ranch started and retire our debt.

One thing I realized was that we needed to recruit a sizable donor family who understood our recurring need for construction and operating funds to adequately care for our growing family of boys. Thankfully, Ken Todd, a Helena businessman who believed in what we were doing, provided us with a really unique "jump-start" on our first mailing.

Ken was District Manager of what was then known as Mountain States Telephone. He could have made a company cash contribution to the Ranch; instead he chose a most unusual and far more fruitful approach. He made the decision to do a one-time-only addressing of 125,000 of our mailing envelopes to his entire customer mailing list for Montana and northern Wyoming!

That mailing included an informative brochure featuring photos of our newly acquired property, photos and brief descriptions of our five Board members, and reprints of warmhearted letters of endorsement from the governors of Montana and Wyoming. Rounding out the materials was an enthusiastic description of our plans for launching our Boys

Ranch and a separate letter requesting people's help. To make things simple we enclosed something truly creative for its time: a pre-addressed return envelope with a flap that contained a blank check. People could fill it out with the dollar amount of their gift and mail it back to us.

Volunteers from Ladies Aide societies, missionary groups and sewing circles kindly agreed to spend evenings hand-stuffing our mailings. It took several weeks because the average group could complete only about five thousand pieces of mail in an evening. Then we took the letters to the Post Office, sent them out, and waited expectantly to see what kind of response we would get.

What a thrill it was to see the responses come back, first by the dozens and then by the hundreds! Many people mailed us dollar bills, while some even sent fives, tens, and twenties. Scores of others used the blank check we had provided for even larger amounts!

One of these checks arrived in an envelope postmarked Libby, Montana, which is some four hundred miles away. The check was filled out in a soft lead pencil. The amount was $500. It was signed Cactus Wade.

At first I thought someone was playing a practical joke on us, but I investigated further and discovered that Cactus Wade was for real. He was a down-to-earth cowboy who had married a classy lady from New York who came West to find romance and somebody who loved horses as much as she did. This couple also shared a concern for kids, and they became regular supporters of the Ranch.

When we reported back to Ken Todd on the success of that first mailing, he was thrilled. He also supplied us with a complete set of phone books so we could develop our own mailing list.

Our first experiment in direct mail was a success, and this first success encouraged us to establish a pattern of donor contact we have followed ever since.

Employee Number One

Getting the Ranch off the ground was challenging enough, but I knew we now faced a decision that was probably more important than anything else we had faced thus far. This was the all-important decision of who we would hire to run our Ranch.

One thing I had observed time and time again during my research visits to various boys ranches and institutions was the critical importance of having the right person as our superintendent. And over time, I thought often about my own job description for the "perfect" superintendent of Yellowstone Boys Ranch.

First, he would have to be a man of character. He would need to be someone who was true to his word, who did what he said he would do, and conducted himself with integrity and clarity of purpose.

Second, he would have to be a man of many hats. Since our Ranch was just starting out and he would be our first employee, he would have to be a teacher, a counselor, a spiritual guide, a disciplinarian, a coach, and an expert on agriculture, livestock, and farm equipment.

Finally, he would need to be a man who shared our passion and vision for kids. He would have to possess a big heart, a deep well of patience, and an ability to love children no matter how unlovable they were.

It may sound like an impossibly demanding job description to fill, but from the moment I began thinking about the Ranch I knew just the person who fit this description. His name was Bob McFarlane, and hiring him was probably one of the best decisions ever made at Yellowstone Boys Ranch.

I had known Bob ever since he and I were students at the same small Bible college. We shared a common commitment to using our lives to serve the world, and believed service was a higher calling than personal wealth or pleasure.

Bob later transferred to Seattle Pacific College (now Seattle

Bob McFarlane, Ranch employee number one, had a rare combination of skills and gifts. His wife Doris worked alongside him, and their children "grew up" on the Ranch.

Pacific University), and after graduation he accepted a job teaching at a Christian school in the Seattle area. I could tell immediately from the way he threw himself into his work that he absolutely loved kids. That's why I recommended him as a high school teacher for the Boys Industrial School in Worland, Wyoming.

Bob started at Worland in 1952, and within a few short years he was the assistant superintendent there. He also served as a teacher in the high school, the coach of their athletic teams, the business manager, and the coordinator of the school's farm, its ranch, and its cannery.

I had many conversations with Bob about our Ranch and how I felt he would make a great superintendent. He was interested in working for us, but understandably cautious early on about exchanging his solid job and secure financial situation for a Ranch that was just being created.

But I kept after him, and as our plans began falling into place in the spring of 1957, I pleaded with Bob to join us. He finally agreed, and we hired Bob and his wife Doris, who would be the Ranch cook and hostess. Bob and Doris moved to the Ranch on May 11, 1957, along with their preschool children Glenn and Gloria.

I wrote an article about Bob for the *Yellowstone Boys Ranch Wrangler*, the Ranch newsletter:

> A Boy's Ranch has boys, most all of them with big problems. Are you trained to understand them and work with them? Do you know how to win their confidence, discipline them, and still hold their respect? Do you know how to play with them? Are you qualified to teach in their high school or coach their athletics? Could you pitch a game of ball, manage a football team, and outbox any boy on the Ranch?
>
> Would you rather dedicate yourself to this type of work than anything else in the world, and would you take a cut in pay to do it at Yellowstone Boys Ranch? Mr. Bob McFarlane meets all these qualifications and more. That's why he is superintendent of the Yellowstone Boys Ranch.

Bob worked full-time at the Ranch for the next twenty-nine years serving us in a variety of roles. Over the years he served as our superintendent, our manager of Program Development and Donor Relations, and as our farm manager before retiring in 1986 at the age of sixty-six.

For hundreds of kids who lived at the Ranch during these decades, Bob was the face and the heart of Yellowstone. He was the person most responsible for translating our passion and ideals into action. And there are many times I have felt certain that we never would have had a Ranch without him.

I said Bob retired, but that probably isn't the best word for it. Bob remains a regular presence at the Ranch, where his son Glenn is now our Chief Financial Officer. Bob is a constant source of inspiration to many of us. He also continues to take on new projects, such as overseeing the construction of a greenhouse on our grounds that has added new capabilities to our agricultural education programs.

Bob also remains committed to helping kids any way he can. I recently sat down with him shortly after he had served his fourteenth year in a row as counselor and "campground grandpa" for third, fourth, and fifth graders at a summer camp for kids operated by his church. As we talked together, Bob thought back to his years at Yellowstone.

"I've always loved kids, and I love to be involved in their lives," he told me. "I had an ideal job at Worland, but I knew there had to be a better way to help troubled kids. At Worland I worked with a boy who had stolen $2.85 from a gas station and was sentenced to a year at the Industrial School. Through experiences like these I came to see the value of Yellowstone and the whole concept of giving kids a second chance by providing care and love instead of merely locking them up."

The First Boy Arrives

Now that we had Bob on board, along with a foster home license from the state Department of Public Welfare, we were finally ready for our first boy. The word soon came from Helena that a boy was on his way, and on June 17, 1957, he arrived. His name was Jim Anderson, and for us he was boy number one.

The first issue of the *Wrangler* told all about it in a page-one story: YELLOWSTONE BOYS RANCH GETS UNDER WAY. Under this article was our drawing showing an aerial view of the Ranch property.

Before long, Jim would be joined by other boys who desperately needed the kind of personal care the Ranch could provide.

After years of work and prayer, our dream had become a reality. Now it was time to hang on for dear life as the Ranch took off and grew in ways we had hoped and dreamed and prayed for so long.

They knew it was a big event, so Jim Anderson and Franklin Robbie got dressed up when Jim, the first boy at Yellowstone Boys Ranch, left the Ranch for good.

Transformed Lives

Jim McCombs: A Second Chance

Jim McCombs was a prime example of the type of boy who motivated Franklin Robbie and others to devote their lives to "finding a better way" of caring for young boys who didn't have the supervision, love and structure they needed at home in order to stay out of trouble.

Jim was a resident at the Montana State Boys Industrial School in Miles City late in the spring of 1962 when the Ranch received a letter from the social worker there. "It is our belief that James is not in need of an industrial school type setting," the letter read, "and that he could profit greatly from your program."

Jim's early life was a heartbreaking series of events which left him and his older sister, Sharon, orphaned and in the care of their grandparents in Malta, Montana in the mid-1950s. But Grandpa and Grandma were not equipped to handle two young children. His grandpa was difficult to deal with and uncooperative in planning for the children. As a result, Jim and Sharon were left unsupervised, and soon they were getting into trouble.

In 1959 Jim's grandmother passed away, and his grandfather would take no responsibility for Jim's behavior. Consequently, in September 1960, Jim was made a ward of the court and sent to the State Industrial School at Miles City.

Reports indicate that Jim was very cooperative while there. He had suffered a severe case of rheumatic fever in 1959, resulting in a heart condition that restricted his engaging in exceptionally strenuous activities. Jim loved participating in sports, but obediently limited his conduct when asked to do so. He had missed a lot of school and had been "held back" several times, but did acceptable work in school while there.

In short, Jim possessed all the "raw material" necessary to stay out of trouble and didn't need to be locked up. That's why the letter from Miles City also stated, "He is a boy, we feel, who would be receptive and responsive to a nurturing, understanding, supporting, and encouraging setting. Because of this we believe his prognosis for remaining out of trouble in the future to be very good."

And so, Ranch Superintendent Bob McFarlane (Mr. Mac) drove over to Miles City and brought Jim McCombs "home" to Yellowstone. Bob remembers, "Jim was a typical All-American boy who was interested in fun, sports and girls! All he needed was a home and a second chance for a normal life."

Jim thrived under the loving care of Bob and Doris McFarlane, Carl and Betty Orth, and the other staff. Jim's love for people, his terrific sense of humor, and his concern for the "underdog" were able to blossom and grow.

Like any adolescent boy, Jim got into mischief at the Ranch. But as his heart condition improved, his energy was redirected into playing the sports he loved. He worked at catching up in school, forged deep friendships with his peers, and developed a strong work ethic.

After leaving the Ranch, Jim stayed in the Billings community and eventually became the owner of J & S Pioneer Service Station. Jim had worked for a neighboring business and the couple who owned the service station were impressed with his hard work and engaging personality. When they decided it was time to retire, they asked Jim if he'd like to take over the business.

Owning his own business gave Jim the opportunity to help many young people get beyond incredibly tough circumstances in their own lives. Jim had personal knowledge of need, hunger, neglect, and of being misunderstood. Yet he never wanted to talk about his past. He just wanted to use the tenderness it had developed in him to help others. Jim wanted to make sure his children were never in the same situation he had been while growing up.

A popular motto today says Live Well, Laugh Often, Love Much.

Jim's life epitomized this phrase, but was cut short when he passed away of a heart attack just three weeks shy of his fifty-eighth birthday. Jim lived life to the fullest, loved his family fiercely, and never knew a stranger.

Jim's wife, Sandy, says, "He never made a lot of money because that wasn't what motivated him. At the station we hired employees who had been in trouble. He felt everyone deserved an opportunity to better themselves, just like the second chance he got at the Ranch."

At his memorial service, one young man shared, "Jim hired me right out of jail when I needed a chance. He was willing to take the risk. I hope I can do the same for someone else someday."

Jim is survived by his wife, Sandy; son Brian and wife Churon; daughters Renee and Stacey; grandchildren, Isaak James and Haley; sister, Sharon, and family; and two "adopted" sons, Jason Clemmer and Jason Horton. They love to reminisce about life with Jim. He was a huge Denver Bronco fan, which was obvious to anyone walking into the service station.

Shortly before his death, Jim posed with his grandson Isaak James.

Jason Horton remembers, "Jim and Sandy took me in when I was about fifteen." Jason was in the same situation Jim had been in, living with his grandmother and getting into trouble. "He gave me a job at the station. I loved watching him with people. If you came into the station once, he never forgot you."

Jim's girls laugh about the time Jason tried to sneak out one night soon after he had moved in. "Dad caught him, of course," says Stacey. "And he didn't even get mad. He just said Jason didn't know any better. He didn't know the house rules yet." Renee adds, "You couldn't put anything over on Dad. He also gave Jason a hard time about what a poor job he did using pillows to make it look like he was asleep in his bed."

It wasn't just that Jim recalled how tough it was to be a teenager; he knew teenagers needed an ally. He was very much their advocate. He was instrumental in helping Jason Clemmer reconcile with his family.

All the kids remember that Jim was not a lecturer. He'd let them make their mistakes, and then they'd sit down and talk about what they should learn from the situation.

Son Brian remembers what great respect Jim had for Bob McFarlane. "Whenever Bob came into the station, Dad would say to other customers, 'I want you to meet my dad, Bob McFarlane.' Any success he had in life, he credited to Mr. Mac."

Reform school really was not the place for Jim. Thanks to the second chance he got at Yellowstone Boys Ranch and what he did with it, Jim is a hero to his kids, and their lives will be proof of the "legacy of caring" Jim lived out for them.

Jim's surviving family members thank the Ranch and Jim's "Dad" Bob McFarlane (pictured at right) for their love and care.

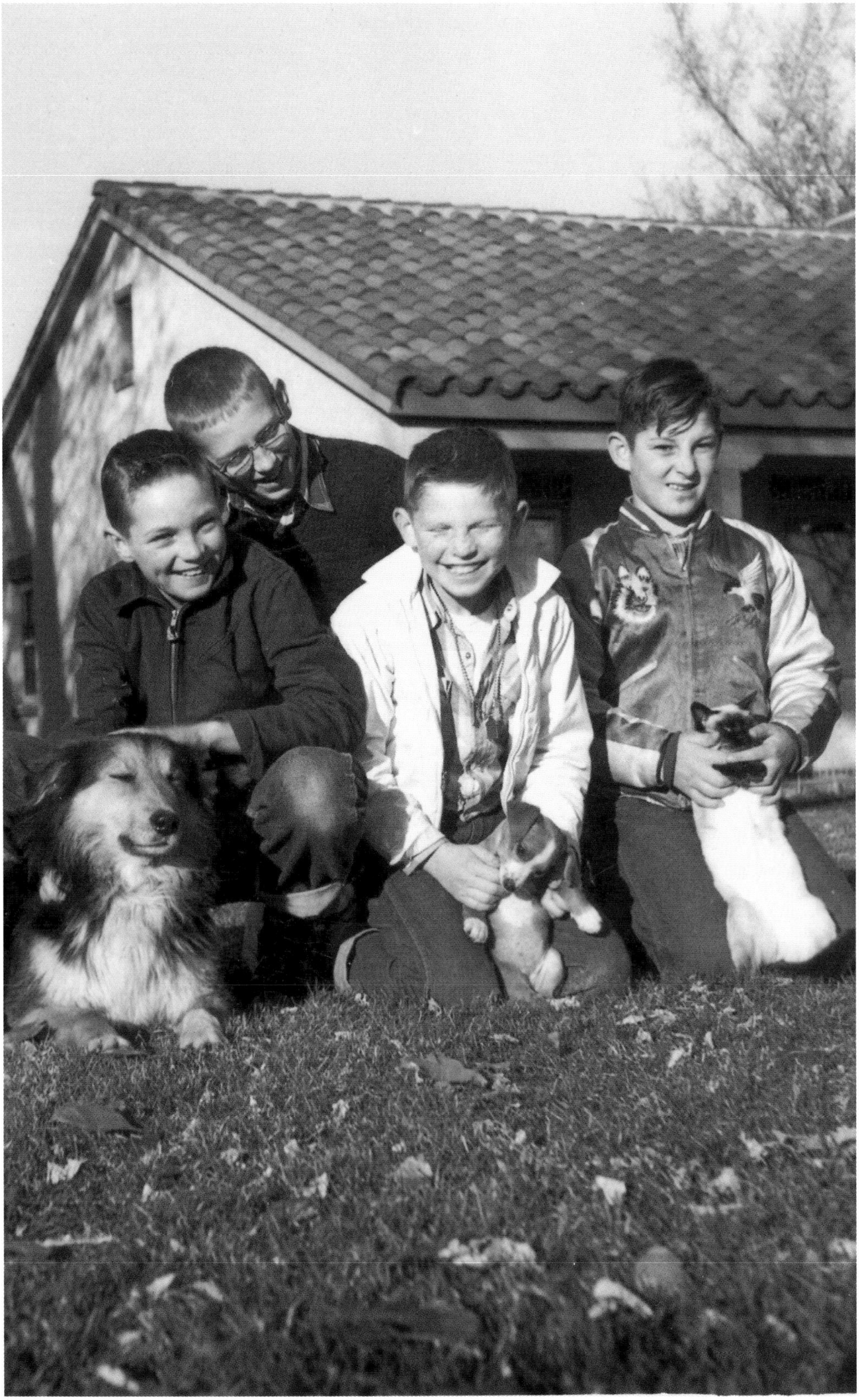

CHAPTER THREE

Growing Pains

Yellowstone Boys Ranch came into existence on September 28, 1956—at least on paper. That was the day our Articles of Incorporation were filed with the State of Montana. But it was in 1957 things really started rolling!

In April we purchased our property. In May we hired Bob McFarlane. And in June we received our first boy, who was referred to the Ranch by Montana juvenile court officials. Then in July 1957 our boy population suddenly quadrupled! It happened when a juvenile court judge in Wyoming referred three brothers, the Johnson boys, to the Ranch.

I had always believed that once the Ranch was up and running it would meet a need in our region. But before now I didn't have any proof of this belief. Suddenly I was starting to see the proof, as more and more boys came to live at the Ranch.

The motto of the characters in the hit movie, Field of Dreams, was: "If you build it he will come." For us, the motto could have been: "If you build it they will come."

We built it. Then they started coming. And over the next fifty years the Ranch would be involved in a continuing cycle of accepting new kids, hiring the staff needed to work with them, and building the facilities required to create a safe place for young people who had no safe place in this world.

By the summer of 1957, it was clear to Bob McFarlane and me that it was time to add staff. And we both agreed that we already knew the perfect man for the job.

Carl Orth's Long and Winding Road

Bob and I had met Carl Orth during one of our research and reconnaissance visits to Cal Farley's Boy's Ranch outside of Amarillo, Texas.

Originally, Carl had been hired as Cal Farley's chaplain. Cal Farley's Boy's Ranch was not even a "religious" ranch like Father Flanagan's Boys Town. But at that time, just about everyone working with troubled kids knew that spiritual issues were an important part of helping them turn their lives around.

By the time plans for Yellowstone Boys Ranch were taking shape, Carl had been promoted to Cal Farley's superintendent. The fact that he had risen from chaplain to superintendent of a ranch for between one hundred fifty to two hundred boys said a lot about Carl's character, his competence, and his professionalism.

When Bob and I first tried to recruit Carl to join us he said he wasn't ready to make a move. We promised to stay in touch. The next thing we knew Carl, his wife Betty, and their sons had moved to Chicago, where Carl had taken a temporary job with the Ford Motor Co. When Bob and I contacted Carl again in July 1957, the strangest thing had happened.

"You'll never believe this," he told me when I reached him by phone, "but my contract with Ford has been fulfilled and, as of thirty minutes ago, I'm available." Fortunately for us, Carl's sudden unemployment at Ford made his sudden employment at the Ranch that much easier. He joined us immediately, serving as the Ranch's assistant superintendent.

This long and winding road Carl traveled down before joining us seemed to be yet another of many cases in the history of the Ranch when things didn't necessarily happen as we thought they should. Rather, they happened according to God's providential timing, and in the end things worked out better that way.

Balancing Love with Discipline

Carl, Betty, and their four boys moved from Chicago to Montana within a matter of days, and lived in my basement until the Ranch could provide a place for them to stay. I remember writing the following sentences to introduce the Orths to supporters of the Ranch:

Carl and Betty Orth brought their sons to Montana in 1957. Shown are sons Skip (top left), Bob (top right), Leonard (bottom left), and Dale (bottom right), who has worked at the Ranch for nearly thirty years.

"Carl and Betty Orth once considered preparing themselves for the mission field. Instead, they prepared for work among troubled boys and found their mission field, not on a foreign shore, but right here in America."

It takes a special kind of dedication for a family to sacrifice their own comfort, privacy, and normal home life to live almost every waking hour among boys whom society has largely rejected. But Carl and his family had that kind of dedication. Plus, Carl had an amazing mix of compassion and professionalism. Time and time again he demonstrated a unique ability to both care for our kids and to do what was best for their long-term development.

Carl also had a deep Christian commitment that was often exhibited most powerfully through his actions, not his words. Many—but not all—of the people who have worked at the Ranch over the past half-century have been people of faith. But our attitude has been one of demonstrating our faith commitment through our care for the boys rather than merely

Carl Orth had love and understanding for Ranch boys.

talking about it. And Carl Orth was that kind of man.

I know that corporal punishment isn't popular today, and I can well understand why it is now illegal in many states. But fifty years ago was a much different time. Carl had a small paddle, which he used sparingly—and creatively. Those of us who saw Carl interact with the boys saw how he intuitively balanced love with discipline and grace with law.

Whenever Carl or Bob were out on the ball field with a group of boys, some of the boys would inevitably forget their jackets or their schoolbooks and leave them out on the field. Carl had a creative way of getting the boys to develop greater concern about keeping track of their possessions. When someone repeatedly left their things at the field, Carl would offer to let him buy it back by receiving a light smack with his paddle.

That may sound cruel to some people today, but I can remember numerous boys who had lived on the Ranch while Carl was there would come back years later for a visit. Many of these boys would specifically comment on Carl and his trusty paddle. At first I thought they might complain about the discipline they received, but they never did. They always described how much they appreciated his firm but gentle prodding.

Carl had such a tremendous capacity to clearly exhibit how much he cared, even when he was firm. As a result, the boys knew where he stood. They also knew they couldn't get away with anything when he was around.

Today we would call this having boundaries. Both Carl and Bob were masters of establishing and enforcing healthy boundaries for boys who had never learned to create such boundaries for themselves. Their approach was tremendously important in those early days at the Ranch.

A Double Blessing

In addition to praising Carl and Bob I need to give credit

to Doris McFarlane and Betty Orth for the pioneering spirit and dedication it took to be "mothers" not only to their own children but also to our growing number of boys.

Doris and Betty cooked hundreds of meals, laundered and ironed thousands of shirts and jeans, canned garden produce, counseled and comforted lonely boys, and heartily supported their husbands in this major endeavor.

Because of the demands of the Ranch schedule it was difficult for the McFarlanes and Orths to get any time off to be with their own families. But when they could, Carl and Betty would take a small camping trailer and head for Yellowstone Park or a campground for some quiet family time.

"I don't remember ever feeling deprived, and I don't think our children minded," recalls Betty. "We were happy because our husbands were happy. We knew they were doing what they loved and what they were gifted to do. It was a wonderful time of camaraderie and dropping into bed each night, very tired, but also very content."

A Tragic Loss

Sadly, Carl Orth was taken from us long before we felt his work on earth was done. A rare and aggressive form of skin cancer took his life at the age of forty-one. His sudden death in May 1963 shocked all of us at the Ranch, and left us feeling a sense of loss and sorrow that took a long time to heal.

The first major building project at the Ranch was transforming a large storage building into a lodge for thirty boys with an upstairs apartment where the Orth family could live. The Ranch board unanimously voted to name this building the Orth Memorial Lodge in Carl's honor.

Many of the Ranch boys expressed their sorrow over Carl's death in other ways. One boy named John spoke for many of the boys in the letter he wrote about Carl:

"Mr. Orth was by far the finest man I have ever known. He not only taught us boys to be useful, well-rounded young men, but he set the best example anyone could possibly set." Today, those of us at the Ranch often think of Carl when we see his son Dale, who has worked with us since 1977. Dale, who is our senior vice president of administrative services, exhibits his father's sensitivity as well as his deep love for kids.

Helpful Hands

As more employees joined the Ranch staff and increasing numbers of boys came to receive help, we quickly discovered there was no way employees alone could do everything that needed to be done.

Thankfully, innumerable good-hearted local people volunteered their labor and provided us with other skills and assistance that we never would have been able to afford without their help.

From the beginning, articles about these selfless acts of caring and sacrifice appeared regularly in the *Wrangler*. The very first issue contained articles acknowledging the help we received from near and far:

BOYS RANCH RECEIVES 14 HEAD OF LIVESTOCK told how local ranchers donated beef and dairy cows. We even had a supporter who hosted a weekly radio program for ranchers, and regularly encouraged his listeners to make livestock gifts to the Ranch.

BILLINGS DOCTORS AND DENTISTS ASSIST BOYS RANCH described how the Yellowstone Valley Medical Association set up a special committee to work with the Ranch in meeting the needs of our boys, many of whom had never received regular health or dental care.

LADIES CLUB HOLDS SHOWERS told about groups from across Montana and Wyoming conducting special activities to collect bedding, clothes, towels, bathroom supplies, and other much needed items.

BAKING AND LAUNDRY SERVICE DONATED described how the

owners of Ideal Bakery and Rex Laundry in Billings made special efforts to meet the Ranch's increasing needs.

And that was only the first issue of the *Wrangler*! Later issues detailed more acts of kindness from individuals and businesses in the area. Let me offer just a sampling of the many things people did for us:

- Department stores in Montana and Wyoming gave our boys clothing.
- Early on western Montana lumber mills donated a railroad carload of lumber (45,000 board feet) needed for our first full sized lodge for boys, with additional donations in later years.
- A wheat farmer who was through with his farm equipment for the season loaned his big truck and front-end loader to the Ranch so we could haul building materials and move dirt and gravel when needed.
- Ranchers donated horses, pigs, and lambs to our growing livestock supply, and veterinarians donated their services to care for our animals.
- Local barbers cut our kids' hair.

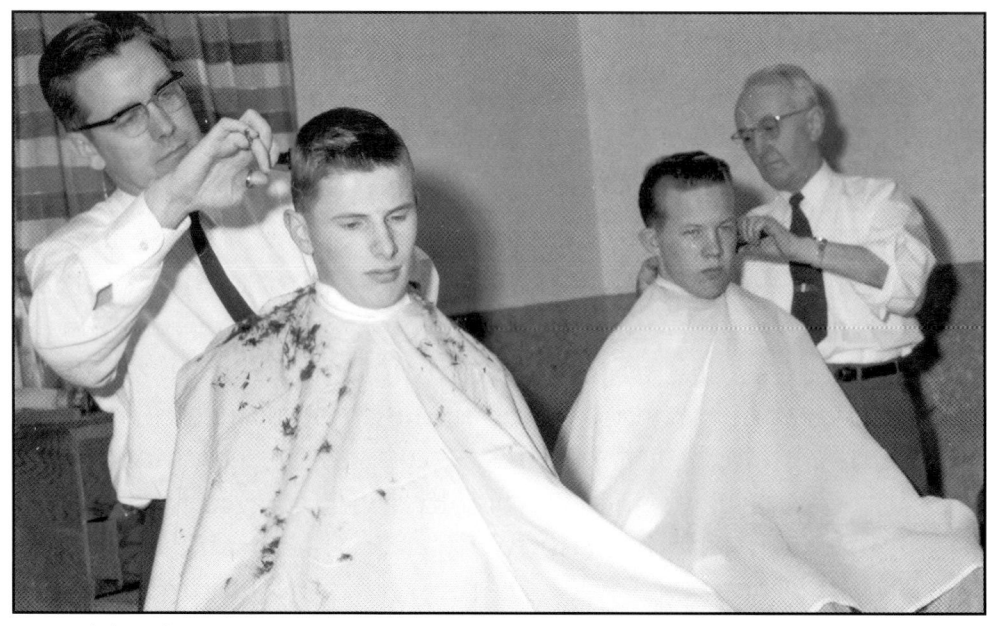

Local barber George Brown (left) persuaded other barbers to volunteer to cut the fast-growing hair of Ranch boys.

And just about everything involved in building and equipping facilities for the boys was given to us over the years, including concrete block, laminated beams, and sheetrock by the truckload!

Initially, I was the primary persuader. I talked with anyone who showed an interest in our work and helped them catch the vision to help us move forward. And sometimes friends, neighbors, and business people, who had experienced the joy of giving, passed the good word along. Recently, a member of the Ranch staff interviewed John Bradford, owner of Bradford Roofing of Billings, who was personally involved in making sure many of our boys literally had roofs over their heads from the earliest days of the Ranch.

"The people at the Ranch are so sincere," said Bradford.

"They don't hold back. They're congenial, and they have a way of talking you into things!"

After their first roofing job at the Ranch, John and his dad decided to make Yellowstone their primary charity. "We wanted to do something that had an impact. If you give $10 here and there, there's very little impact. But putting a roof on a new building to help take care of kids, that's an impact. We were always very proud of it. And my sons who run the business today are still proud of it."

He continued: "Franklin always told me he'd find the materials and all I'd have to do is get the job done. We developed a great working relationship and a great friendship that has endured until today.

"There were only a few roofing companies in Billings in those days, and everyone came on hard times once in awhile. So when there were those times, I was able to convince the roofer's union to donate time and we would supervise it.

"Then we'd get roofers from every roofing company in town to work on a roof at the Ranch. And it was kind of fun for them. It was like a challenge, whose roofing company was faster and better. The guys really enjoyed those times. It built camaraderie in the business and gave Yellowstone great exposure.

"The Ranch is a fantastic organization, and what it is doing is an asset to the Billings community," said Bradford. "They're dedicated to what they do, and they're dogged about getting it done."

Another local company that played an important role in our early years was Lew Chevrolet. There's a picture in a 1958 issue of the *Wrangler* showing the dealership manager handing me the keys to a brand new Chevrolet station wagon. The staff at the Ranch drove that car every day for a year and then traded it back in for a new model. Lew continued this pattern of generosity by giving the Ranch the use of a new Chevy wagon every year for ten years! McIntyre Motors would perform a similar service, loaning us a new Pontiac every year for twenty-three years for my fund raising travels!

Another interesting gift arrived after a Redstone, Montana, semi-professional baseball team went out of business. One of their final actions was to "will" all of their uniforms and equipment to the Ranch. With a little help from our "clothing room tailors," our boys looked pretty classy on the field for the next few years.

My heart was touched so many times over these past fifty years as people gave us whatever they could. For example, Maude Maring of Billings made weekly trips out to the Ranch to pick up a big box full of clothes in need of mending. The following week, she would return the mended clothes and pick up more in need of repair.

Maude wasn't wealthy. And she didn't own a business. Instead, she gave us what she could: her loving labor that kept our active boys from growing out of their clothes. Her gift makes me recall the words of Jesus as he praised the poor widow who gave two small copper coins to the temple treasury (Luke 21:1-4).

Initially the only housing for our growing family of boys was a small tenant's house which, with an added bedroom and kitchen would accommodate nine boys. Our hope was to remodel a large machine storage building into our first full-sized lodge with planned accommodations for 30 boys. We had received that first carload of lumber, had a donated floor plan, but were in desperate need of an experienced carpenter/supervisor to manage the project.

That's when Mr. Roy McNeal of Basin, Wyoming drove to the Ranch, met Bob McFarlane and said, "I'm a carpenter and cabinet maker. I'm past 65 and on Social Security. I have a complete set of tools and time on my hands. You are taking Wyoming boys so I would like to offer my services free of charge to help you get your new lodge built so you can take more boys."

His generous offer certainly fit our limited budget so it was quickly accepted. He even brought his own camping trailer to sleep in, joined the boys at mealtime and watched with approval the way Bob and Carl worked through the problems of our growing family of boys. Our urgent need for that new lodge was so intense that Mr. McNeal only went home to visit his family for a day or two about twice a month.

This went on for about 8 months when he came back from one of his weekend home-visits and confessed to Bob and Carl that his son, David, the youngest of 11 children, had been expelled from high school because of behavior problems similar to those of some of the boys he saw in our care.

Mr. McNeal wondered if we would consider admitting David and helping him get straightened up. He said with deep feeling, "If Carl will become his father figure, I promise to stay out of the way."

David came and Carl practiced his persuasion with outstanding success! David was big for his age and anxious to get on with his life so he didn't quite finish high school, but got his G.E.D. and joined the Navy.

Anxious to keep Mr. McNeal on the job, we began paying him the $100 a month he could earn beyond his Social Security and he stayed on for another year. When Mrs. McNeal learned we needed a full-time cook, she volunteered to fill in until we could find a professional. By then the new lodge was nearly finished, David was in the Navy, and after another year of faithful service, the McNeals resumed their retirement somewhere in Wyoming.

Friends in High Places

Another person who supported the Ranch in those early days was Montana Governor J. Hugo Aronson. I had always believed that outreach to government officials was important, so I made many trips to Helena in those early days.

Governor Aronson, who visited the Ranch on a number of occasions, embraced the work of the Ranch with such enthusiasm, sincerity, and warmth that many of us were pleasantly surprised. Clearly he was doing more than playing politics. He even agreed to serve as the Chairman of the Boys Ranch Advisory Committee.

He wrote us a letter after one of his visits:

> You and your co-workers are certainly to be commended on the job that is being done at the Boys Ranch. As Governor, I have been asked to be honorary head of a great number of things, but few have made me as proud or given me as much pleasure as being Chairman of the Advisory Committee of Yellowstone Boys Ranch.

Governor Aronson was not the only top state official to

Montana Gov. Hugo Aronson was the first of many state officials who have supported the Ranch over the years.

help the Ranch. Former Montana Governor Judy Martz serves on the Ranch Board of Directors and Montana's current Lt. Governor John Bohlinger served on the Ranch Board from 1993 to 2001.

Over the past half-century, those of us who worked at the Ranch would invest much energy in explaining our work to government officials in various arenas of public life in both Montana and Wyoming. And over time, government officials and those who worked with juveniles came to see that the Ranch was a place where caring people would give all they had to help kids who had somehow got off on the wrong track.

"It Sure Makes a Difference…"

Yellowstone Boys Ranch was now a reality. We had staff. We had a growing number of boys coming to live with us. And soon some of them were "graduating" from the Ranch and returning to the "real world."

I wanted to know whether or not the Ranch was having a positive impact on the boys who were sent to live with us. Were we helping those boys who were entrusted to our care? What was happening to them once they left us?

After his time at the Ranch, Sheldon Kelly enlisted in the Army. And when he received his first furlough, he returned for a visit.

Sheldon, who years later joined the *Reader's Digest* as a staff writer, also wrote numerous letters to Bob and Doris McFarlane, who had cared for him while he was with us. One of Sheldon's letters revealed his keen sense of humor as well as the affection he felt for all at the Ranch:

> Dear Ma and Pa McFarlane:
> Sorry I haven't written sooner but what spare time I do have I spend shining my boots or cleaning my rifle.
> I sure do miss the Ranch, especially getting up at a decent hour in the morning and eating real food. But I guess that's the Army. And if we put all our complaints on paper the paper surplus would be solved.
> How is Jim and how are all the other boys?
> Well, here comes my sergeant and his expression is very unfavorable. How can I explain to him my rifle is clean!
> Write soon!
> Love, Sheldon.

During the next fifty years we would receive hundreds of letters like Sheldon's, but Sheldon was unique. He was the first "success story" we ever featured in the *Wrangler*. But he was far from the last. From now on, each issue would carry a story, a photo, or a letter from boys who had lived on the Ranch.

People liked reading these stories, but they were especially important to the entire Ranch staff, for we wanted to make sure the work we were doing was making a difference in boys' lives. And letters like Sheldon's helped us see that we were having an impact. One by one, we were turning around the lives of the boys who had stayed with us.

These demonstrated results proved that the Ranch slogan was more than mere advertising hype. It was true. That slogan stated the mission of the Ranch in one simple sentence: IT SURE MAKES A DIFFERENCE WHEN YOU KNOW SOMEBODY CARES.

Now that we were seeing the fruit of our work in boys like Sheldon, all the hard work seemed completely worthwhile.

Transformed Lives

Russ White:
The Place I Call Home

Rusty White was a pretty normal kid. He'd been adopted as an infant and had a fairly good home life. But when his adoptive father died just as Rusty was entering adolescence, things began to change. He became quite aggressive, and if he didn't want to do what his mother said, she couldn't force him.

Back in the late 1950s and early 60s the medical approach to belligerent kids wasn't all that sophisticated. A local doctor put Rusty on a strong sedative to keep him under control. Rusty may have been heading toward a lifetime in a mental institution had another doctor not told his mother about Yellowstone Boys Ranch.

One day Carl Orth, assistant superintendent at Yellowstone, showed up at his hospital room in the mental health ward and began asking Rusty questions.

"Carl Orth saved my life," says Russ, now fifty-six years old and retired from a career as a detective with the Las Vegas Metropolitan Police Department. "Carl could see that I wasn't mentally ill, that I just

Christmas shopping as a child at the Ranch. These experiences later inspired Russ's "Shop With A Cop."

needed strong male leadership in my life. He believed in me. He took me to Yellowstone Boys Ranch where I met all kinds of strong, committed men who taught me what it meant to really be a man."

Russ has fond memories of his time at the Ranch. He learned to sling hay bales with Jim Soft when Jim worked summers at the Ranch while he was in college. He also learned to work alongside Loren Soft, milking cows, mending fence, and doing other chores. Farm manager Irwin Eleson invited Russ to join his family for holidays. "Irwin made me feel like I was one of his sons," says Russ. "He let me stay at his home with his remarkable wife and children. Those times are among my happiest memories. He also taught me about ranching, farming and handling heavy equipment."

Russ lived in Paul Stock Lodge where he was mentored by Dan and Sharon Hansen. "They were much more patient and understanding with us kids than I would have been. Dan was one of the most fun people I've ever been around. He was a great role model."

Lodge life was like living in a dorm. "We boys played pranks on one another, just like any kids would. But we became brothers. We shared everything. We cried together, fought together. We were actually closer than a lot of kids who are truly brothers and sisters. Because I didn't have a real family, they became my family."

Sunday was Russ's favorite day of the week. Unlike a lot of the other guys, he actually liked going to church. Then, after Sunday dinner, the boys and staff would play football, weather permitting. "We'd play all afternoon, until we were so tired we could hardly put one foot in front of the other. It was our one free day, and we loved being able to do what we wanted.

"There were always chores to do. I remember I was on the milking crew so my day started pretty early. We all learned the value of an honest day's work. We also learned to share with others; how to be aware of the feelings of others; and how to function in a family. I think these were the values they were trying to instill in all of us. I am so grateful for Franklin Robbie, Bob McFarlane, and Carl Orth. If it weren't for their vision and wisdom in selecting staff, I would not be where I am today."

So, where is Russ today, and what did he do with his life?

He takes great pride in his primary roles as husband to Sharon for thirty-two years, father to Russell and Jenefer, and grandfather of three.

Russ always dreamed of coming back and working at the Ranch someday. His other passion was law enforcement, so he decided to exchange the dream of working at the Ranch for a career as a police officer.

Early in his career Russ realized how easy it is for kids to have a negative view of police officers. When police are called to handle a domestic violence situation, they often have to remove young children from their parents for the children's protection. Russ remembers thinking, "What is this child's memory going to be of police officers? They only know that a policeman took them away from their parents."

An idea began to percolate in Russ' mind that would give underprivileged kids a positive experience with policemen. In 1986 Russ started a program known as Shop With A Cop. Growing up at Yellowstone, one of his favorite holiday memories was the annual Christmas shopping trip to JC Penney, paid for by an anonymous "Santa." Shop With A Cop provided a similar shopping experience for kids and cops, one-on-one.

Shop With A Cop's major goal is to bring needy children and local law enforcement officers together in order to better understand each other. Now with hundreds of chapters nationwide, thousands of disadvantaged children have the opportunity to get to know police officers in a positive way.

Russ's official Police officer photo.

Russ received several commendations during his career. He was Las Vegas Police Officer of the Year in 1988. In 1995 he received the Las Vegas Metro Police Department Community Service Award, and, in 1996, the Las Vegas Chamber of Commerce Community Service Award.

Russ spent part of his career field training new officers. This involved taking an officer through "real life" situations for several months, teaching them to react quickly by putting their police academy training into action. They trained with several veteran officers, spending one month with each.

Recently, Russ learned that one of his star trainees, now a seasoned officer, had been killed in the line of duty by an extremely troubled young man. When Russ heard the news, his first thought was, "If someone had been able to get that young man to a place like Yellowstone early in his life, maybe this tragedy could have been avoided, and I wouldn't have lost my good friend."

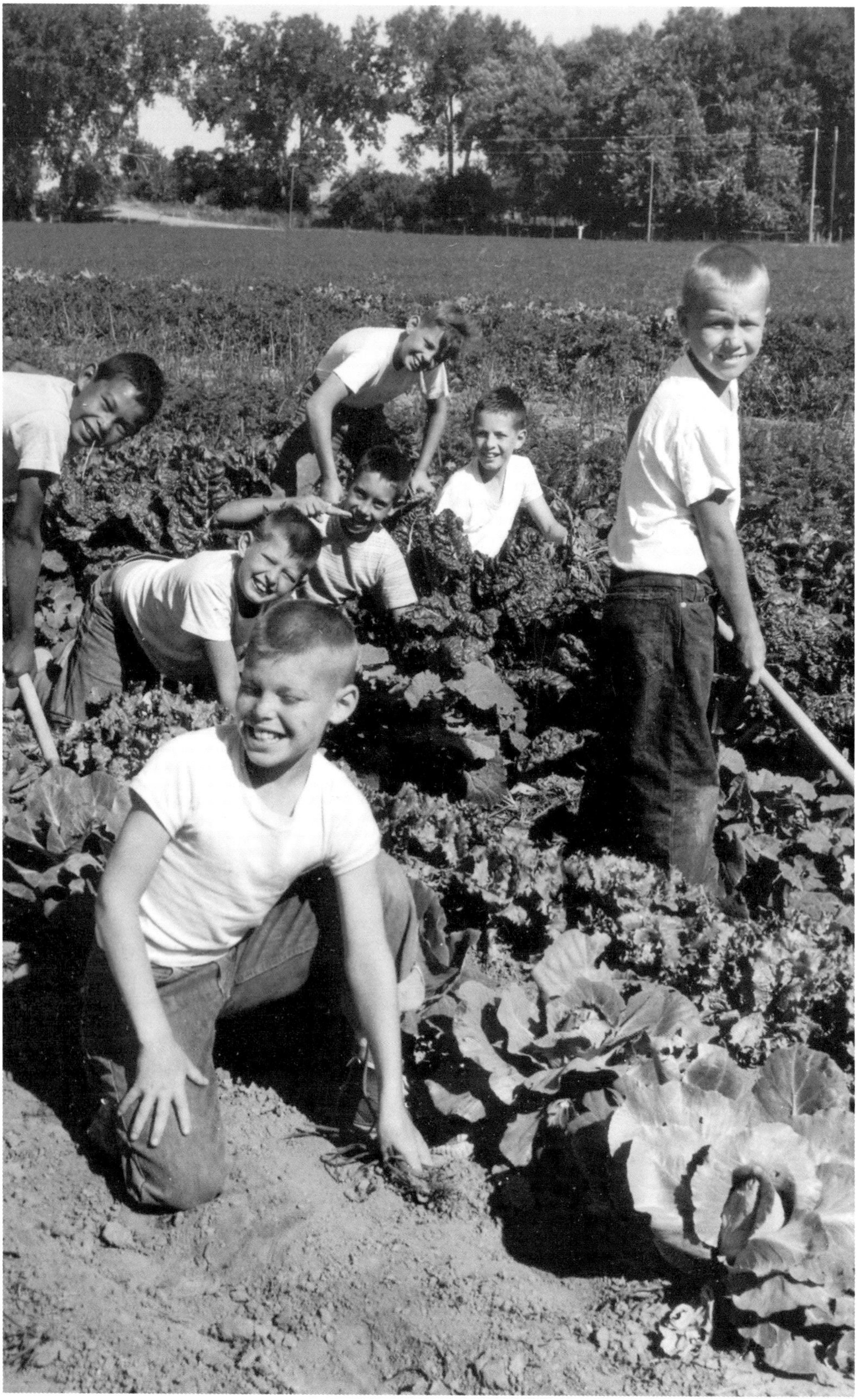

CHAPTER FOUR

An Evolving Program

As more and more boys came to the Ranch, we were increasingly challenged to translate our ideals into practical activities and programs that could help these boys work through and move beyond the problems that had brought them to us in the first place.

I explained this challenge in one of the early annual reports to our Board:

> "Yellowstone Boys Ranch is not only the name of a corporation, for with it are identified a group of people who have taken upon themselves the moral obligation of sharing in the eternal destiny of other human beings, namely the boys both big and little, who have been placed in our care.
>
> "Not only do these dependent children look to us for daily bread, clothing, and shelter, but from us, too, they must also receive the parental teaching and guidance, both social and spiritual, which one day will help them to take their place in the world as good Christian citizens.
>
> "As a Board, we have been drawn together, not by

desire for personal gain or prestige, but by a common concern for brokenhearted little boys whose desperate plight was dark indeed until we stepped into their lives."

Filling the Rest of Their Day

One important thing to remember about the first few years of the Ranch is that we did not have a school on our property as we do today. Our on-campus school, known years later as Yellowstone Academy, came along soon enough. But back then, the boys we took in attended Elder Grove School, about a mile away.

In those days, mornings would start with Bob rousing sleeping boys from the bunkhouse and guiding them to a steaming hot breakfast cooked by Bob's wife, Doris. After breakfast, Doris would pack a lunch for each boy, and Bob would drive them to school. When they got back to the Ranch after school, they would begin ranch chores, recreational fun and games, and other activities that filled up afternoons and evenings until bedtime.

Each evening, when our ever-growing Ranch family gathered around a big table for dinner, Bob—and later Carl Orth—would perform the role of father for this rowdy, but, mostly respectful assembly of young boys.

Bob recently described the operating philosophy that was at the core of his interaction with the boys:

"We tried to put together a program of activities that mirrored God's plan for human life, including the body, the mind, the heart, and the soul," he said. "The Ranch was filling the role of parents for these boys—a role that had been sadly lacking in most cases—so that we could help them be all that God meant them to be."

I can appreciate the plight of boys who never had the benefit of parental involvement in their lives. That's because I had good, compassionate parents who guided me and drew out the positive things within me that might not have been developed without their concern.

The "Big Ditch" running through the Ranch property provided hours of fun on hot summer days.

My own parents encouraged me to reach high. When I told them about my dreams and ambitions, they supported me rather than dragging me down. Sadly, many of the boys at the Ranch never had a mother or father who prayed over them, or tried to bring out the best in them, or lovingly disciplined them, or spoke to them over dinner. But Bob, Carl, and the others who came to work at the Ranch did that, becoming substitute parents for these boys.

"Much of it consisted in finding activities that were of interest to the typical rebellious adolescent," said Bob. "We just took each boy as he was and worked with him to make things better. And for most of these boys, the only way to go was up.

"The fact that we were on a big ranch gave us plenty of raw material to work with. There were numerous opportunities for recreational activities, including organized team sports as well as 'unorganized' activities like climbing trees, fishing in a creek, swimming in the big irrigation ditch that ran through our property, and playing softball in a corner of an open field.

"But this being a working ranch, there were also limitless chores to do, including everything from gardening, to caring for the animals, to helping out in the kitchen, to lending a hand on all the various construction projects that always seemed to be underway."

The activities varied from day to day and from season to season, but the goals of these activities were always the same. We wanted the boys to work together rather than fighting each other. We wanted them to learn to receive direction and guidance from others rather than resisting and rebelling against anything that seemed to encroach on their distorted sense of personal freedom. And we wanted them to learn skills and social graces that would help them survive and thrive once they left the Ranch.

The Ranch staff took advantage of every opportunity to seize "teachable moments" as they arose. And no matter how fast our numbers grew, we always tried to maintain the kind of warm and affectionate family atmosphere that meant so much to the boys who had never known this kind of love before.

Testing from a Troublemaker

Many of the boys we worked with in those early years were basically good kids who had gone off the track somewhere along the way. But you wouldn't say that about Steve, who was the sixth boy at the Ranch. Steve was an ornery, cantankerous, rebellious youngster who was sent to us by a juvenile officer who wanted to test our resolve.

Steve was a street-wise kid who grew up in a contentious, chaotic home with virtually no parental supervision. He began hanging out on the street when he was seven, and by the time he came to the Ranch at age twelve he already had a dozen episodes of petty crime on his arrest record. If Steve hadn't come to the Ranch he would have gone to an industrial school like the ones where I had visited boys in the past.

The police officer who sent Steve to us was a cynic who didn't think very much of so-called "do-gooders" like us at the Ranch. The officer was convinced we were in over our heads when it came to working with troubled kids, and he felt certain Steve would help us come to our senses.

I went to the judicial hearing where Steve was sentenced to spend time at the Ranch. It was the first time I had met Steve, and as I tried to impress on him the importance of the fact that he had been given a second chance, all he could do was make faces and mimic the judge.

Steve was supposed to arrive at the Ranch the next day, but he didn't show up. Instead, he had somehow eluded the police and hopped a freight train. They tracked him down in Helena, 225 miles away. When he finally arrived at the Ranch he was hungry and sick with a bad case of the flu. His face looked like that of a ghost hidden under a swirling mass of tangled red hair.

Steve immediately brought a new level of chaos to the Ranch. When Bob invited Steve to join a group of boys he was taking to a Sunday morning service at a nearby church, Steve said, "Hell, no. I ain't goin' to no church meeting!"

"That's okay," said Bob. "We won't force you to go."

Instead, Steve had his eyes set on riding one of two new burros that had been donated to the Ranch by Dick Logan, a rancher after whom the Billings airport was later named.

When Dick made his gift to us, he owned four burros. Two had been broken to ride, but the other two hadn't been and were still wild. They all looked so much alike that when Bob went to get our two, he mistakenly got one of each instead of getting the two who were tame. Wouldn't you know, the burro Steve chose to ride that Sunday morning was the wild one.

After a very brief ride Steve was thrown into the air, landing with a thud on the ground. The fall broke his arm. When Bob returned home from church with the other boys, Doris was caring for Steve.

As Bob explains, "Our slogan says, 'IT SURE MAKES A DIFFER-

Steve was a troublemaker who finally met his match in a wild burro.

ENCE WHEN YOU KNOW SOMEBODY CARES!' And in Steve's case we were certainly being put to the test. We had demonstrated this from the moment he arrived. Now we were helping him nurse a broken arm."

Steve finally acknowledged how much people like Bob and Carl cared for him, and, in time, he decided to receive that affection instead of fight it, and even return it as well as he could.

"I think that as long as there's life, there's hope," Bob told me recently. "No matter how bad off a kid is, he can turn around."

Steve certainly turned his life around. Before leaving the Ranch he graduated from high school. Then it was off to Vietnam with the U. S. Marines, where he survived a dangerous tour of duty. When he came back to Montana, Steve decided to attend college. He had his G.I. Bill funding, and we made a contribution from our modest Scholarship Fund.

He graduated from Eastern Montana College in Billings (now Montana State University–Billings) with a double major in history and psychology, took two more years to get a master's degree in psychology, and settled down in nearby Hardin, Montana, where he worked as the school psychologist and director of Special Ed in the local public school. After fifteen years in the school system, Steve resigned and established his own private practice as a mental health provider and school psychologist. After receiving further schooling and more credentials, he became the first registered play therapist in Montana. He recently completed a two-year postgraduate program in neuropsychology, and is currently working on his doctorate program in clinical psychology.

I visited Steve in Hardin recently, and he talked about being the only member of his family to even get to college. He said wonderful things about what the Boys Ranch meant to him.

I also caught up with the juvenile officer who years earlier had sent Steve our way. He no longer thought of the Ranch as a bunch of naïve, pie-in-the-sky do-gooders. And over the next few decades, officials in Montana, Wyoming, and other states would send us some of their worst kids, hopeful that if anybody could turn their young lives around, we could.

Counsel from a Wise Doctor

Our programs continued to evolve at the Ranch as we received many new boys, including some who had serious emotional problems. One especially troubled young lad frightened our staff so badly that we later adopted new procedures for assessing anyone who was referred to us.

Kip came from a broken and troubled home in western Montana. After his father deserted the family, his mother quickly remarried an angry and temperamental man who murdered Kip's mom before turning his gun on himself in an act of suicide.

Kip witnessed this carnage firsthand. When he came to the Ranch he was loaded full of troubles that were too deep and too destructive for us to clearly see. At first Kip seemed to get along great with the other boys, even joining the chapel choir we had at the Ranch.

But Kip was a ticking time bomb, and one day he exploded. He broke down, spent hours crying and screaming. He kept sobbing and asking, "Why didn't I bump his arm? Why didn't I make him miss?" As he acted out his anger and grief, he put himself, the other boys, and our staff at risk.

We placed a call to Dr. Donald Harr, a Billings psychiatrist, who evaluated Kip and referred him to a psychiatric treatment center in California where he could get the kind of help he needed. Then he gave us a sober warning:

"Kip is a very troubled boy, but he's not the only one," said Dr. Harr. "There are more boys in the juvenile justice system who are just like him, and you need to develop a way to assess the kinds of boys you are getting."

Dr. Harr could clearly see how we were feeling our way along with the more deeply emotionally disturbed youth, and he willingly provided medical assessments, training and consultation. However, his busy private practice prevented him from giving us all the help we really needed.

Nevertheless, we were challenged to begin thinking about

Psychiatrist Donald Harr (seated left) met with Ranch leadership to discuss procedures for assessing the needs of deeply troubled youngsters.

ways the Ranch's programs would need to evolve even more in the future if they were going to offer significant help to deeply troubled boys like Kip.

Better assessment of new arrivals was surely part of what was needed, but that would require staff with additional skills plus secure facilities for long-term care–all of which would require additional funding.

Transformed Lives

**Rubin Ackerman:
A "Love" Story**

Rubin's dad was the primary influence in his early life, and he was a good one. "Dad was a pretty strict disciplinarian," Rubin remembers. "He kept us in line, and we had a good home life. My mom was not in the picture, though."

When Rubin's dad died, Rubin and his older brother were sent to live with their mother, and things didn't go so well. "There was lots of alcohol abuse; lots of people in and out of the house. Consequently, we just lost control of ourselves. With no one there to keep an eye on us, we pretty much came and went as we pleased."

For two boys, twelve and fourteen, that meant skipping school. Before long, their truancy came to the attention of the authorities, and Rubin's older brother was referred to Yellowstone. Rubin followed soon after.

Rubin dancing at a pow-wow.

"At the Ranch, I was finally able to have a normal childhood," says Rubin. Being on a work crew taught him accountability, promptness, and how to do a job right. At chapel Rubin learned that God loved him and had a plan for his life. He also remembers Mrs.

Baker and her etiquette class. "It seemed kind of silly at the time," he says, "but I learned things like table manners, which fork to use when, and to stand when a lady came into the room."

Rubin is grateful for the many wonderful staff whose patience and compassion touched him, but landscaper Joe Love had a particularly strong influence. He had several pretty daughters who would come out with him on weekends to ride horses. That definitely caught the attention of the boys!

There was a lot more to Joe than his pretty daughters, though. After Rubin left the Ranch, he spent quite a few years "sewing wild oats." Whenever he got in trouble or needed to talk, Joe and his wife Jerry were there for Rubin. "It didn't matter what time of night it was; if I called or rang the doorbell, they would take time to listen."

Joe and Jerry's strong faith helped them have a heart of compassion toward Rubin. They say, "When someone's down and out, that's when you have to help them. Rubin had spent a lot of time with our family as a teenager, and the influence rubbed off."

Daughter Jody remembers, "When I was growing up, I was always kind of outside the circle of my older siblings. When Rubin was dating my older sister I always wanted to be the chaperone, just so I could be around him. And I'd go out to the Ranch with my dad on Saturdays, hoping to catch a glimpse of him."

Years later Rubin returned to Billings to attend college and realized Jody had grown into a beautiful young woman. They spent a lot of time together and knew there was an attraction, but didn't want to admit it.

It was especially difficult for Joe and Jerry. Rubin was pretty heavily involved in drugs and alcohol, and they feared for the hard life Jody would have if she and Rubin married. "We loved Rubin," Joe says, "but we felt he would have to come back to the spiritual commitments he'd made at the Ranch if he were ever to have a chance at overcoming his family's strong history with alcohol and drug abuse."

Torn as Jody was by her parents' concern, she had been praying for Rubin for many years and felt God had given her a "vision" of what they could accomplish as a couple among his Native American people. So, they married, without her parents' blessing.

For the first couple of years, Joe and Jerry's reservations were valid. "When I look back now," Rubin says, "I remember that when I got in trouble, my mom would come and see me. Bad attention was better than no attention. It was one way I could get her to pay attention to me." Rubin does not excuse his behavior. He takes full responsibility for the bad choices he made, but feels he now has an understanding of the false reasoning alcoholics will use to justify their behavior.

Soon after Rubin and Jody's first child was born, father-in-law Joe and Rubin agreed that Rubin should go away for a while. He needed to learn to take care of himself and his own issues before he could be a faithful dad and husband. Rubin left for a time and finally hit bottom. "At my lowest point I had decided that suicide would end my and everyone else's misery. It was at that point, November 7, 1985, when the Lord miraculously delivered me. He removed all my addictions to drugs and alcohol and gave me back my life."

"While Rubin was gone, I began attending Al Anon," says Jody. "I'd had no exposure to alcoholism growing up and knew I needed to learn about this disease." The timing was perfect. When Rubin returned home, Jody was ready to use tough love to help him rise

Rubin with his family today. Jody (back left), Randy Jo (back right), Elisha (front left) and Yasha (front right). Not pictured: Wesley, Dustin, Marquita, Karen and Rubin, Jr.

above the habits that had sent him back to drinking in the past.

Rubin and his family now live in Wolf Point, Montana. Rubin works as a resident supervisor at the Spotted Bull Treatment Center for Youth Drug and Alcohol Rehabilitation on the Fort Peck Indian Reservation.

Jody is the administrative director for the Boys and Girls Club of Fort Peck where Rubin also mentors children. They are both involved in leadership positions at their church and volunteer to help raise funds for their local Annual Tribal Pow-wow. In 2006, Rubin will serve as the headman dancer at the Pow-wow in Wolf Point, held the first weekend in August.

When asked how he blends his Indian heritage with Christian faith, Rubin says, "I just pray about each activity as it comes up. If I feel the Lord says it's okay, I participate; and if I feel He's saying 'no,' I don't. People here know what I stand for. They respect my beliefs, and I don't try to pressure anyone."

Rubin and his mom were able to experience a full reconciliation before she passed away. "She had carried a lot of guilt for many years," he says. "My own struggles helped me to understand her addictions, and we had great conversations where we were able to forgive each other for the ways we had hurt each other deeply."

Rubin and Jody now have a wonderful relationship with her family. Rubin calls Joe "Dad," and Joe considers Rubin his true son. Since no family attended their first wedding, Rubin and Jody celebrated their ninth anniversary by renewing their vows with all the family present. They hope to celebrate their twenty-fifth in 2008 at Yellowstone Boys and Girls Ranch, where the adventure began.

Being a dad is one of the most important things in Rubin's life. Rubin has four children with Jody and four from previous relationships. Jody has embraced all his children as part of their family. "How can I deny him the desire to be a dad to all his kids when he realizes how important the influence of a dad is?" she says.

Rubin has brought each of his children back to the Ranch to show them where he was finally able to have a home and childhood.

Rubin and Jody have a strong relationship and a ministry that Jody had prayed for years ago. Rubin's only explanation for why he is alive and doing so well today is, "God never let go of me! And He gave me a strong, wonderful woman with whom to share my life."

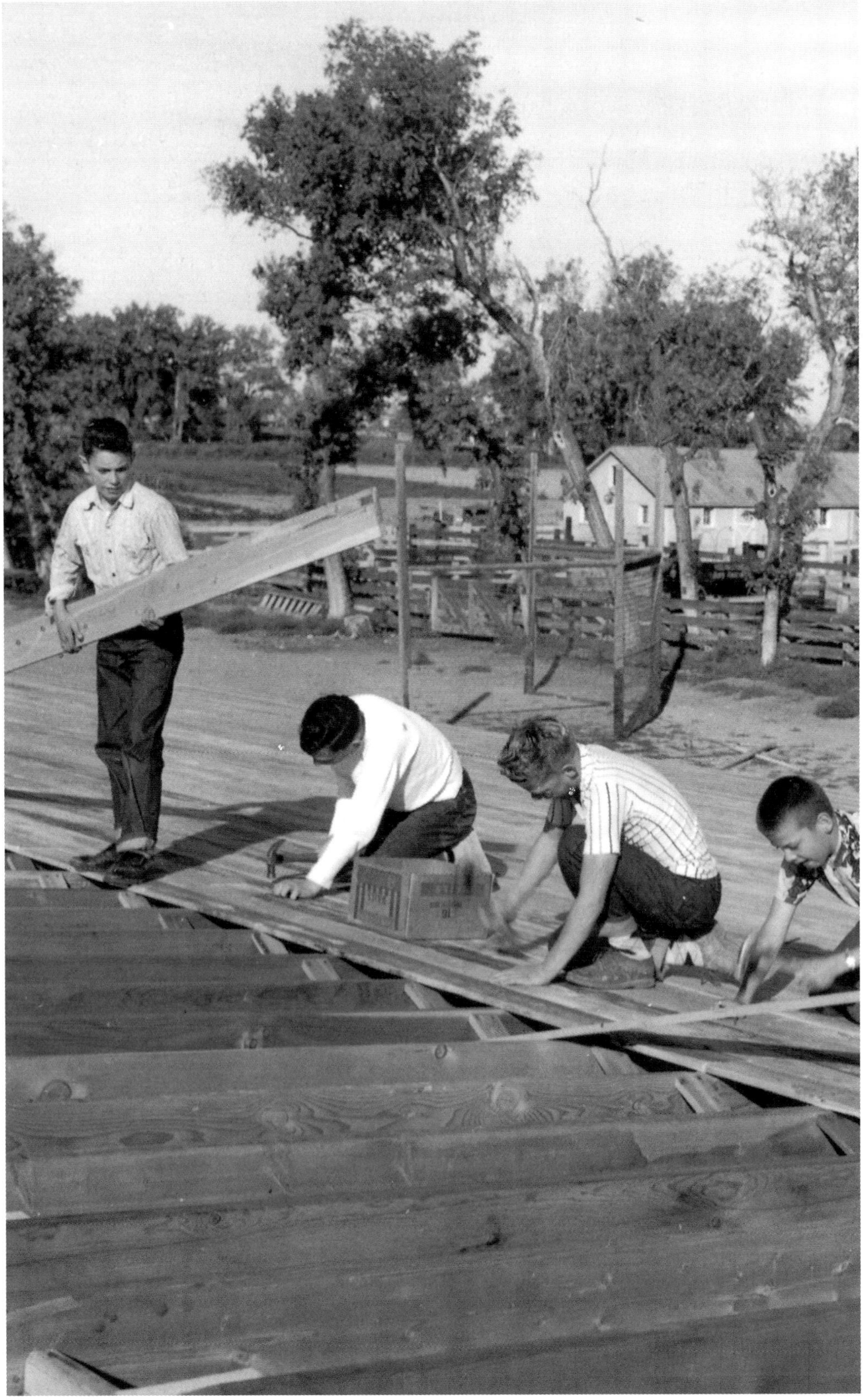

CHAPTER FIVE

Adventures in Fund-Raising

Thanks to the wisdom of our Board and the skill and commitment of staff members like Bob McFarlane and Carl Orth, the day-to-day operation of the Ranch was in good hands. This meant I could turn my full attention to raising the funds needed to keep the Ranch running. There was a growing payroll to meet and bigger stacks of bills to pay. And government agencies were sending more boys to the Ranch, necessitating another round of campus expansion.

Raising money for the Ranch was a heavy burden on my shoulders during its first three decades. We were not supported financially by any institution, organization, or religious denomination. As a result, we would sink or swim on our own. This meant we had to give high priority to attracting and winning the loyalty of kindhearted friends who cared deeply about troubled kids, and could be persuaded to become repeat, long-time donors.

Some people have the gift of preaching. Some have the gift of making beautiful music. These were not my strong points, but when I sat down with a donor and explained what the Ranch needed, or wrote about our needs in solicitation letters, I was able to convey our needs in ways that brought us both short-term support for current projects and long-term friends who would help us repeatedly through the years.

Tips from a Pro

I received some of my earliest lessons in fund-raising from Bob Pierce, the man who founded World Vision, which is now one of the largest relief and development organizations in the world.

During my days with Youth for Christ I invited Bob to speak at some of our YFC rallies in Montana. On one occasion we had to drive from a rally in Great Falls to the next night's rally 250 miles away in Kalispell. A heavy snowstorm didn't make the long drive any easier.

It took all night to reach Kalispell through the blowing and

Bob Pierce, the founder of Christian relief and development agency World Vision, spoke at our Youth for Christ Rallies and shared his tips on fundraising with me.

drifting snow, but along the way Bob helped me understand some of the basic principles of fund-raising he had used so effectively.

"I'll tell you the formula for writing a successful fund-raising letter," he said. "It boils down to three things: project, price tag, and deadline." He went on to say, "the project, which must be described in adequate detail, becomes the obvious reason for writing the letter. The price tag covers bottom line costs, with discount or challenge grant or completion grant advantages, enthusiastically described. And the deadline includes time limits on challenge grants and suggests urgency related to completing the entire project."

He then concluded by saying, "My best letters also included language which suggested an immediate or at least a very prompt response and I always included a postage paid, self addressed reply envelope."

I put this simple but effective formula to use hundreds of times during the coming years, raising crucially needed funds and establishing an important communication link with many donor friends. Whether we needed a new lodge for another dozen boys or a new fire truck to protect the Ranch in case of fire, this approach for communicating with our donors enjoyed consistent and encouraging success.

For example, in July of 1958 construction on a new lodge had come to a standstill due to lack of funds. I told our small but growing family of donors about this crisis and asked for their help:

> For the past nine months we have been working very hard to complete our new lodge to make room for another 32 boys…but two weeks ago we had to suspend construction due to a lack of building funds. It has been somewhat of a heartbreak for all of us, but the hardest part, I think, is breaking the news to eight new

boys we had promised to take in July...

If we can raise $10,000 in the next three weeks, we can still finish our new lodge before school starts and maybe save these boys from reform school.

Having explained the project (construction of the new lodge), I moved on to the completion price tag (a final $10,000) and the deadline ("the next three weeks").

Photos could help make the case for support. There were plenty of photos of buildings under construction, as well as photos of the finished projects, which we used to thank those who had made contributions.

Another letter from 1958 encouraged new, first-time donors to send the Ranch one dollar. That amount sounds ridiculously low today, but back then when postage stamps cost only 3 cents, every dollar mattered:

"On behalf of some problem boys who cannot speak for themselves, may I ask—'Will you help us complete our new lodge with a gift of JUST ONE DOLLAR?'"

The goal was two-fold: generating immediate cash flow to complete that desperately needed first new lodge, but also to solicit first-time gifts from new donors so we could thank them warmly, send them the next issue of the *Wrangler*, and, in due time, encourage them to give again for future projects.

We sent out thousands of letters like this one to donors and potential donors. Plus, I was on the road nonstop visiting individuals and business owners whose giving potential was substantially more than a dollar. As we will see in a later chapter, some of these bigger donors are now memorialized in the names of buildings all over the Ranch campus.

Telling Our Story

In addition to the three-step formula for fund-raising I had learned from Bob Pierce, there was another three-step formula we employed for communicating about Ranch happenings in the *Wrangler*.

Early editions of the *Wrangler* informed our friends and supporters about our growth and construction projects.

The first priority was reporting on the various projects we had asked our supporters to help us with. This let them know we meant what we said when we sent out requests for funding, plus it demonstrated that we had used their money for the specific projects we had asked them about.

The second priority was sharing with supporters some of the many success stories we developed from our work with the kids at the Ranch. Such stories provided powerful evidence of the success of our work, and passing these stories on to donor friends was one way to inform them about the "return on their investment" in us.

Since most of our thousands of donors lived too far away to ever visit our campus personally, I was determined that the *Wrangler* would carry our success stories to them with pictures and happy, optimistic reporting. Our care-based approach continued to deliver powerful results with the boys, and I felt we had the responsibility to let people know about these amazing stories.

The third priority in the *Wrangler* was preparing people for what's coming next. This included describing new projects and why they were needed. We would include advance notice on challenge grants and significant material gifts (like another carload of lumber) along with bargain-price numbers on what the discounted price might be. Thus, they were better prepared for our next appeal letter.

Two Important Words

All of us like it when people thank us for something nice we have done. On the other hand, we sometimes feel unappreciated if the good things we have done are not acknowledged. Even Jesus was disappointed when only one of the ten lepers he had healed returned to thank him (Luke 17:11-19). The two words "Thank you" are very important in life, and these words have played an important role in helping the Ranch develop lifelong relationships with our many support-

A Legacy of Caring

ers and friends.

From the beginning, I was determined to do a good job of

> **Yellowstone Boys' Ranch**
> BOX 1841 · PHONE 252-5301
> Billings, Montana
>
> From the desk of
> Franklin Robbie
>
> *Just a line or two along with the enclosed receipt to say thanks so very much for your recent gift to Boys Ranch.*
>
> *These are days of special meaning for our boys and your gift helps us prove that indeed there are people who care about boys who know they have done wrong.*
>
> *We sincerely hope your Holiday Season will be a happy one in knowing you have added joy to ours.*
>
> *J. F. Robbie*

The Ranch has always appreciated donor gifts and has made a point of saying so.

saying thank you to donors, regardless of the size of the gift, because all the gifts were so vitally important! Many donors have told me how much they appreciated our thanking them for their gifts (see example, previous page). And some even said our gratefulness was a factor in increasing their giving to us.

Saying thank you in the right way meant sending an official receipt for every gift, accompanied by a warm and friendly thank-you letter reporting progress on the project to which donors had given. I also usually included other good news about how things were going with our growing family of boys.

Larger gifts often required a more comprehensive expression of gratitude. For instance, the sizeable gifts of lumber used for our new buildings often came from a dozen different lumber mills. So we took photos from the very beginning to the final completion of every project. We then selected the best photos and put together a scrapbook type report several pages long, full of pictures with brief notes of explanation where needed. It began with a warm, chatty cover letter and ended with some handwritten comments on the last page. Each was obviously a handmade original and every lumber mill that helped us got one.

Invariably, I could see the positive impact of these reports the next time I visited lumber companies who had helped us. I was often greeted warmly by an owner or manager who was quick to inform me about how he had appreciated our reports. "Over the years we've given away lots of lumber," said one owner, "but nobody has said thank you the way you folks at Yellowstone Boys Ranch do! We passed that picture thing all around the mill, and then sent it on to the headquarters office back east."

As the years went by and our campus kept growing, I went back to these and other mills for more than forty years, and my records show the donated lumber in all our buildings, corrals, and feedlots would total more than eighteen railroad carloads worth tens of thousands of dollars!

Also, taking time to answer donors' questions and telling them exciting stories about our boys always strengthened the bond between us. Visits with Leonard Hamilton, whose lumber mill was located just south of Missoula, Montana, let us know that he admired the fact that we aggressively sought out donated and discounted goods, and he was always willing to help.

When it came time to build a new staff residence on the Ranch campus, I went to Leonard first, even though he was approaching eighty years of age and hinting about retirement. Leonard gave us the lumber we needed along with a $10,000 gift we used to purchase other materials. Today the Hamilton House is where current Ranch chaplain John Jamison and his family have lived for more than twenty-five years.

One Good Thing Leads to Another

When the Carl B. & Florence E. King Foundation made a very substantial grant toward the construction of our physical education building, Mrs. King was so pleased with our personalized report on the project that she kept it on her coffee table and showed it to all her friends. Her favorite part was the action photos showing boys playing basketball or bowling or swimming in the facilities she had helped make possible.

Our "thank you" touched her so deeply that she personally paid the entire cost of a Ranch group home in Billings for older boys and paid half the construction cost of a much needed administration building on our campus. Then she also insisted that the King Foundation stay involved in other projects throughout the Ranch over the next several years.

Memorial Gifts Add Up

In the early years, memorial gifts made upon the death of a friend or loved one were our most dependable source of income. In fact, memorial gifts paid most of the construction costs on our next two lodges for boys and a substantial part of our chapel construction financing.

Many of our donors liked memorial giving because it allowed them to recognize the passing of a friend or loved one in a tangible way by making a gift to help kids. The donor's memorial gift would be promptly followed by acknowledgment cards we sent to them and to relatives of the deceased, and we published the names of the deceased and the donors in issues of the *Wrangler*.

We printed up a simple brochure listing all the benefits of memorial giving and distributed these brochures by the thousands. The results were increased giving and positive connections with hundreds of new friends and supporters.

For example, there were two brothers who lived near the Ranch. Their uncle from Minneapolis would sometimes visit us when he came to town. When he passed away, his nephews each gave $5 memorials in his name. After his widow received our acknowledgement cards, information about our work and a copy of the *Wrangler*, she wrote back requesting more back issues of the *Wrangler*.

We added her name to the *Wrangler* mailing list but didn't hear from her until we received notice that we had been mentioned in her will. Her remarkable bequest of more than $50,000 came to the Ranch long after we had received her husband's memorial gifts, but in this case one gift inspired another.

A Solution to Overload

As the Ranch grew, the efforts to fund it grew, too. In time I became increasingly burdened by the amount of work required to keep the income flowing. I began looking for an assistant or understudy who could help share the load. Little did I know that the search would lead me straight to my own twenty-two-year-old son, Wesley Franklin Robbie.

Our son Wes was ten when I moved the family to Billings to launch the Ranch, and for much of his youth our evening dinner conversation focused on financing the Ranch. Then I would often head back to the office to research and write more appeal letters or spend a weekend putting together another *Wrangler*. By the time Wes graduated from high school, he was understandably overdosed on the Ranch. He headed for college at Montana State University in Bozeman, determined to get a degree in General Business and prepare for a career in life insurance.

But the sudden death of a close family friend in Vietnam changed Wes's perspective on life. All of a sudden he took a different view of his dad's commitment to human services, and asked me, "Where can I go to graduate school to learn how to do what you do?" We decided together that the best way for him to learn was to become my "shadow," working alongside me and picking up what he could.

With the full approval of the Board, Wes was hired on a trial basis and began helping me with the heavy load of funding the Ranch. In time, Wes learned to do everything I did: writing the appeal letters, preparing the reports to donors, and writing and editing the *Wrangler*.

During the thirty-three years he worked with us he also made many improvements in our procedures, increasing the effectiveness of our appeal letters by adding compelling details, securing new mailing lists that enabled us to find new donors, and taking photos of

Wes Robbie was introduced to the Ranch family of donors in 1972.

Ranch activities so he could prepare personalized project reports for major donors. He also took over the daily routine of managing our business office. This enabled me to spend much more time on the road meeting with donors and developing solutions to our long-term income challenges.

One benefit of my having more time to travel was explaining to cattle ranchers how their livestock gifts helped us in several ways. Not only did they put meat on the table for our growing family, but extra animals would also go to our feedlot to be cared for by our older boys and then to market as a "cash crop" to help the budget. When ranchers understood this, hundreds of them gave a calf every year for several years in a row!

And the most amazing and rewarding benefit came years later when an occasional ranch couple would decide to will their entire ranch to us. We would sell the ranch, adding the proceeds to our Endowment Fund. The income from this fund is used for the care of hurting boys and girls needing our treatment.

A Blessing Bestowed

We have always insisted that all our fund-raising efforts be honest and ethical. We don't lie to donors about what we need or how we spend their money. This leads to the kind of trust that is impossible to buy.

Hard work, generous friends, and God's continuing blessings have made it possible for us to keep paying the bills at the Ranch, thus enabling the people who work there to fulfill our ultimate mission: to help troubled kids.

Transformed Lives

**Vince Wagner:
Kick-Starting a Life**

When nine-year-old Vince Wagner arrived at Yellowstone, nobody predicted he would go on to successful stints with the Minnesota Vikings and Seattle Seahawks, become the owner of several successful businesses, end up with an incredible wife and family, and give back to his community in meaningful ways.

"I remember the day he arrived," says Dan Hansen, who along with his wife Sharon were Vince's houseparents in Paul Stock Lodge. "He was a wild-eyed little guy who couldn't communicate much and was obviously bewildered by his new surroundings."

Vince showing Rubin Ackerman (story page 86) and others the proper technique for holding a football.

Sharon Hansen remembers, "His adoptive mother dropped him off at the Ranch. She revealed a lot about what his home life had been like when she told him to go with me to check out his new room before saying good-bye. When Vince and I returned, she had left without even a word of comfort or farewell!"

His official placement at Yellowstone had come through his school district. They just couldn't handle him any longer. Vince was disruptive in school, picking fights on the playground and creating havoc in the classroom. What he needed was a more structured environment and more individualized attention than his school was able to provide.

The special education program at Yellowstone Academy was just right for Vince. He'd never fallen behind his grade level and was a capable student, but emotionally he was too splintered to succeed in a regular school. Once Vince settled into the structure, schedule, and security of Ranch life, his behavior at school straightened out, giving him time and attention for his passion: sports.

"I remember pleading with the other boys to play any sport with me. It didn't matter whether it was playing catch, shooting hoops, or throwing a football," Vince recalls. "I just lived to have a ball in my hands."

The Ranch provided as many sports opportunities as it could for

Kicking in a Vikings game.

athletically inclined boys through Little League and intramurals. Vince thrived in this environment, training hard and playing hard. He was coached by several Ranch staff members who in their own ways built character into Vince's life.

"By the time I was in high school, I knew that sports and education were going to be my ticket to a better life," says Vince. "I went to public high school in Billings, but Boys Ranch kids weren't exactly the most popular kids in school. We were dubbed 'the convicts' and other even more derogatory terms."

Vince harbors no bitterness. In fact he is especially proud of his Boys Ranch upbringing. But it meant another hurdle he had to overcome. No colleges were looking at him. He had to pursue them.

The Hansens were instrumental in urging Vince to apply to Northwestern College in Minneapolis. Football Coach Mel Boehland was willing to give Vince a chance to prove himself. The rest, as they say, is history. Vince became a star player, earning several MVP awards and helping his team win three conference titles and one small college title during his four years on the team.

He was drafted by the Minnesota Vikings and kicked a 51-yard field goal against the Washington Redskins at RFK stadium in Washington, D.C., during the second preseason game of his rookie year in 1981. At the time it was the second longest field goal in the Vikings' history.

Vince with "Dad" Dan Hansen at Vikings training camp.

Vince thought he had it made. "I wanted to be the star all little boys look up to," he says. But competition from other kickers and injuries resulted in his being traded back and forth between the Vikings, Seahawks, Buccaneers, and Oilers over the next five years. After experiencing the devastation of being the last player cut at training camp more than once, Vince finally accepted the fact that a long football career was not in his future.

"Every time I got released from a team it was awfully painful. I'd worked so hard and had overcome so many hurts. I couldn't understand why God was allowing more disappointment in my life. I became bitter and angry."

Vince wandered for several years and made lots of poor choices. He landed in Tacoma, Washington, working hard, but at a dead end.

The turning point came one day when he woke up, looked in the mirror and didn't like what he saw. "You're going nowhere!" Vince said to himself. "Do you want to be a husband, and father? Do you want to own a business and a home someday? You're not going to do it this way. Straighten up, get yourself back on track spiritually, and get on with your life!"

Signing autographs.

Yellowstone and the Hansens had laid the foundation. His mentors at Northwestern had built upon it. The work ethic, discipline, and spiritual instruction Vince had received through the years brought him back to building the life he'd always wanted.

Vince met his wife, Patti, while playing on a coed softball team. She was a single mom with three children who needed the love and guidance Vince had learned how to give through the role models he'd observed at the Ranch. They have since added two beautiful daughters to their family. "I don't know where I'd be today without Patti," says Vince. "She and my five children are the light of my life."

With his quick mind and commitment to integrity and hard work, Vince has achieved success in several small businesses in Tacoma.

He is also the co-founder and executive director of Defender of the Faith Ministries (DOTFM), whose motto is Upholding & Defending the Values of Faith, Family & Freedom.

His passion for sports continues. He's been offered a number of coaching positions over the years, but has elected to coach at a small Christian high school that not only competes, but wins, against teams from schools three times its size.

"It's sort of like David playing against Goliath," Vince quips. He adds that it's a great opportunity to pass on the life lessons he's learned. "I tell my players, don't waste your valuable time and energy blaming others if things don't go the way you'd hoped. Instead, dare to believe in yourself and be bold enough to prepare for the certain challenges you will face. And when new opportunities come, expect results!"

Vince feels he's a much more effective coach for having gone through the disappointments he's had in life. "Yellowstone seemed like an easy way out for my adoptive parents. They pretty much left me on the doorstep. But it turned out to be the best thing that ever happened to me."

Today, Vince considers the Hansens his real family. Dan and Sharon take great joy in seeing the changes in his life from the "wild-eyed" little boy who blasted through the front gate at Yellowstone Boys Ranch back in 1969. On a recent visit in Tacoma, they accompanied Vince to football practice.

When a young player began asking Vince about his pro days, Vince replied, "That's not important right now. What's important is how you're doing."

That's quite a change, from the young man who wanted to be everyone's hero, to the mature man who now cares more about developing character in the lives of the next generation!

With wife Patti, and daughters Jazzlyn and Kaleah. Children Brent, Mindy and Hillary are grown.

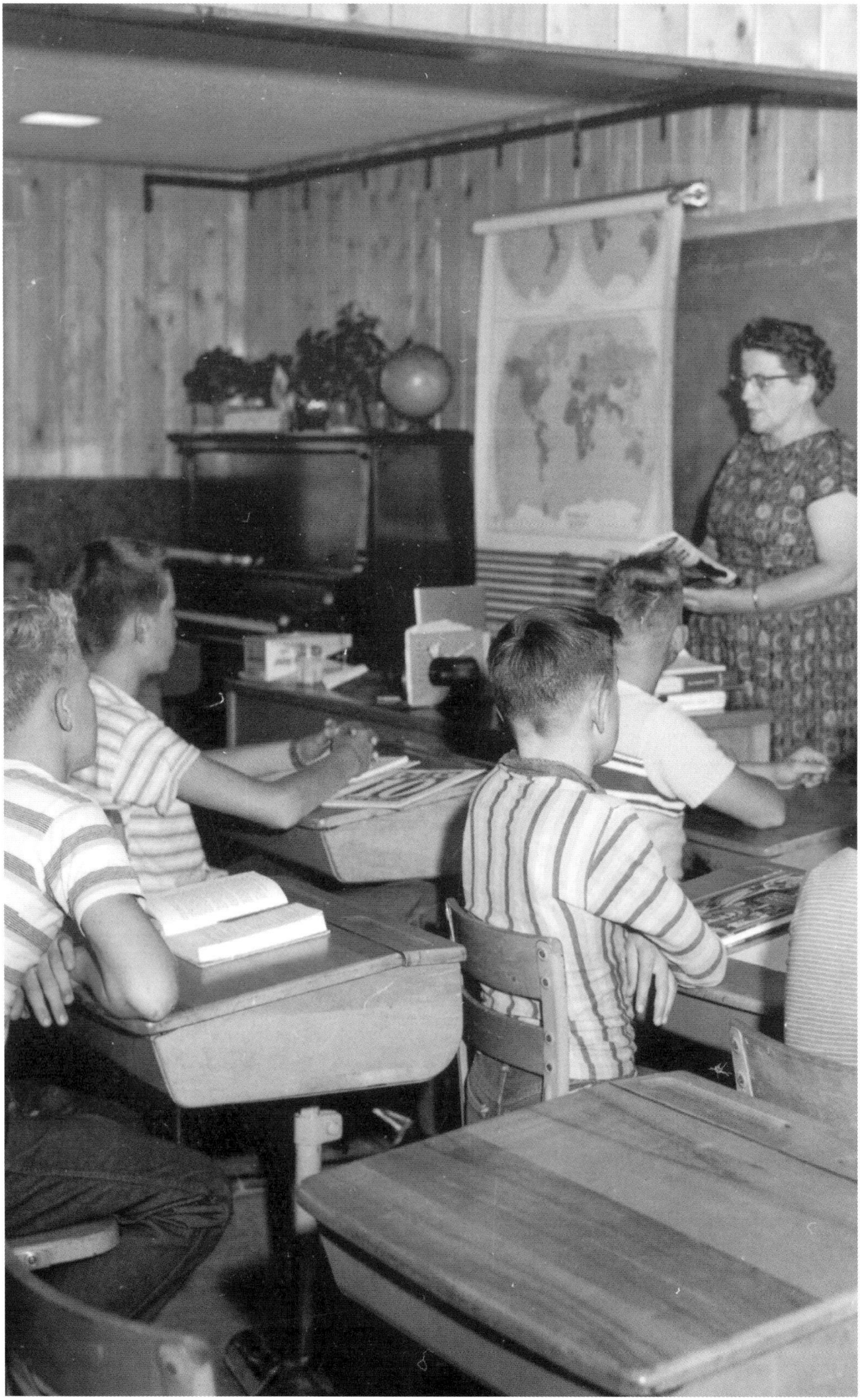

CHAPTER SIX

School Days

It makes a big difference how young people are schooled. The years kids spend in school do more than show how well students do in traditional academic subjects like reading, writing, and arithmetic. They also indicate how well these young people may do in the future as they develop careers and start families.

We knew from the very beginning that education would play a significant role at the Ranch. But, in those early years, we were focused on issues like recruiting staff, constructing buildings, and developing programs and activities that would help boys during the hours they weren't in school.

Getting the Ranch off the ground and ensuring its success and survival were difficult tasks that took all our energies. During this embryonic period we were largely content to let nearby public schools educate the boys.

But our rapid growth in the 1960s forced us to rethink these assumptions. In 1963 Bob McFarlane welcomed the hundredth boy to the Ranch. Not only were we taking care of more boys every year, but also the kinds of boys we were working with were changing in significant ways.

Bob McFarlane welcomed the 100th boy to the Ranch in 1963, but with growth came demands for the Ranch to develop its own educational programs.

    As we saw in an earlier chapter, some of our new arrivals had longer arrest records or more destructive psychological troubles than originally anticipated. Nevertheless, we were more than willing to receive these boys, and were committed to helping them turn their lives around.

    But it quickly became evident that not all of our neighbors were as excited as we were about our working with these "bad" boys. Apprehension only increased when these neighbors' own school-aged children sat across the aisle from these Ranch boys in English class. In time, some came to feel that our boys were interfering with the education of their own children.

    We were committed to being good neighbors. After all, we were the new folks on the block.

    So instead of turning a deaf ear to local residents or fighting back, we listened to their concerns, and began the process of accelerating our plans to establish our own school on the Ranch.

In the long run, we discovered that by running our own school we could actually do a better job of educating our kids than the local schools, which struggled to teach Ranch kids in ways that effectively addressed their unique educational and emotional challenges.

Finding a Win-Win Solution

Early on our elementary-aged boys attended Elder Grove School, which was located about a mile down the road from us, while the older boys attended junior high and high school in Billings.

In June 1960 a boy named Robert became the first Ranch boy to graduate from high school in Billings. Robert, who had lived with us for two and a half years, proudly wore his cap and gown at graduation ceremonies before starting a summer job at Eddy's Bakery in Helena and then attending Carroll College there the following fall.

Robert's graduation was the first of many celebrated at the Ranch, but we still wanted to move ahead with starting our own school. In part, this was because we were sending more than a dozen boys to Elder Grove, which was a large number for such a small rural school.

Progress had been made in 1959 when the Ranch's license from the State of Montana was changed from a foster home license to a child care license. This now meant that boys were seen as legal residents of the Ranch and thus entitled to an education at local schools.

I began making frequent trips to Helena to talk with education officials in the state government about what we should do. One possibility was that we give money to Elder Grove so the school could expand its buildings and program. The school board eventually vetoed that idea. There were other ideas, too, that did not work out due to a variety of logistical problems.

We had promised our neighbors we would do something, so in the fall of 1959 we gathered together a bunch of antique school desks that had been rescued from an old, abandoned schoolhouse. We set them up in what had been the recreation area at the end of the boys' lodge, hired Mr. Harold Wright as the first teacher, and officially declared grades six and seven of the new school open for business

Over the next few years, growth at the Ranch would lead us to add other grades to the school. After Mr. Wright became ill we hired a new teacher named Mrs. Dorothy Cooley. Mrs. Cooley was both firm and loving with her students, and she served our school for many years.

Before long, we were building a schoolhouse for our growing student body.

Beyond a One-Room School

The Ranch grew rapidly during the 1960s. By the fall of 1961 a new Memorial Lodge was up and running. This additional facility meant that boys who had been on a waiting list could now join us at the Ranch. It was definitely time for the Ranch to begin building its own grade school.

The expenses of teachers and other salaries at the school were covered by the various sending school districts, but the costs of building the schoolhouse were the Ranch's sole responsibility, so we began asking our supporters to help provide the necessary funds.

As usual, our supporters responded liberally, including members of the Montana Sheriffs and Peace Officers Association, who gave the Ranch a $3,000 check for building expenses. Long interested in the work of the Ranch, these law enforcement officers became more committed to us after they saw our work first-hand during a special August open house.

Others chipped in as well, including local companies that donated services and expertise on construction and heating as well as thousands of dollars worth of building supplies, which enabled us to stretch every dollar donors sent in.

By the fall of 1961 the new school building was well under way. And by 1962, fifteen boys had graduated from the eighth grade of our Ranch school program. A photo from the *Wrangler* shows thirteen of these boys at their fashionable best. Their neckties and suits are clean and crisp, and their hair is nicely combed as they stand holding their diplomas.

It was a proud moment for us, and even a prouder moment for them. But our local challenges with neighbors and school officials were not yet completely resolved.

The Birth of School District 58

The Ranch was doing more to take a greater responsibility for the education of our boys. The new schoolhouse was only four years old, but was already bursting at the seams. However, according to some people, we still weren't doing enough.

Even though we had built a school and were adding new grades as fast as possible, some of the leaders at Elder Grove complained that they were required to handle all the administrative details for our school. They didn't want to carry this burden any longer, so I began exploring new options with the legislature in Helena.

The result was a unique 1965 state law that never mentioned Yellowstone Boys Ranch but was custom-designed for us and our unique educational needs. The law made it possible for "a non-sectarian, licensed child-care institution to petition for the creation of a new elementary school district within an existing district."

That's exactly what we did. The state created a new school district for us. The headline and story on the cover in the October 1965 issue of the *Wrangler* told it all: BOYS RANCH GRANTED NEW SCHOOL DISTRICT. As far as we know, School District 58 is the only government-approved school district located on the property of a private, not-for-profit organization.

This new school district not only lifted the burden of management from the shoulders of the neighboring school district, but it also set the stage for us to develop a highly specialized school with extra help for every Boys Rancher who needed it. The district's geographical boundaries precisely matched the boundaries of the Ranch property. And as for the state law mandating that school board members of any district reside in that district, this meant that some of our own staff would be school board members of the newly created District 58.

The boys in grades four through eight now numbered thirty-six, including Ranch boys and one child of a staff member. The teachers at Boys Ranch School No. 58 were certified and approved by the County Superintendent and the State Department of Education.

From the beginning, teachers like Dorothy Cooley, Jean Ketterling, and Loren Soft were devoted to caring for our boys and were sensitive to their unique needs. Loren, who joined the Ranch staff in 1963, found more than a teaching job here. He found a life-long career.

Loren would go on to work with the Ranch for thirty-three years before retiring from his position as the Ranch's CEO in 2004 after twenty-two years in that position. He still remains very active with various projects at the Ranch as well as maintaining an involvement in numerous other not-for-profit human service agencies.

A Ranch-Style Education

Taking total responsibility for the educational needs of the Ranch boys was the best way for us to ensure they got the kind of education they most needed. After all, many of our boys had trouble with school as well as other areas of their lives. Now we could do a better job of helping them address the various issues that had held them back.

Our educational philosophy and programs have grown and

evolved over the years. Still, our current statement of educational goals is consistent with the motivations that led us to start our school in the first place:

1. Each student will develop academic skills in core subjects such as math, science, reading, writing, speaking, listening, and will be given the opportunity to work in an individualized curriculum.

2. Each student will develop habits and skills necessary to maintain optimum physical fitness and mental health.

3. Each student will learn the rights and responsibilities of citizenship while learning to live in harmony with others.

4. Each student will explore career opportunities and capabilities.

5. Each student will develop and apply standards for judging his or her own behavior.

6. Each student will acquire a positive attitude toward lifelong learning and develop intellectually, socially, emotionally, physically, and spiritually.

7. Each student will have the opportunity to be educated in an environment that will be physically and emotionally safe.

An Evolving Educational Program

Throughout the 1960s and the 1970s, we provided our supporters with updates on the evolution of the Ranch's educational programs.

For example, in 1966 we dedicated the school's new library, which contained nearly eighteen thousand books and other resources, as well as other programs introduced by new school principal, Loren Soft. One of these program offerings was a remedial reading program for those boys who needed it.

The next year, the *Wrangler* contained reports from four of the school's forty-six students about their daily activities.

"The best studies I like are math, spelling, reading, and social studies," wrote a fourth grader named Robbie, who added this comment about his non-academic interests: "Every morning I watch the time because I like recess."

By 1971 we were offering an impressive curriculum of vocational-academic classes, thanks to Ranch employees and a local school official. Harry Sawatzky, who had become principal of the school, together with Loren Soft, who was now Ranch superintendent, and William Serrette, assistant superintendent of schools for Billings, secured federal funding to purchase equipment, hire staff, and establish a vocational education program for the Ranch students.

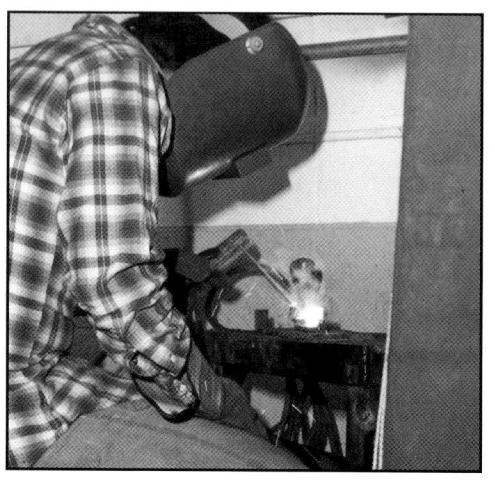

Students could take vocational classes in five different subject areas: offset printing, building trades, metal shop, drafting, and small engine repair. Over time additional courses were offered in custodial services, food services, and landscaping.

By 1972, our second year of this program, the Ranch's initial "vo-ag" courses received state accreditation. As we told our supporters at the time:

> Most of the boys referred to the Ranch have been having trouble in school in their home towns. They are usually two to three years behind their age group when they arrive at Boys Ranch. But with an individualized program and lots of personal attention from the staff, a boy is started on his way to learning new attitudes and skills.

Ranch School Gets Good Grades

The educational programs at the Ranch continued to evolve as the needs of the growing Ranch population changed over time. It was always our desire to hire staff who not only had a deep care and concern for helping troubled youth but also were well trained and had the skills needed to ensure that the services we provided were of the highest quality.

Throughout the Ranch's history, the educational component of the program has been under the leadership of people who brought specialized skills and talents to the work place which continually raised the bar for our educational programs. Leaders like Don Black, Jim Bryngleson, Ron Hatcher, Bob Western, Doug Neihart, Ken Adams and Ed Zabrocki helped to build a "school without failure" for students who had been all too familiar with failure in school prior to coming to the Ranch.

The educational programs at the Ranch continued to evolve as the needs of the growing Ranch population changed over time. One thing that has remained constant, though, is the thankfulness and support of students, parents, and educational officials who have seen our school programs up close.

"I'm so happy you made it possible for me to graduate," wrote one happy student. "I will not blow my second chance in life and education."

"I have seen such a great change in my son," wrote one parent. "It is the first time he has been successful in a classroom and received an A."

And one official whose district now sends students to our school wrote, "I don't know what our district would do with our troubled students if we didn't have access to Yellowstone."

No matter where they work, good teachers love to see their students succeed. But success is especially sweet at the Ranch, where many students who arrive to be with us already have so many strikes against them before they enter our classrooms. It's thrilling to see these troubled kids make solid academic progress while they are in our care. It's even more exciting to see them begin to take concrete steps toward future success, like the young woman who recently wrote to update us on her progress:

"I am currently attending The Art Institute of Seattle for a degree in Graphic Design," she wrote. "I will be graduating next winter....Yellowstone gave me the skills that I need in everyday life. I want to thank you for giving me a second chance—over and over again."

In 1960 Robert became the first Ranch boy to graduate from high school in Billings. Two years later more than a dozen boys "graduated" from eighth grade at the Ranch's own school.

Tyler Stephens:
Too Smart for His Own Good

Passive-aggressive (def.): behavior which expresses resentment, aggression, and attempts to control others in unassertive, passive ways such as through procrastination, sullenness, moodiness, and stubbornness. The passive-aggressive person often has a strong need to feel accepted, yet feels he cannot please the person or persons whose acceptance he craves.

This was Tyler when he arrived at Yellowstone: almost sixteen; unwilling to communicate with his parents in a civil manner; particularly anti-social at school; a brilliant, brooding adolescent who was a ticking time bomb.

Tyler's mother, Judy, explains, "Our entire family unit had broken

Tyler at Yellowstone Academy graduation with parents, Ron and Judy.

down. Tyler was extremely defiant at home, sullen and moody. He would hardly come out of his room in the basement. We knew he was having problems socializing at school, but he was not at all receptive to any suggestions we would make. Finally, a serious problem at school which brought a probation officer into the picture convinced school district officials that he needed residential treatment."

Tyler adds, "Much of my behavior toward authority figures was classic passive-aggressive – stubbornness, procrastination, and refusal to follow rules. But I definitely had anger management problems, too, and occasionally exploded into a rage. As I became more reclusive at home, what little communication I did have with my parents often ended in a shouting match."

Tyler felt that no one really understood him, and his efforts at "fitting in" with his peers always seemed to backfire. He was trying so hard to be liked, but not letting people see the real Tyler. He was proud of his intelligence, but also uncomfortable with it. Other kids didn't respond to the false front he would put up, and their rebuff just added to his feelings of rejection.

At Yellowstone, Tyler continued to struggle with social skills and submitting to authority. Counselor Matt Chaney remembers, "Tyler was a smart kid who tried to manipulate people and circumstances. He never got into any serious trouble because he knew where to draw the line. But he would stir things up with the other kids in the lodge, then sit back and get enjoyment out of watching what he'd created. A good example would be that all the kids in a lodge must walk to school in a group each morning. Tyler would take so much time getting ready for school, he'd make everyone late. It didn't bother *him*, but everyone else was mad at him and frustrated before their school day even began."

The challenge for his counselors was helping Tyler to see that, even though he wasn't technically breaking the rules, he was still responsible for creating unnecessary havoc in his own life and the lives of others; and that his actions were not socially acceptable.

Tyler is quite analytical about his time at the Ranch and says it fell into three stages. "In the beginning stage, Kevin Swalley, Deb Perrigo, and other staff in the Emotional Growth Program helped me to see I was going down the wrong road and tried to steer me down the right one," he says.

"In the middle stage, Cameron Smith, Matt Chaney, and others in

Fortin Lodge provided the tough love and guidance I needed to make the necessary changes in my life.

"And, in the final stage, Peggy Swalley, Sheryl Metzger, and the entire King Group Home staff helped me in my transition from the structured life at the Ranch to the 'real world.' They provided me with the life skills I needed to survive on my own. Sheryl helped me learn to cook and taught me how to make really good hamburgers!"

Peggy Swalley, Unit Manager at King Group Home, remembers Tyler's insightful sense of humor. "Just when I was about to get frustrated with him, he'd say something to make me laugh. But Tyler was learning to use his sense of humor in a healthy way, rather than trying to avoid responsibility."

Yellowstone helped Tyler learn to be comfortable in his own skin. He realized that as he grew to accept himself, others would accept him as well.

As Tyler learned how to relate better with his peers, he also became receptive to working on his relationship with his parents, Ron and Judy. Family Therapy saved their relationship. Because they lived far away, Ron and Judy were not able to come often for visits, but weekly phone conversations with Tyler and his therapist facilitated working on family issues. "Setting measurable goals was always a part of family therapy, and it was very beneficial," they say.

Later on in treat-

At work at Erdman Anthony Associates.

ment, Tyler would occasionally fly home on a pass. "We would always get a call ahead of time," says Judy. "They would say, 'Now this is what we would like you to do. Judy, you do this with Tyler one-on-one; and, Ron, you do this with Tyler one-on-one; and then do this as a family.' Everyone had an assignment, and we would try to do what they said. It was so good that we had one-on-one time and then family time."

Today, their family relationship has changed dramatically. Tyler and his parents can laugh and joke, and they enjoy one another's company. They are also able to listen to each other's point of view and respect their differences. "If we do have a disagreement," says Tyler, "we know how to walk away, think about it, then come back and work it out."

Tyler graduated from Yellowstone Academy, and went on to graduate cum laude from Central Pennsylvania College on May 6, 2005, with a Bachelor of Science in Information Technology–Application Development. He is currently in charge of Information Technology at a branch office of Erdman Anthony Associates, Inc., an engineering firm where his father is an engineer.

"Computers have been a love of mine ever since I was little, and now I finally have the opportunity to make a career of it," he says. "At Erdman Anthony I am a jack-of-all-trades. I have done everything from swapping out hardware components to creating web pages for clients. I thoroughly enjoy my job.

"The time I spent at the Ranch was necessary and helped me to grow into the man I am today. The Ranch provides a safe place for kids to grow up and mature in a structured environment that encourages them to make right decisions and choices."

Family involvement in treatment at Yellowstone is expected, encouraged, and supported. Staff at the Ranch are often heard expressing what a privilege it is to be a part of reuniting families, and are especially grateful that Tyler's family gave them that opportunity.

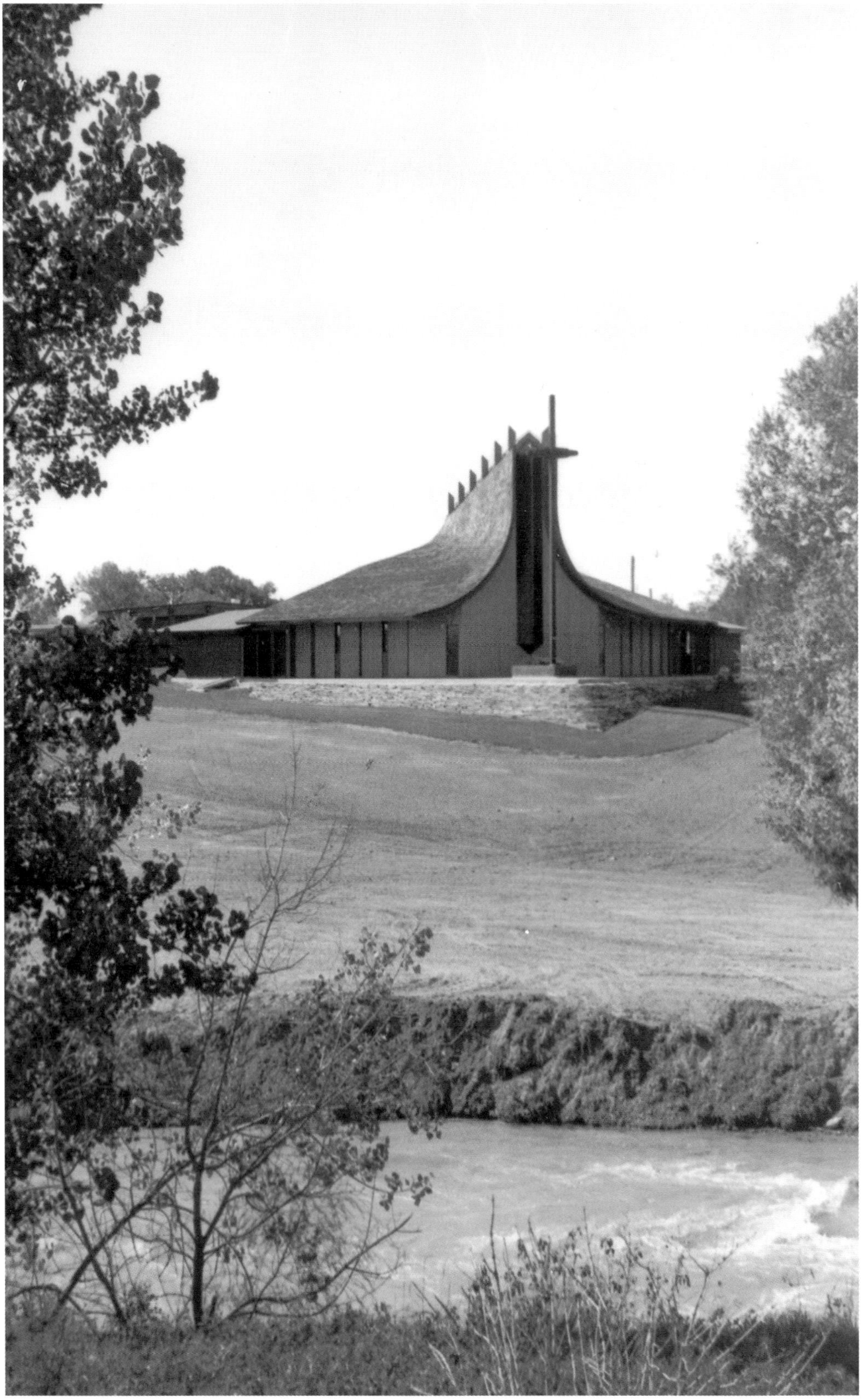

Chapter Seven

The Soul of Yellowstone

The Ranch grew rapidly during the 1960s and 1970s. We were caring for more boys than ever before, and we were offering them a wider range of helpful programs and services each year. But amidst all this growth and change, one core conviction that remained solid was the belief that if our Ranch were truly going to make a difference in young people's lives, it would need to incorporate a powerful spiritual element.

Religion wasn't a crusade for us. After all, we were a boys ranch, not a church. Still, there was a conviction among many of the Ranch's founders, leaders, and employees that true transformation involved more than improving minds and bodies. We believed that lasting change often required something deeper within the core of our kids.

I addressed this conviction in the October 1962 issue of the *Wrangler*:

> In accepting a boy from a juvenile court there is nothing in the court order outlining the necessity or importance of religious training, but it becomes part of our moral responsibility to strive to meet all the needs

of each boy given into our care.

That includes more than providing food, clothing, shelter, education, and recreation. It embraces trying hard to take the place of parents in defining and teaching moral and spiritual values as well.

We are keenly aware that "man doth not live by bread alone but by every word which proceedeth out of the mouth of God," (Matthew 4:4) and we have many encouraging evidences of the value of the religious emphasis included in our daily program at Yellowstone Boys Ranch.

I had a belief in the importance of spirituality for turning around the lives of troubled boys long before I ever became involved in the Ranch. In fact, this belief arose from difficulties I had experienced myself. Allow me to explain by recounting an episode of personal transformation in my own life.

My "Life of Crime"

As I've said, my father was a pastor who worked in many small churches and who supported his family through free-will offerings of his congregations. This meant that whatever small donations people were inclined or able to drop in the offering plate was all our family had to live on.

The people in my father's churches were often poor folk who gave what they could. But that wasn't very much, and as a result I was raised in poverty. I can remember times when if we hadn't had a big vegetable garden in the yard, a productive milk cow in a shed, a weaner pig eating table scraps, and corn gleaned from farmers' fields, we wouldn't have had enough food to sustain us.

Outwardly, my father bore these hardships with strength and faith. But I chafed under our family's poverty. When I got into high school I became obsessed with trying to get a little more money in my pocket. Over time, that obsession led to my giving in to various temptations. To put it another way, I became a petty thief.

I was a pretty small-time crook as crooks go. And, thankfully, I never got caught, or I might have wound up in a reform school like the one in Miles City where I first met the young boys who helped inspire the founding of the Ranch.

But I was amazed to see how my anger over being poor and my desire for a little pocket money led me to steal things that I had no rights to.

In one case I snuck into my high school library one day after school and helped myself to a couple of dollars from the librarian's desk drawer which held payments for overdue book fines. In another case I had been asked to sell tickets to a school basketball game. By stealthily reselling a few tickets I was able to skim an extra dollar or two. And, in my biggest haul, I grabbed five dollars from a bag full of money students had paid for their class rings.

It was a relief having some money in my pocket, but deep down inside me there was a feeling of guilt about what I had done. That guilt came to the surface when I was at Bible college. We had a special speaker talk to our students one year during the annual spiritual emphasis week. When this man spoke to us, it was as if his message about sin and repentance was directed straight at me.

Sitting there in the auditorium that day, I suddenly became aware of the sense that God was telling me to make restitution for those thefts I had committed, so when I returned home from Bible college the next summer that's exactly what I did.

Making Things Right

Working for a farmer who paid me a dollar a day, I slowly saved up some money for paying back my victims. One of the first people I visited was my former high school principal. I remember going to his house, knocking on his door, and telling him I wanted to pay back the five dollars I had taken from the class ring money bag two years earlier. He started to cry right there at his front door.

One by one I visited the other victims of my adolescent crime spree, and they all reacted with a combination of surprise and joy when I confessed my wrongdoing and made things right.

Many years later I would hear President George W. Bush talking about a similar transformation in his own life. I remember a reporter asking the president why he felt so strongly about giving federal dollars to faith-based charities that worked with people who were struggling with drugs or alcohol. The president responded that it had been faith-based groups that finally enabled him to overcome his long-running problems with alcohol.

We have all seen how 12-step groups like Alcoholics Anonymous have been able to help people overcome their dependencies through relying on a "higher power."

Similar motivations have played a role in America's criminal justice system from the earliest times. Many people don't realize this, but the reason penitentiaries have that name is because it was hoped that inmates would experience penitence for their crimes. Penitentiaries were not designed as places where criminals would be locked up for life. Rather, it was hoped that time behind bars would lead criminals to see the errors of their ways, repent of their crimes, and undergo a process of inner transformation that lessened their tendencies toward further criminal behavior in the future.

This kind of transformational spiritual emphasis was a building block of the Ranch from the very beginning, and over the decades we would continually assess how we could best integrate these principals into the life of our growing institution.

Lessons at Home and at Church

People who work at the Ranch often operated more as family members than as employees of an impersonal institution.

From the earliest days we have done that by seeking teachable moments with the boys as they played games together, worked together on chores, or sat together around the evening dinner table.

On Sundays, we would pack up as many boys as we could, and take them into town to attend the local churches of their choice.

There were some benefits of this ecumenical approach. For one thing, boys could go to the Methodist, Presbyterian, Baptist, Lutheran, or Catholic churches they were most comfortable with, and those boys who had no church background could go with the other boys they were closest to.

Most of the Billings area churches welcomed our boys. But as our numbers grew, and as we began transporting more and more boys in cars, a van, and, ultimately, an old bus to a dozen or more different churches, it became harder for us to manage this process. It was also becoming more difficult for local churches to accommodate all the rowdy boys we were bringing them.

Plus, there was always the challenge of talking to the different boys about all the different things they had heard at the various church services and Sunday school classes they attended. There were certain lessons about life and behavior we were trying to teach our boys, and not all of these messages were addressed every Sunday by the various churches they attended.

One other problem discovered by Bob McFarlane in the early days was the in-and-out approach to church. Bob would deliver a handful of boys to a church and watch them enter the church's front door. Then, a few minutes later, he would see the same handful of boys exit through the church's back door. They never got into any serious trouble during their Sunday morning periods of hooky, but we felt we needed to exercise greater control about where they were and what they were learning.

Ranch-based chapel programs like the Ranch choir provided ample opportunity for moral, spiritual, and character development.

In 1960, Jack Dabner worked with me in the Ranch's business office. After completing a full day of work, Jack would often spend his free time with the boys talking to them about their lives. In time, Jack was leading Bible studies with the boys, and working with them to sort through some of the spiritual issues in their lives.

By the summer of 1962 the Ranch had twenty-nine boys, and we decided we needed to start organizing our own Sunday services. Jack led many of these services, and he did a wonderful job. It was great having someone like Jack who deeply cared for the boys and was committed to their spiritual growth. But we had also created a problem for ourselves.

The Ranch was growing rapidly, and every dollar was being stretched to pay for new buildings and staff. Somehow we were slow in getting around to coming up with the finances needed to create a chapel where we could hold our services

A Legacy of Caring

and the chaplain could better focus his energies on spiritual growth.

Over the next two decades we would confront these challenges and place our spiritual programs on a much more solid footing.

A Church without a Home

The Sunday morning services we began organizing at the Ranch in 1962 were held wherever we could find the space. Initially, we held these services in our small classroom facilities located at the end of one of the boys lodges. We would move aside the heavy metal desks, bring in some chairs, and have church service there in the classroom.

Within a few years we had moved our services to a new and larger boys lodge. And by the time our new dining facility was completed in 1966, we hosted Sunday services there for ninety boys.

Aesthetically, all these arrangements left much to be desired. And the men who served as chaplain under these conditions – Jack Dabner, Wayne Rohrs, Dallas Demmett, Bob Koerner and Larry Slaughter – struggled to keep the boys minds on higher things when they were surrounded by the school desks or dining

Chaplains Wendell Wilson (top right), Bob Koerner (left), and Larry Slaughter (right) served Ranch residents in a variety of ways.

room tables they used seven days a week.

The first real step toward realizing our goal of having a dedicated chapel facility happened when a donor, Dr. Harold Schwartz of Butte, along with three of his children, made a significant gift to the chapel building fund.

Other gifts came in, too, including a sizeable donation from the Kresge Foundation, which was operated by the family that would later start the Kmart retail chain.

We started taking tentative steps, and at the April 1964 meeting of the Ranch's board of directors, architect Willard Johnson presented us with a scale model for a proposed chapel structure.

As much as we wanted to press ahead and build a chapel, other needs somehow always seemed more pressing and the project wasn't completed as quickly as we hoped. The Ranch was growing as more and more courts sent troubled boys to the Ranch. And each year brought new demands for expanded facilities and a larger and better-trained staff.

Nevertheless we persevered, and the All-Faith Chapel was finally completed in 1970. Scores of people filled the pews for an October 11, 1970, dedication service that included several local pastors among the invited guests.

Chapel Programs Provide New Opportunities

Wendell Wilson was the Ranch's first chaplain to serve in our newly constructed chapel. We could immediately see the positive results that came from having a dedicated staff member serving our kids' spiritual needs in a dedicated facility. In addition to regular chapel services, Wendell began hosting a voluntary youth group program on Sunday evening for interested kids. He incorporated a variety of fun activities at youth group, all designed to hold the attention and catch the imagination of our active boys.

Wendell also introduced the idea of having boys act out episodes from the lives of different Bible characters. Over the years this active, hands-on approach helped boys recognize and appreciate some of the profound moral issues found in the Bible.

In time these activities led to the creation of a very effective Ranch drama group. Many kids who have participated in the drama group through the chapel program have been able to deal with some of the very deep issues in their own lives. As a result, Wendell's drama activities were more than an acting class. They were a way for kids to get in touch with feelings that may have otherwise been too painful to pursue.

Chaplain Wilson also had the vision for a Boys Ranch Choir. The choir not only participated in Sunday morning chapel services but also performed in other settings and even went on tours. The Ranch Choir performed in communities all over Montana, Wyoming, Colorado, Minnesota, and Canada, bringing audiences doses of entertainment and inspiration while doing great public relations work for the Ranch. A photo of the choir taken in 1972 shows Chaplain Wilson directing the choir, which featured a dozen and a half boys who look almost angelic in their beautiful choral robes.

By 1973 Chaplain Wilson's Ranch Choir was twenty voices strong. The members wore stylish matching vests made by Mr. Wilson's wife, Anne, for their successful spring tour, during which they traveled more than five thousand miles and performed thirty-five concerts to delighted audiences.

Subsequent chaplains, George Hoherd, Dan Hansen, Tom Carey, Tom Wilson and John Jamison would continue to focus on the spiritual growth of our boys, and the benefits from this program would enrich many areas of Ranch life.

Faith and Flexibility

Spirituality remains a core component of many Ranch programs today, but the ways we incorporate spirituality into our varied activities have changed over the years.

As we received more boys who came from a wider range of

The Boys Ranch Choir, shown performing at the Montana State Capitol building, traveled more than 5,000 miles in 1972 to perform 35 concerts.

cultural, ethnic, and religious backgrounds, we worked hard to find ways to adapt our programs to their individual needs without compromising our basic Judeo-Christian values.

In addition, old ways of teaching have been modified so that today we continue to capture the imaginations of our kids.

Times have changed, but the spiritual principles that have formed the basis of the Ranch have not. And even though we have continually improved the ways we apply these principles to the changing population of the Ranch and our kids' unique spiritual needs, we are more committed than ever to the belief that spirituality plays a central role in changing the lives of troubled kids.

Transformed Lives

**Jeanette Shannon:
Careening Toward Destruction**

Jeanette Shannon became a local celebrity at age twelve – but for a tragic reason. Both her parents died within three months, leaving Jeanette and her older brother John, just eighteen, orphaned and alone. They never had had much, because her dad took in odd jobs at home so he could care for Jeanette's chronically ill mother. Jeanette and John were left with virtually nothing when their dad suddenly died of a heart attack, just three months after losing his wife.

John was determined to see that he and Jeanette stayed together. He was just starting his freshman year in college. The University of

Jeanette (far left) enjoying a special dude ranch outing designed to reward young men and women who are making exceptional progress in their treatment.

A Legacy of Caring

California at Riverside mercifully bent the rules, allowing them to live in campus apartment housing.

A former teacher brought them to the attention of local media. The *Riverside Press-Enterprise* did a series of stories on the two, resulting in an outpouring of community support. The first story mentioned that their apartment lacked a rug. The next morning, a van passed by, and a new, sky-blue rug was thrown onto the front lawn. The people drove off with a wave. John didn't even get a chance to say thanks. "It was a drive-by rugging," John said, laughing.

Jeanette mentioned a love for horses in the article. It caught the attention of Bob and Alice Fusco, both child psychologists, who also happened to love horseback riding. They contacted Jeanette, asking if she'd like to go riding sometime. The Fuscos remained in close touch with John and Jeanette, providing encouragement where they could.

Jeanette doing some Christmas shopping with Bob Fusco and brother John.

John and Jeanette stayed together in their apartment, doing an adequate job of making it on their own. They were frugal with money that had come in from the community and the financial aid John had received for

Jeanette with Deb Perrigo (left), Chaplain Jamison and a fellow peer the night before leaving treatment.

school. He made countless sacrifices to parent Jeanette, exhibiting the character his father had modeled.

Jeanette was lonely and vulnerable, though, and eventually began looking for companionship through the Internet. She says, "I met a boy named Keith. He was older, charming, and manipulative. He smoked marijuana and influenced me to do the same. He convinced me to have sex with him. Still dealing with the pain of losing my parents, I gave in to his powerful influence.

"I became depressed when John, the only family I had, expressed his disapproval of our relationship. I was skipping school to see Keith and eventually attempted suicide. Frantic for my safety, John knew he had to do something. He went to our friend Alice, the child psychologist, and she suggested professional help."

Alice already knew of Yellowstone Boys and Girls Ranch, having referred several children through her practice. She felt this was the perfect place for Jeanette, but there was no money for treatment.

Alice related Jeanette's story to Ranch CEO Loren Soft. Loren discussed her case—and her inability to pay for care—with his management team. Yellowstone has offered charity care to a few youth over the years, and, somehow, Loren felt that Jeanette was one they should consider. His team agreed. Alice wept with relief when he called her and said Yellowstone would take Jeanette.

Now John had to do some quick thinking to get her to the Ranch. He convinced Jeanette to accompany him on a vacation to Montana. When they landed at the airport in Billings, several Ranch staff were there to meet them.

Jeanette was furious with John. He begged her forgiveness, saying he knew she would have run away if he'd told her what he had in mind. She understands now, but at the time his plan only seemed to add to the feelings of abandonment she had experienced after her parents' deaths.

At first, Jeanette expressed her anger by claiming she had no problems. She tried to stay in touch with Keith and was obstinate. She also claimed to be an atheist and wanted nothing to do with God or chapel.

However, she was intrigued by the drama group that was offered as part of pastoral care; and one of her favorite counselors, Deb Perrigo, also helped with drama.

Deb recalls, "Jeanette was a natural actress. She wanted to be involved in drama and put her heart and soul into it. She glowed when she was in character."

Through some of the dramas they performed, Jeanette began to deal with her issues. One particularly meaningful drama was entitled "Why, God?" Jeanette cried out "What kind of God would take a twelve-year-old girl's parents from her?" In the drama Jesus appears and has a conversation with her. This experience opened her up to begin to understand some of her feelings of abandonment and blame. She also began to accept the fact that things happen for a reason; that maybe even losing her parents, tragic as it was, had the providential result of bringing her to Yellowstone so she could find God.

When Jeanette returned home several months later, she was a very different young girl. She says, "I believe that when I left the Ranch I had completed what I was sent there to accomplish. I had let go of the guilt surrounding my parents and I had broken my co-dependency on Keith. But the most important change I had made was coming closer to God.

Jeanette attending her Senior Prom two years after leaving YBGR.

"When I first came to the Ranch, I considered myself an atheist. By the time I left, I was very close to the Lord. I feel this was the most important change I made, because allowing God into my life gave me the strength to let go of all the bad feelings and bad things I'd done and replace them with love. The void in my heart which was there through years of heartache was filled with God."

In a letter Jeanette wrote to Loren Soft the night before leaving treatment, she said,

Most of all, I would like to thank you for allowing me to come to this wonderful place and giving me a second chance. Thank you that you helped this little lost girl find her way to a brand new self. I also want to thank all the other people who decided to let me be admitted to Yellowstone. I will pass what I've learned to my children and them to theirs, and so on. So think of it as if you've helped to save many precious lives.

Realizing how close the Ranch had come to not accepting Jeanette because of a lack of funding, the Yellowstone Foundation has determined to look for special gifts to the Endowment Fund, which can be designated for children of families with financial need. It is hoped that in the future, many more Jeanettes will have access to treatment at Yellowstone.

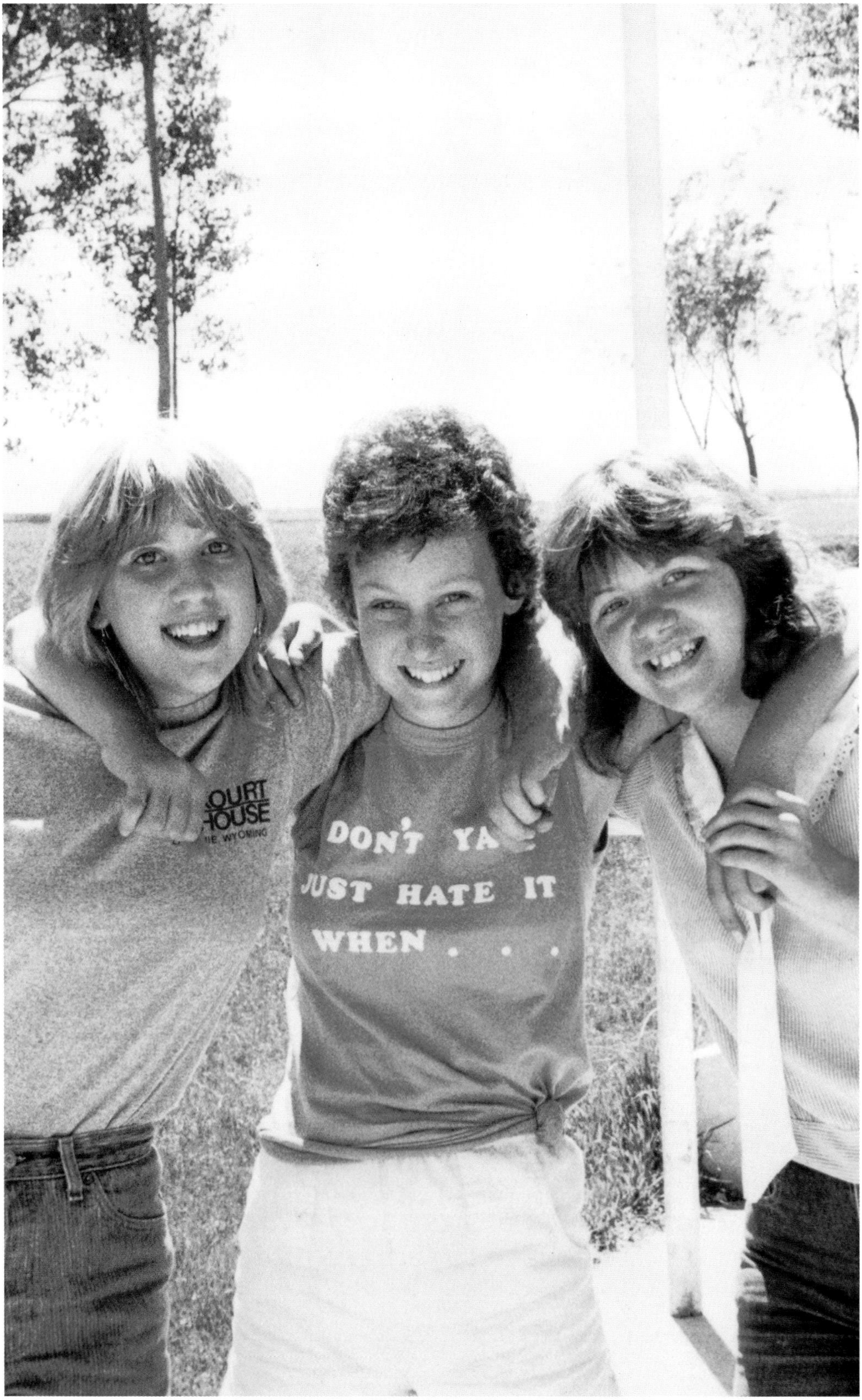
DON'T YA
JUST HATE IT
WHEN . . .

CHAPTER EIGHT

Girls at the "Boys" Ranch

The year 1980 was full of world-changing events. The Soviet Union invaded Afghanistan. The U.S. mission to rescue U.S. hostages in Iran failed. Ronald Reagan was elected president. And Mount St. Helens erupted in Washington state.

It was also a year of change at Yellowstone Boys Ranch. We announced one of the major changes in the *Wrangler*:

> After 23 years of exclusive service to boys only, and after years and years of increasingly urgent pleas to remember the little sisters who also have needs, Yellowstone Boys Ranch has finally prepared for a major change. Our new treatment programs have been carefully designed to serve girls as well as boys.

This change required another. The "Boys Ranch" name we had used for so long no longer fit, so we renamed ourselves Yellowstone Boys and Girls Ranch. There was a strong desire to maintain a connection with the identity the Ranch had built up over the past twenty-three years while accurately describing our commitment to serving girls, too.

Opening the doors of our facility to girls had been long in coming, but was actually just one facet of broader changes at the Ranch as we prepared to celebrate a quarter century of service.

A Place for Troubled Girls

Welcoming girls to the Ranch wasn't a new idea born in 1980. In fact, we had discussed helping girls from the earliest days. There is even a brief mention of girls in the first annual report that I prepared for the Ranch's board way back in 1958.

> In another field, more and more people are asking what is being done for problem girls, and both Montana and Wyoming face some very real problems in this area. As I look to the future, I can say without hesitation that I would like to see us develop this field.... I am also uncovering some very substantial interest and possible financial support in this area, and I am wondering if I should at least be willing to discuss it, or should we say emphatically that we never intend to enter that field?

If we were interested in helping girls that long ago, then why did it take us more than two decades to develop programs for girls? There are a number of answers.

For one thing, in the early years it seemed that there were far more boys who were in trouble than there were girls. Montana did have the Vocational School for Girls similar to the Boys Industrial School that had inspired me to start the Ranch, but the girls school had a much smaller population.

Also, the problem of juvenile delinquency in the 1950s was largely defined as a problem involving boys. Sure, there were girls who got into trouble, but somehow or other, it seemed that girls with problems were more easily overlooked.

In some cases, it was hoped that their parents would take

care of the girls. Plus, there were differences in the ways boys and girls acted out their anger and rage. Boys were more defiant and more destructive in their delinquent behavior than girls were. Both boys and girls dealt with some of the same problems, but it seemed boys more often acted out in ways that led to them creating more destruction or getting in trouble with the law.

Furthermore, working with girls at the Ranch would have required separate housing, and our continuing financial pressures demanded that we stay with the simpler all-boys approach we had begun with. After all, we were already challenged in our efforts to raise the funds required to meet the needs of an ever-growing population of Ranch boys.

Clearly, the interest I had referred to in my 1958 annual report seemed to run ahead of the financial support I hoped would materialize from our supporters. And we decided that we would rather succeed at doing one thing well (helping boys) than fail by stretching too far and trying to do two things (serving boys and girls) less successfully.

We also wondered what kind of impact bringing girls to the Ranch would have on our boys. Today, there are many schools for boys in troubled urban areas, and the people who run these schools believe that focusing only on males makes things easier and more productive. That was certainly what we thought in the early years of the Ranch.

But over the years, a number of the social workers who referred boys to us would say, "By the way, there are girls who need this kind of help, too."

It was particularly frustrating for us when state juvenile offices wanted to refer a brother and sister to us. In these cases we could accept the brother but not the sister. When you knew the families these kids came from, it was clear the sister needed our help as much as the brother did. But there was nothing we could do. In cases like these, I felt we had abandoned these girls and turned our back on them.

Ultimately, it was the state government of Montana that enabled us to do what we had hoped to do from the beginning. Basically, state agencies could only give us certain kinds of kids, namely boys with certain kinds of problems. But by the late 1970s, states were dealing with an increasing number of girls in trouble, as well as growing numbers of more deeply troubled kids. The State of Montana helped us finally open up our programs to girls by offering to fund a girls pilot program for a full year.

This practical offer encouraged us to expand the Ranch's range of services, as well as the kinds of kids we could offer these services to.

In order to accommodate girls at the Ranch we expanded our campus to a new building on the east side of 72nd Street. This East Campus boasted a new Residential Assessment-Treatment Center that symbolized the positive steps we were taking to meet the needs of more deeply troubled kids.

Taken together, the admission of girls at the Ranch and the development of the new treatment center demonstrated that the second twenty-five years of the Ranch would be much different than the first twenty-five years. Our goal of caring for kids hadn't changed, but the ways we reached this goal were changing rapidly as we reached this important mid-point in our history.

Boldly Going Where No Girl Had Ever Gone Before

If you have ever sympathized with a lone daughter who grows up in a family of many sons, then you can feel for the young girl named Lisa who was the first girl to be welcomed to what had previously been known as Yellowstone Boys Ranch.

The face of courage: In 1980 Lisa became the first girl at the "Boys" Ranch.

Lisa arrived in the spring of 1980, and by the following fall she was doing surprisingly well. She wrote about her experience in the October 1980 issue of the *Wrangler*:

> I am the first girl in the whole establishment and I think the system's OK. I've been here for about six or seven months now and I have learned a lot. Whether I wanted to or not!!
>
> If I can come here to YBGR with the attitude that "I'm not gonna get anything out of this place and they are just holding me until I'm 18" and I still get more out of it in seven months than I got out of anything in my entire life, then it must be a pretty good system! I mean if I can learn something from it—anyone can!
>
> I'm not saying that everything's peaches and cream. Don't get me wrong. I've got my bad days and moods and I still have problems. I'm still learning. But there are days when I feel almost at home!
>
> And it's all because of some very understanding, patient, loving people who work here with me and because of all my great new friends.
>
> I'm beginning not to be so lonely and down. YBGR is a haven!

Our experiment with girls seemed to be working, at least from Lisa's perspective. But how did the boys react to this new development? Some of us had worried that the presence of girls might bother the boys. Were we ever wrong!

When we had been Yellowstone Boys Ranch, the young men who lived with us didn't always comb their hair as often as they could have. And they didn't worry about extravagant things like wearing a clean shirt. After all, boys will be boys, especially when boys are all you have. But after Lisa and other girls arrived at the Ranch, there was a noticeable increase in use of combs.

Though it had been a long time coming, the addition of girls to the Ranch turned out to be a healthy move, not only for the girls but for the boys as well.

Riding a Wave of Change

Shortly after welcoming girls to the Ranch we began experiencing the same kinds of growth challenges we had seen with boys. By the fall of 1980 we were turning down new girls because we had already reached our capacity. A new girls lodge was under construction, but we could have filled it as soon as it was finished.

The perennial challenges of funding our growing operation continued as they had from day one. Only now, the need for funds was escalating year after year. Fortunately, donors stepped forward with considerable gifts that helped us construct our new assessment-treatment building and two new girls treatment lodges.

There were other important changes at the Ranch that shaped us in significant ways in the years leading up to our twenty-fifth anniversary.

One of the benefits of establishing a program for young men on a ranch-farm setting was that it provided the opportunity for us to teach another valuable life skill to the youth, that of learning about the world of work. In September of 1963, a young couple, Dan and Sharon Hansen joined the Ranch family. Dan started out supervising the youth on work projects and activities.

In February of 1964, Dan and Sharon became houseparents in Paul Stock Lodge, where it was obvious they both had a "heart" for children. Dan quickly became known around the Ranch as a man who could be both firm and tender at the same time, as someone who had a great sense of humor and a hearty laugh and as a person who would challenge young men to be their best in whatever they did.

Following their years as houseparents, Dan and Sharon were challenged to take new roles and responsibilities. Dan became program director and athletic coach of the Ranch bas-

Dan Hansen (above at head of table at right) and his wife Sharon (shown with a youth in the kitchen) pioneered the Ranch's group home approach to housing and caring for kids.

ketball team. As program director, Dan developed something for the boys called the Earn While You Learn Work Program.

Job descriptions were developed; application blanks were created and the boys had the opportunity to apply for the job of their choice. An allowance/salary was established for each position.

The boys were required to keep time cards to record hours worked. Work supervisors were instructed how to fill out work satisfaction reports on the youth assigned to them and could even give raises to the workers if it was merited. Or, if the work performance was less than satisfactory, the youth could be "demoted" to a less desirable work site.

This program actually became a model used in a number of other ranch programs throughout the country.

In 1970, the concept of community-based group homes was on the rise across the country. The Ranch, striving to ever be on the cutting edge of residential group care, decided to open a group home in Billings. This was a brand new program for us and as we searched for just the right couple to begin this new service, Dan and Sharon stepped up to be the first group home parents in our newly purchased Svarre Group Home.

Over the years Dan and Sharon filled other roles at the Ranch. Sharon developed the "Fine Fittery" clothing room where the youth could purchase their clothing needs at greatly reduced prices, well within the allowance/salaries they earned in the Earn While You Learn Work Program. She also had a significant role in the interior designing and furnishing of new lodges, the administration building and staff homes built during the 70s and early 80s. Her warm, homey decorating style set the Ranch apart from other "institutions."

Dan continued as program director for several years, coached the basketball team, assisted in the chapel program, was Ranch administrator and later served as Ranch chaplain. Dan and Sharon were wonderful examples of young people who dedicated their lives to helping us establish the foundation stones for a safe and caring place for young people.

The Ranch also continued its involvement in the National Association of Homes for Boys and the National Association of Homes for Children (now known as the Alliance for Children and Families).

We learned much from these groups' meetings and conventions, and soon we were contributing our own wisdom by leading workshops and even hosting annual conventions in Billings, where we taught other administrators how to achieve the success we had achieved at the Ranch. In 1963 I was elected president of the NAHB, and I would continue to serve the organization in many capacities over the next twenty years.

The governors of Montana continued to be good friends to the Ranch, and in 1966 Governor Tim Babcock and more than 450 other people visited the Ranch for the dedication of our new Donald Nutter Memorial Dining Hall, which was named after the governor who had played such an important role in the early years.

Movie star Rex Allen also participated in the dedication ceremonies, and other celebrities like bestselling author Norman Vincent Peale and country music stars Glen Campbell and Charley Pride visited the Ranch or participated in public service announcement campaigns that introduced the Ranch to people throughout the region.

But it wasn't just celebrities who befriended the Ranch. As in the early days, we continued to receive tremendous support from the local community. The clearest evidence of this could be seen at our annual open house events, some of which attracted nearly two thousand people to the Ranch for a Sunday afternoon of activities, guided tours, and refreshments.

Film and TV star Rex Allen was one of many celebrities to visit the Ranch.

In time these events grew so large we feared they would overwhelm the Ranch. Ultimately, though, it was privacy concerns about many of our troubled kids that led us to make the Ranch

Open house at the Ranch always attracted many visitors and featured lots of activities.

less accessible to the public than it had been in the early days.

Of course, our favorite visitors were former Ranch residents who returned to see us when they could. It was so exciting to see what these young men who had lived with us earlier were doing now. It was also very gratifying and moving to realize that the Ranch had played a crucial role in their lives, a role that many of them profusely thanked us for when they made their return visits.

New Needs Inspire New Programs

Year after year the Ranch expanded, and not only numerically. We were also expanding the range of programs we were offering, including new programs for younger boys as well as off-campus group homes for older boys who had done well enough at the Ranch to be given greater independence.

The Svarre Group Home and King Group Home in Billings were the perfect places for some of these older boys to test their wings and make their first ventures into the "real world." Though still under Ranch supervision, the control was less strict than it was at the Ranch, and many of these older boys were able to hold down jobs while getting good grades at school.

Readers have already met the Kings. The Svarre Group Home was paid for by Ingvaard Svarre, a successful cattle buyer with a large feedlot operation in Sidney, Montana, who influenced dozens of eastern Montana ranchers to be regular livestock donors to our Ranch. Ing also served on our Board of Directors for nine years and, through his will, left a substantial gift to our Endowment Fund.

The boys' group homes were so successful that a former Board member donated the money needed to purchase an off-campus group home for girls. This Board member preferred to remain anonymous and encouraged us to name the new facility the Dennis Wear Group Home in honor of a former Ranch resident who had died serving his country in Vietnam.

Eventually, the Ranch added more group homes, including a co-ed facility in Dillon, Montana, and a boys' home in Lewistown. In each case, the activities and supervision at the group home were tailored to the needs of the youth who lived there.

We also continued to enhance our school programs, adding academic courses that helped poor students become better students as well as creative vocational programs that would give our boys and girls some of the advantages they would need to succeed in the job market.

We added extracurricular activities, including crafts, music, and art to develop the creative nature of the youth, many of whom had never been encouraged to express themselves artistically before they came to the Ranch. There were some who were already very creative and in some cases their intelligence and creativity had contributed to their problems. Our programs gave them positive outlets for expression many of them had never enjoyed before.

And who can forget the baseball, basketball, football, and soccer teams that challenged so many of our boys in those early years and even won the Ranch a number of competitive trophies? Like everything else we did at the Ranch, sports teams were seen as opportunities to seek out teachable moments, and many boys learned valuable lessons about teamwork, discipline, and dealing with pain through their involvement with our teams.

None of the positive developments I have been describing would have happened without the one thing that is most needed in order to make the Ranch work: an excellent staff. Each time we added a new program or facility, we also added new staffing requirements. The more we grew the more of a challenge it became to find employees who had just the right balance of professionalism and care. Thankfully, we did very well in recruiting people, surprisingly large numbers of whom have worked with us for a decade or more.

Let's not kid ourselves. The work at the Ranch is demanding. Grueling might even be a better word. The amount of time and emotional energy our employees invest in the boys and girls here is amazing. And without their selfless giving of themselves to these kids, nothing of any real value would happen here.

From a "Ranch" to a "Treatment Center"

Clearly one of the most significant developments in the first twenty-five years of the Ranch was the opening of the new Residential Assessment-Treatment Center.

The "juvenile delinquents" of the 1950s and 1960s were a far cry from the deeply emotionally damaged young people we began seeing with increasing frequency during the 1970s and 1980s.

At the urging of the state agencies with which we worked, we began accepting more of these broken and hurting kids and developing the programs to meet their needs. One sign of our growth in this area was the certification we received from the Joint Commission on Accreditation of Healthcare Organizations. Actually, our certification came from the JCAHO division called the Council for Psychiatric Facilities.

Our philosophy of care remained the same as it had in the beginning when we chose our slogan: IT SURE MAKES A DIFFERENCE WHEN YOU KNOW SOMEBODY CARES.

But the means and methods we were using to care for kids were changing. We were rapidly evolving from our original house-parent approach to a state-of-the art, full-service comprehensive program to help emotionally troubled youth. Along the way there were many growing pains, but the pains were worth the improvements we could bring to the service we provided to the precious lives entrusted to our care.

Transformed Lives

Nicki Jenkins: A Place of Refuge

"I hate you kids." "I don't want you." "I wish you were dead."

These were the phrases that rang in Nicki Jenkins's ears throughout her turbulent childhood. Nicki's mother just couldn't handle the responsibility of parenting. Untreated mental illness put her over the edge when it came to relationships, including several failed marriages.

Nicki's grandparents, who lived just across a field from their daughter, did their best to provide love and stability for Nicki and her siblings when their mom was abusive. But her mom resented their efforts and lashed out at them as well.

Nicki, thinking she was most of the problem, tried to ease the pressure on her grandparents by going to live with her dad. More heartbreak followed when she was sexually abused by his girlfriend's sons. When things weren't working out with either

Nicki playing floor hockey.

parent, Nicki was sent to live with relatives in Montana.

Nicki says of these relatives, "In their minds I was supposed to be able to forget my past, put it all behind me, and be a normal person. They had lots of money and gave me anything I wanted. Things were okay for about six months, then I just fell apart."

After a suicide attempt and a number of hospital stays, Nicki was placed at Yellowstone. She was suffering from depression, posttraumatic stress disorder, feelings of abandonment and rejection, and several other self-destructive behaviors.

At Yellowstone Nicki learned a better way to handle all the pent up frustration and self-hatred that consumed her. Recreational therapy played a major part in Nicki's treatment. Lisa Frazier, head of Yellowstone's Recreational Therapy department, provided individual therapy for Nicki. "Lisa not only gave me healthy outlets to vent my frustrations," says Nicki, "she also showed me I could trust in someone again. She challenged me both physically and mentally. As I accomplished activities I didn't think I could, my belief in myself began to grow."

Lisa says, "I remember the first time I met Nicki. She had come to the Uihlein Recreation Center (UC) to swim with her lodge and refused to get in the water. The consequence for refusing to participate was time alone in what we call a 'quiet room.' After awhile, when Nicki realized she couldn't manipulate me, she decided maybe she would swim. That was the beginning of Nicki realizing what recreational therapy could do for her. She admitted that she hated rules and discipline, but knew they were good for her."

Before long, Nicki was working hard to reach her treatment goals in the lodge so she could earn the reward of going to the UC to

One of Nicki's "Super Stars" blue ribbons. Super Stars is a ranch-wide competition that has been ongoing each year for more than 20 years.

Nicki (second from left) having light-hearted fun in the lodge. The girls put on a "beauty pageant" using dress-up and silly things they had on hand.

work out with Lisa. Self-confidence was Nicki's major hurdle, especially with physical challenges. Lisa says that's true of many of the youth who come to Yellowstone. Once they grow in self-confidence, they make great strides in treatment. When children learn that a difficult past doesn't automatically guarantee a difficult future, they can finally take ownership of their mental health.

Nicki's confidence grew to where she played on the girls' volleyball team. She also joined the intramural soccer and indoor hockey teams. She still has all her team pictures and other mementos. They are reminders of the place where she finally felt the safety and security of people who truly cared about her.

It wasn't just Lisa who helped Nicki learn to believe in herself. One of the things that impressed her most was how everyone at the Ranch works together for the good of the youth. "You always felt that everybody was rooting for you. Every person wants the same thing for each kid, and they all work together to achieve that."

Chaplain John Jamison and his wife Carolyn have remained a source of support and encouragement. "I remember when I was first at the Ranch," says Nicki. "I was determined to hate going to chapel. I had always heard my mom blame God for the death of my older brother, so I was sure I didn't want anything to do with such a God. The Jamisons were incredibly patient with me – and all of us. They never forced anything. They just made themselves available to answer questions and talk about spiritual things." The Jamisons eventually became Nicki's close friends, and she still considers them her spiritual counselors.

Nicki's life was not easy after she left the Ranch. She returned home for a while, but it just didn't work out. Nicki felt she would lose all she had gained at the Ranch if she stayed in that environment. She was sixteen and virtually on her own. So, she contacted Lisa Frazier and asked if she could return to Billings and live with her. "I know I was still very immature. I didn't make very wise choices. But Lisa stuck by me and loved me in spite of my choices," Nicki remembers.

"Graduation from high school was our major goal," says Lisa. "I took her in and gave her the disciplined home she needed to reach that goal. She became the daughter I never had."

Nicki (right, front row) on the girls volleyball team. Lisa Frazier is pictured on the far right.

At age twenty, life changed dramatically for Nicki when she became pregnant. "That was my wake-up call. Suddenly it wasn't just me any more. I couldn't keep doing the same things I'd been doing. It was time to change. Becoming pregnant with my daughter, Taylor, made me grow up."

Nicki went on to earn an Associates Degree in Criminal Justice. She now owns her home, has a career, and is doing a great job of raising two daughters, Taylor and McKenzie.

Nicki says the Ranch taught her how to work through and "live with" her problems while still having the responsibilities of everyday life. "At the Ranch you have a schedule to keep, school, activities, and then specified times to work through your issues. This routine made a much easier transition to life outside the safety of the Ranch."

With Taylor and McKenzie on a trip to Washington D.C.

Fortunately, Nicki and her father have worked hard at their relationship in recent years, and today it is on much more solid ground.

Yellowstone was and continues to be a place of peace and serenity for Nicki. "My life would have been filled with pain, and I would never have known happiness if it weren't for the Ranch," she says. "It still feels like home to me, and my girls love to visit 'Grandma Lisa' out there. Sometimes I go to the Ranch just to be there. The atmosphere is so serene. I walk around and collect my thoughts. It's a wonderful place to get my perspective back."

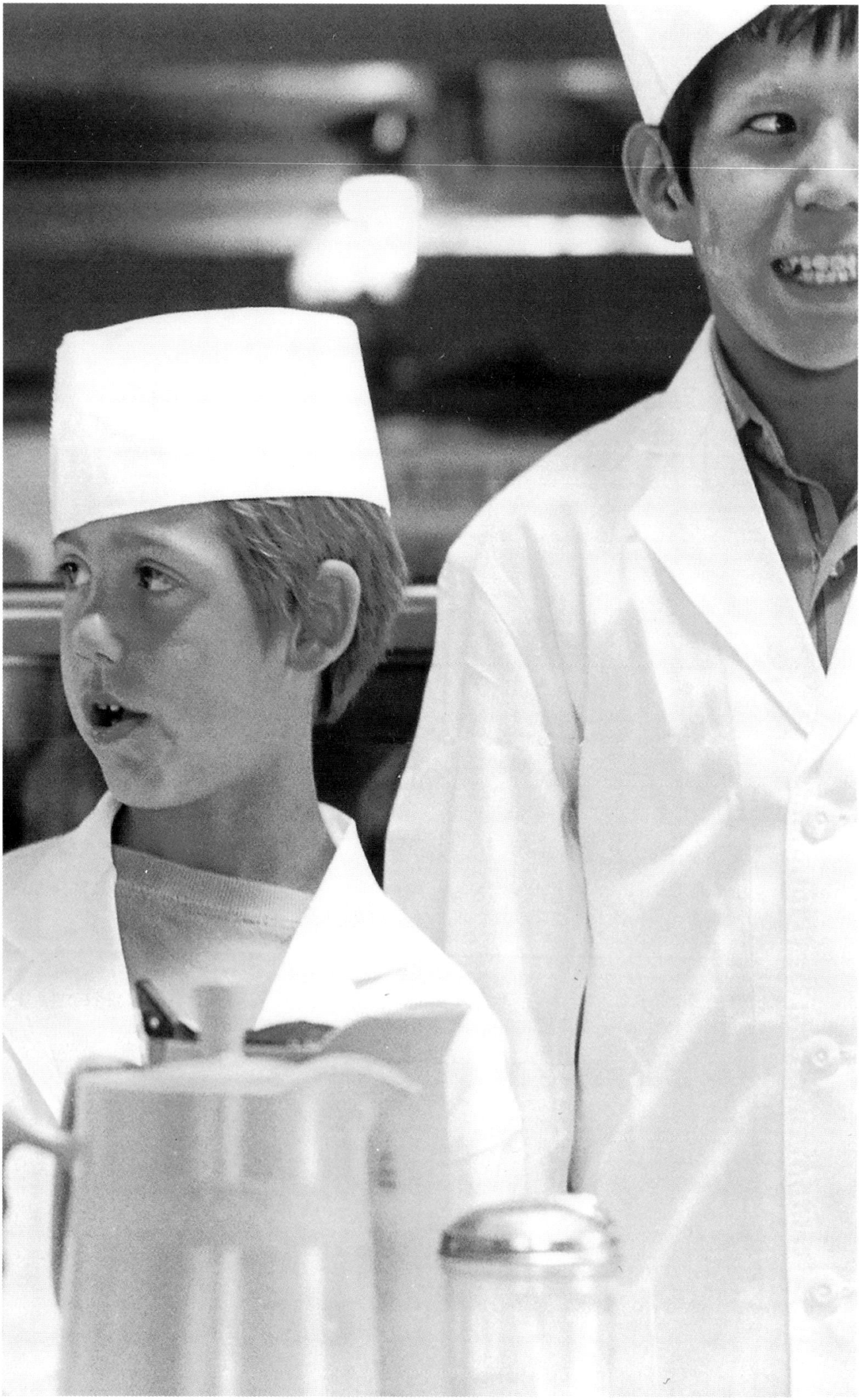

CHAPTER NINE

The Great Escape and Other Stories of Ranch Life

Even the most normal families can provide endless interesting anecdotes about togetherness and tension, laughter and tears. Just think of all the unusual things that have happened in your own family over the years.

But our "family" here at Yellowstone Boys and Girls Ranch is far from typical. When you put more than a hundred struggling kids and dozens of caring adults together on one campus, you have the raw material for more than the normal number of humorous stories about what happens when people live together.

Everyone who works at the Ranch brings a combination of professional competence and compassion for kids. But the experiences of the past fifty years also show that one of the most important qualities people here can have is a sense of humor. The following stories illustrate this point.

Life Imitates Art

After long days of classes and work, young people at the Ranch want to do the same thing people in the "outside world" want to do: enjoy a relaxing time during the weekends. In the 1960s we responded to this need by hosting monthly movie nights in our dining hall.

Kids would come bringing their blankets and pillows and make themselves comfortable on the floor or in big beanbag chairs. Our staff would cook up big batches of buttery popcorn. And young volunteers would help us load the movies into our old reel-to-reel projector.

Every movie night would begin with a few cartoons before the screening of our featured presentation. And our kids were never hesitant about giving us their "thumbs up" or "thumbs down" on the films we selected. Over time we began to learn that their favorite movies were those with plenty of drama and action like *Ben Hur* or *The Guns of Navarone*.

By 1969, the duty of picking out the monthly movie fell to a man named John Jamison, who worked in many capacities at the Ranch before becoming our chaplain. John would study

John Jamison, shown here with his pumpkin twin, thought showing *The Great Escape* would entertain the Ranch kids. It did more than that!

catalogues from rental companies until he found something he thought the kids would like. One of the films he picked out was a critically acclaimed movie that year, and it had a bigger than anticipated impact on our Ranch audience.

The film featured an all-star cast including Steve McQueen, one of the era's more popular actors, along with James Garner, Charles Bronson, James Coburn, and others. The action was riveting. The script was fast-paced and interesting. And there was much dramatic tension between McQueen and his group of Allied soldiers and the German guards who ran the prison camp where they were being held. The name of the movie was *The Great Escape*.

The kids loved the movie. They gasped when the Allied prisoners feared being caught, and they applauded when things went well for the heroes. Even after the movie the kids seemed unusually animated.

After the movie was over kids and staff each went to their rooms for the night. That's when things started going crazy. First one and then other small groups of kids decided to imitate the heroics of Steve McQueen and the other stars by running away from the Ranch. Before the night was over we had rounded up more than a dozen young people who had tried to stage their own great escapes. Most of them didn't get very far, perhaps because their pajamas and slippers didn't provide very good insulation against the cold night air.

We learned a lot that night about the kinds of films that made the best movie night for our kids. From then on we considered films like *Great Expectations*, *The Greatest Show on Earth*, or *The Greatest Story Ever Told*. But we never again unspooled a prison break film like *The Great Escape*.

Traveling Mercies

It's natural that some young people who live at the Ranch are intent on running away. A number of kids have come to be with us after making many attempts to run away from their parents or other institutions where they were cared for. Today, the most troubled young people who live in our secure residential units would find it impossible to get away from their supervisors, but some of the kids who live in less secure environments still make occasional attempts to run away.

For some kids, talking about running away is so exciting that they never see the need to put their threats into action. In the 1950s Carl Orth responded to one young man named Ricky who threatened to run away one too many times.

Ricky was one of the roughest and rowdiest kids we ever had at the Ranch. Ricky's dad was a copper miner who worked the night shift in a mine near Butte and spent his days in a bar. Unfortunately, he took young Ricky along with him on his daylong drinking binges.

Ricky said that when his dad was feeling particularly ornery, he would involve Ricky in his practical jokes.

"Hey, son," he would say. "I want you to go over to that guy at the bar. I want you to kick him in the shin. And I want you to tell him he's an S.O.B."

The recipients of this treatment would typically turn around ready to punch whoever kicked them. But they backed down when they saw it was six-year-old Ricky.

By the time he got to the Ranch at age eleven, Ricky had already been to reform school. And one of his favorite responses to our direction and discipline was to threaten that he would run away.

Finally, Carl Orth had enough of his threats.

"Ricky," said Carl, looking him straight in the eyes. "I'm sick and tired of hearing you talk about running away. So here's what I propose. Today is the day you can run away. So go ahead and do it. Run away. But I'll tell you this. Here at the Ranch we believe in something called unconditional love. And what that means is that if you leave this place, I will find you and bring you back."

Ricky didn't run away, and he never mentioned the idea

again. But others tried. I remember driving from Billings to the Ranch one day. As I got close to the Ranch I saw one of our boys named Billy walking down the road away from the Ranch.

I honked my horn, pulled over to the side of the road, and spoke to Billy.

"Where you going, Billy?"

"Oh," he said, "I don't know Mr. Robbie."

"Well, in that case, would you like me to drive you back to the Ranch?"

Billy looked at me with his big blue eyes.

"Yes," he said. "I would like that."

Once Dan Hansen saw a boy named Robert riding his bike on campus. Robert had already tried to escape on foot once or

Sports and recreation were a high point for many Ranch kids. Softball and soccer are among the kids' favorite sports.

Co-ed soccer and indoor hockey are popular intramural sports at the Ranch.

twice, and Dan didn't want him trying with a bike.

"So, Robert," he said, "you're not going off campus with your bike, are you?"

"No, Mr. Hansen," he said.

An hour or two later, one of our staff found Robert pedaling as fast as he could down Hesper Road. When Robert was returned to the Ranch, Chaplain Hansen talked to him.

"I thought we agreed that you wouldn't leave the campus on your bike," he said.

"I didn't," said Robert. "It's not my bike!"

Some Ranch escapees were able to make it to a nearby town before they were found. One called us from his new location with a request.

"I left so quickly that I didn't pack," he said. "Could you send me my clothes?"

"Sure we will," we said. "Just let us know your address."

But others didn't get so far. One of our obsessive/compulsive kids would decide to run away and make a few steps toward the gate, but then would turn back, unsure of herself.

And one of our boys who wanted to flee ran into difficulties. Literally.

When Jim Soft worked at the Ranch as a college summer staffer in 1966 in one of our boys lodges, a boy named Terry tried to make a speedy getaway from one of the other lodge counselors.

"I was standing outside of Fortin West Lodge," says Jim. "Suddenly I saw the door fly open and heard Terry screaming his head off saying, 'You'll never catch me.'

"Unfortunately, Terry was looking back over his shoulder while running full-speed ahead. A few feet outside the door he ran straight into a big wooden light pole, knocking himself unconscious."

That was Terry's last escape attempt.

Where There's Smoke There's Fire

Until about 1985 the Ranch operated its own fire department, in part because our two closest government fire departments in Billings and Laurel weren't able to respond to fires or other emergencies at the Ranch in a timely manner.

Our fire department had a fire truck that had been phased

The Ranch's home grown fire fighting team came in handy more than once!

out of service by one of the local municipalities. We also had a crew of firefighters. These were staff living on campus who had been trained by the Billings Fire Department. As a result of having a fully equipped fire truck and trained personnel, the Ranch qualified for a small amount of state funding to help support ongoing upgrades to our fire equipment.

But acceptance of these funds also required the Ranch Fire Department to participate in the Yellowstone County Fire Suppression Agreement. This meant our crew was required to respond to fires on any of our neighbors' property within a ten-mile radius of the campus. The gradual growth of Billings, which has come closer and closer to the Ranch over the years, finally led to the abandonment of this Agreement.

The Ranch fire department came in handy more than once. Like the time a group of kids hid under the bridge on 72nd Street to smoke a cigarette. We never knew there was a natural gas leak under that bridge until those kids lit up. The small explosion didn't hurt anyone, but it nearly scared those kids to death. And our fire department was on the scene in moments, ready to provide first aid if needed.

We were also glad we had a fire department the day in 1994 when some kids jammed pencil leads into an electrical outlet in Leuthold Lodge. The prank caused electrical arcing that resulted in a fire. The building wasn't damaged, but it rapidly filled with smoke. We were easily able to locate the culprits. All we had to do was look for watery eyes and sniff around for the telltale smell of smoke.

Dinner for Two

Lyle Seavy has more than two decades worth of counseling experience in a variety of mental health settings. In 1994 he was named our vice president of Residential Services, and in 2005 he was named vice president of Strategic Planning. We're glad that we have executives like Lyle who have significant front-line experience with our kids. Lyle's experience includes an unusual situation that arose with a boy named Merlin.

"Back in 1984 I was a counselor in Fortin West Lodge," says Lyle. "When it was time for dinner we would eat together at a table with seats for me and nine kids.

"Dinner was always a fun time, but I noticed that something strange seemed to be going on. Whenever I turned and looked at Merlin after talking with one of the other boys, I would notice that he was hiding his hands under the table and giving me a guilty look. A couple of times, I even saw Merlin removing food from his plate and putting it in his pockets.

"I wondered what Merlin was doing with his food, so I followed him back to the lodge after dinner one night. He entered his room and headed straight for the closet. There seemed to be a strange noise coming from that closet, and when Merlin opened the door a kitten hopped out and ran to his cupped hand.

"Unlike many normal families, we have rules against kids having pets in their rooms at the Ranch. Merlin knew that, and when I confronted him about his cat he expressed his frustration by cussing me out in a big, long blue streak of words.

"After things calmed down, I made Merlin a promise.

"'I'll take care of your cat for you, Merlin,'" I said.

"'Will you, Mr. Seavy?' he said, with a grateful look in his eyes. 'Oh, that would be great.'"

"I took that cat home with me from work that night. We kept her and took care of her until she died seventeen years later."

Just the Beginning of the Story

Just as old soldiers swap war stories when they get together, those of us who work at the Ranch now or worked there in the past frequently compare anecdotes about some of the more unusual episodes that have happened here over the years. If a tape recorder had been running when we told these stories, I could fill an entire book with episodes that are every bit as funny and unexpected as the mass exodus that happened the night John Jamison showed *The Great Escape*.

But I think the stories in this chapter give you an idea of the type of environment we have here. Even though kids don't want to be sent here, and some continue to express their displeasure for some time after they settle in, we try to create a community that has the same kind of warmth, support, and love that a good family would provide. And for many of our kids, their time here with us is the first time in their lives they have ever experienced such love.

As you will see in the second half of the book, changing times brought with them new pressures for the Ranch to become more professional and more clinical. But as we adjusted to the times and developed new programs to meet the needs of different kinds of kids, we never lost the family feel that makes the Ranch a warm and caring place.

Timeless Ranch Traditions

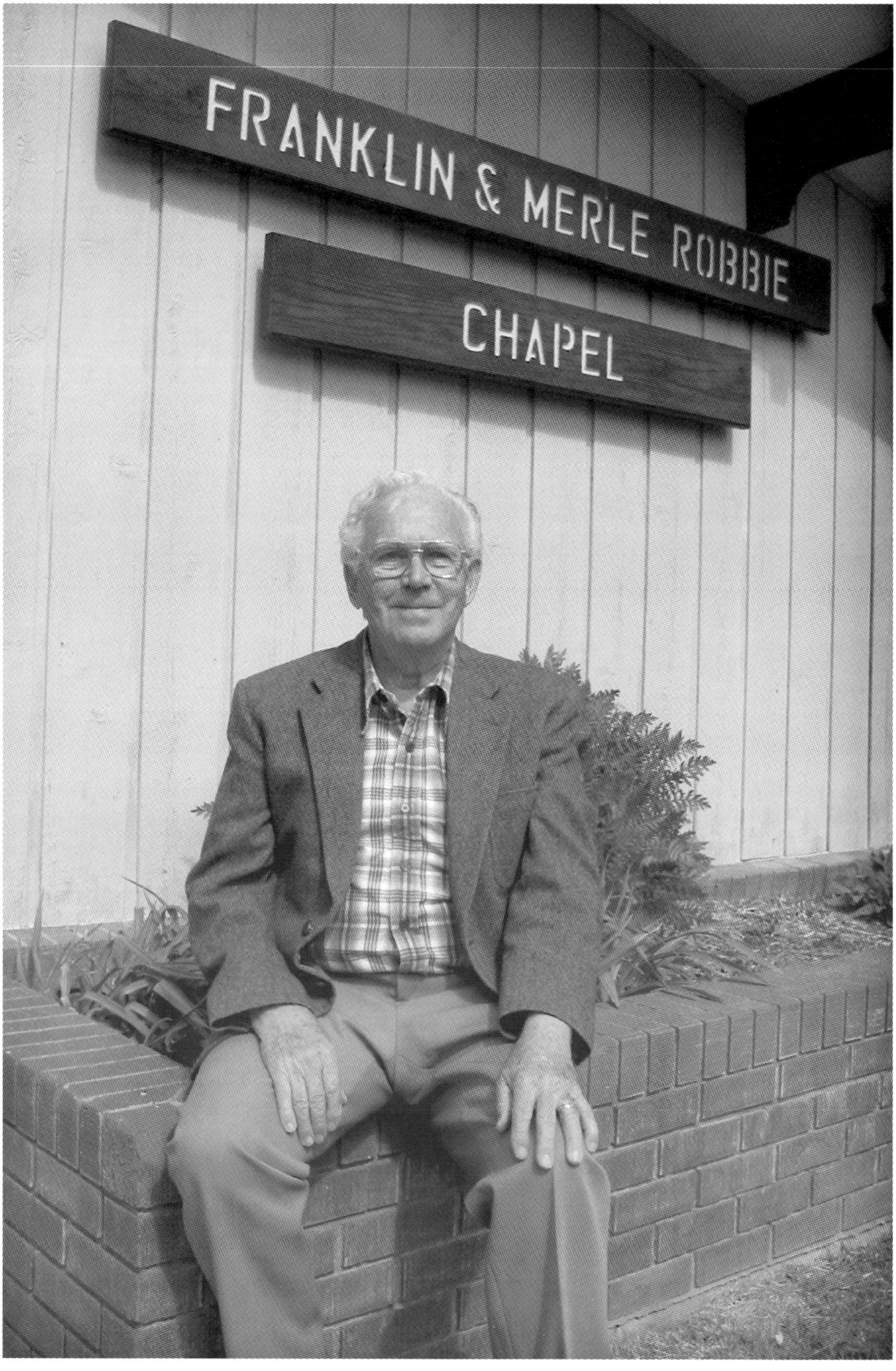
FRANKLIN & MERLE ROBBIE
CHAPEL

Section II

The Vision Matures

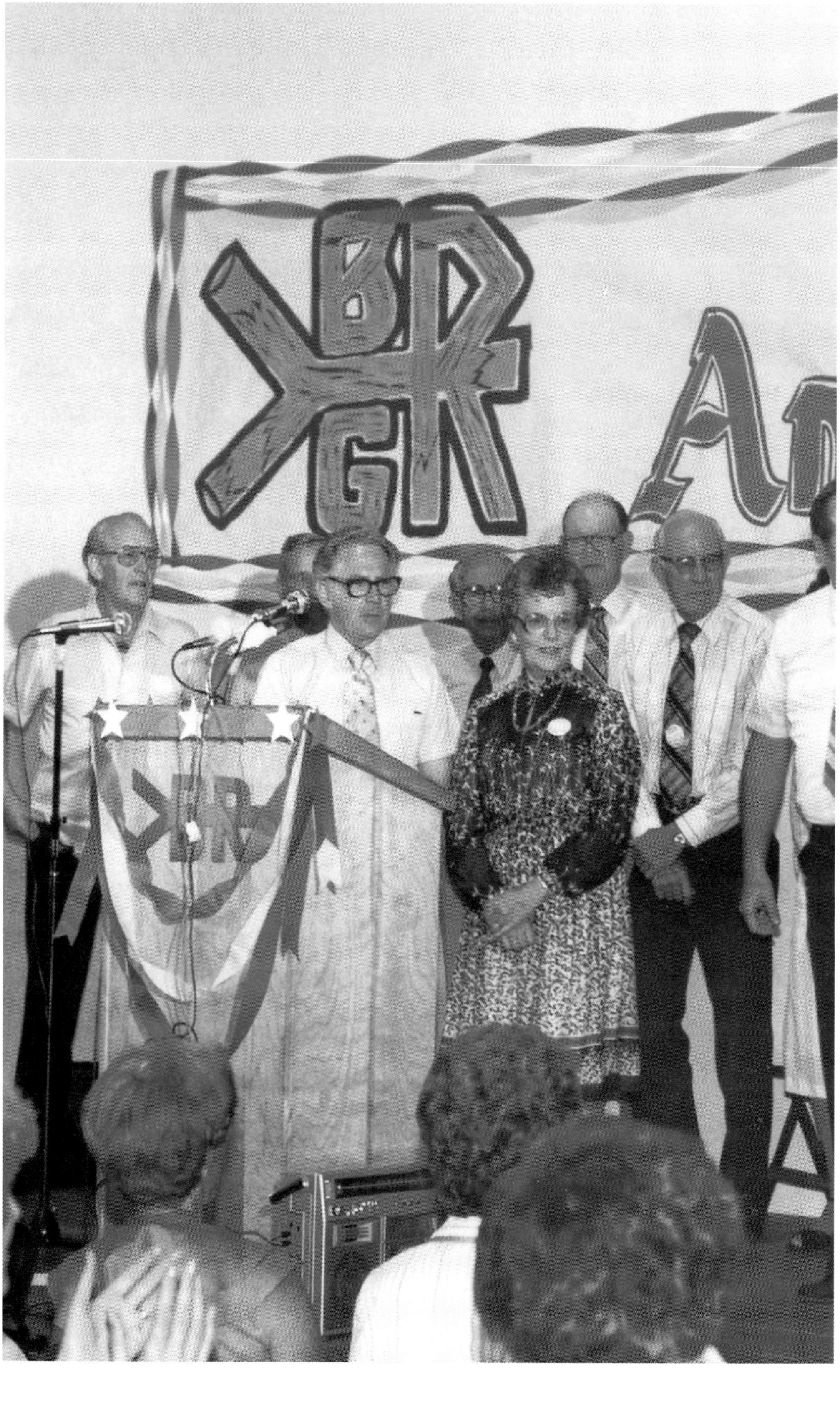

Chapter Ten

A New Day, with New Challenges

Millions of Americans were involved in patriotic celebrations during the 1982 Fourth of July weekend. Meanwhile, those of us involved in the work of Yellowstone Boys and Girls Ranch were having a major celebration of our own.

Our staff, board of directors, youth, and many friends and supporters gathered to commemorate the Ranch's twenty-fifth anniversary. We were also pleased to welcome many boys who had graduated from the Ranch, and these alumni provided a constant reminder of the vision that had brought the Ranch into existence.

That vision was to help troubled young people make the transformation they needed to put their past behind them and prepare for a future of possibility and hope. The simple slogan we came up with in the early days still expressed our vision as well as anything could: IT SURE MAKES A DIFFERENCE WHEN YOU KNOW SOMEBODY CARES.

In many ways, the Ranch itself was going through a similar transformation from past to future. At the Saturday evening banquet that weekend (pictured on facing page), I was pleased to welcome four men who had been members of the Ranch's original board: (pictured from left behind Merle and me) Forrest Crum, Bill MacKay, Les Shryock, and Ted Keating. These men had given the Ranch their time, their wisdom, and their financial support, and without them the vision of helping young people might never have become a reality.

During chapel the next morning, I was keenly aware that the future success of the Ranch depended on a number of people in the audience whose expertise and skill would guide it through many challenges during the next twenty-five years.

If this book were a thousand pages long, it would make sense to salute each of the many leaders and staff people whose dedication and compassion helped the Ranch survive and thrive in its second twenty-five years. Instead, the following pages will focus on a handful of key people who made the difficult decisions and invested the hard work that would ensure that the Ranch would continue to evolve and grow into its fiftieth year.

As I spoke on Sunday morning at chapel, I was addressing my comments to these leaders as well as the scores of other people who came to celebrate our anniversary. And I turned to the Old Testament book of Joshua, which describes an important period of transition from thousands of years ago.

Just as Joshua faced an important period of transition when Israel prepared to enter the Promised Land, Yellowstone was facing its own major transitions as it entered its second quarter century of service.

The Ranch was undergoing a major shift in its approach to childcare, moving from its original foster-parent model to a more clinical emphasis designed to help more deeply troubled youth. While many of our approaches were undergoing significant and necessary change, I wanted to make sure we were not turning our back on the core values of compassion, caring, and concern that had guided us from the beginning.

Thankfully, the emerging leaders who sat in the chapel pews that morning would make sure the Ranch's founding vision was safe and secure. Even more, the foresight and dedication they would exercise over the next twenty-five years would ensure that the Ranch grew and improved its staffing, programs, and services in ways that amazed those of us who had been there from the earliest days.

People of Passion

There are now nearly four hundred employees at the Ranch, and a large number of these people have been with us ten years, twenty years, or even longer, even though the work that is required of many employees at the Ranch can be very demanding. Why do they stay with us for so long?

I believe the answer to this question is passion. The one thing that keeps our employees motivated year after year is their passion for kids and their commitment to helping them overcome the tremendous problems they face.

We depend on them all, but if I were to name one person who has probably had the greatest impact on the work at the Ranch in its second twenty-five years, it would be Loren Soft. Loren came to us as a teacher and principal in 1965 after graduating from Eastern Montana College in Billings. Shortly after our twenty-fifth anniversary celebration in 1982 he became our CEO, a position he held until

Loren Soft always enjoyed giving awards to boys and girls at the Ranch.

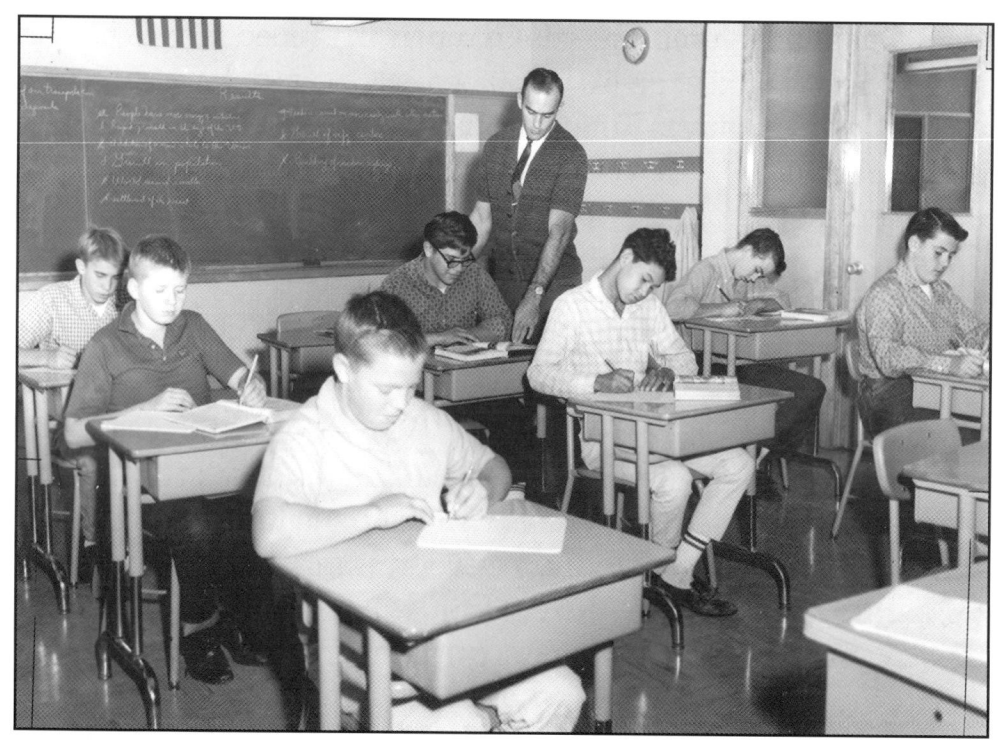

Loren Soft came to the Ranch as a teacher in 1965, and retired as CEO four decades later.

his retirement in 2004.

Retirement is probably not the best word for Loren's current state of life. He still works with the Ranch on various projects, and helps direct the work of the Yellowstone Resource Center, which provides consulting and training for boards and staff of other not-for-profit human service agencies. He serves as an administrator for a church here in Billings.

Even when Loren first joined our staff, he did far more than just teach. "Back then everyone on the Ranch did everything," he says. "The days were long, and we all worked with the kids from 5:30 in the morning when we milked the cows until 9:30 or later at night when we put everyone to bed."

Kids always looked up to Loren. They had to, and not only because he is over six feet tall! Like many of the other workers and leaders at the Ranch, Loren has that rare combination of gifts that allows him to be gentle when kids need him to be and firm when they need someone to set and enforce boundaries.

Loren not only taught the academic subjects in our Ranch school, but he also coached our kids in their various athletic activities, oversaw their work around the Ranch, and listened when they needed someone to talk to about their problems. His growing role in counseling kids led him to get a master's degree in counseling from Eastern Montana College in 1973. Soon after that he became the ranch administrator. Then after a number of years he became our CEO.

As our senior executive, Loren used his counseling background to help the Ranch in its painful transition to a more intensive treatment center for severely emotionally disturbed young people.

"During the 80s and 90s, I saw my job as being similar to an orchestra conductor," he said. "I was trying to make sure that everybody was on the same page, playing the same music, hopefully, beautiful music."

Loren was also a visionary who knew how to transform his ideas into practical programs that others could understand and put into practice. And outside the boundaries of the Ranch he was a tireless advocate in the political and legislative arenas for the needs of children and families.

From 1995 to 2001, Loren served in the Montana State House of Representatives, which meets from January through April of every other year. We sorely missed his presence during his months with the legislature in Helena, but his work there allowed him to serve not only the kids at the Ranch but also work on behalf of all the people of our state.

"Frankly, serving in the legislature was one of the best things that ever happened to me," he says. "I never represented Yellowstone Boys and Girls Ranch during my time in the legislature, I represented the field of human services. But during my tenure I was able to sponsor nearly thirty bills that would benefit people who depend on these services, and all but one were enacted into law."

Loren's experience in the halls of government would play an important role in the life of the Ranch as we increasingly received troubled children from state agencies both in Montana and nationwide.

Like many present and former employees, Loren still regularly receives phone calls at his home from former Ranch kids who update him on their latest struggles and triumphs.

"They always call and say, 'Hi, remember me?' And I nearly always do," says Loren.

Loren is a man whose passion for caring for kids remains strong and powerful, and the Ranch was in exceptionally good hands during the twenty-two years he served as our CEO.

Getting the Hard Work Done

Too often, history books focus solely on the leaders who make all the big decisions and set all the policies that others will follow. But here at the Ranch, all the good policies in the world wouldn't make a bit of difference in the lives of troubled kids unless there were caring, professional people who could put these ideas into action.

When I spoke at the Ranch's twenty-fifth anniversary celebration, there was a young man in the audience who, in many ways, represents the kind of care and compassion that makes the difference in so many of the kids who come through here.

His name is Mike Hammer (see photos, next page), and he joined us in 1979 as a child counselor. At that time he thought he would work at this job for a year or two before a better opportunity opened up elsewhere. Now it's more than a quarter century later, and Mike is still here investing his life in our kids.

"I've been through cycles during my time at the Ranch," says Mike. "There are times when the demands are tough and the burnout is high. And some people can't take it very long. But when I have looked at my options, there's nothing else I could consider doing that would have as much worth and impact as what I'm doing here."

During his years at the Ranch, Mike has had his share of opportunities to move from front-line work with kids to administrative positions. But Mike found that when he worked behind a desk he missed the one-on-one work with the kids.

"When I stepped out of direct child care, I realized that I needed to go back to counseling because administration wasn't what I came here to do," he says. "For me, even though the work is rough, being able to work directly with difficult kids every day helps me feel I am contributing. There's nothing else that makes me feel more like I am being used by God than when I am

Mike Hammer started helping kids at the Ranch in 1979 (above) and is still serving here over a quarter century later.

working with a kid and helping him work through his problems."

The work hasn't always been easy. Recently I sat down with Mike and three of the other front-line counselors who work most closely with the Ranch residents. Every one of these counselors can detail difficult situations in which kids cursed them, hit them, kicked them, bit them, threw things at them, or spit on them.

"I can remember the first time a boy clenched his fist at me," says Mike. "I told him, 'Please don't do that.' Then he popped me on the jaw."

Mike and the other counselors who work with troubled kids at the Ranch could find easier jobs. They could also react with anger when anger is directed their way. But for Mike and the others, those tense situations in which kids act out their buried anger and rage are perfect opportunities to show compassion and grace.

"The challenge when you receive abuse from a kid is to put your own feelings aside and maintain a loving and caring approach. Or as we say around the Ranch, each crisis or trauma situation is a teachable moment. And that's how we choose to react."

Organizational values—like the Ranch's commitment to providing professional and caring assistance for hurting kids—are little more than platitudes unless there are people throughout the organization committed to carrying them out. And without people like Mike and all the other counselors and therapists who deliver that care to very difficult kids, the Ranch would fail to deliver on the promises it makes.

A Doctor in the House

Another person who was sitting in the audience during our twenty-fifth anniversary celebration was Joe Rich. Since then, Joe has earned more professional credentials and awards than most people could imagine.

He is a medical doctor and psychiatrist. He is a former president of the Montana Psychiatric Association and a Distinguished Life Fellow of the American Psychiatric Association. He serves as a member of the Domestic Violence Fatality Review Commission appointed by the Montana Attorney General. And he has been named an Outstanding Doctor in both the state and the nation.

In 1977 Joe was a psychiatrist in private practice who came to the Ranch two days a week to help us out. Back then we were starting to receive greater numbers of more significantly troubled kids, and we weren't always sure what to do with them.

At that time, Dr. Rich was not able to offer his services on a full-time basis, but his consistent part-time services from 1977 to 1987 made a big difference. He helped us design some of our early assessment and treatment programs. He also did a great job on staff training, and constantly admonished us to "think clinically" about the behavior and needs of the youth in our care. In 1987 the Billings Deaconess Hospital developed a Psychiatric and Behavioral Health Center and recruited Dr. Rich to become its medical director, a position that occupied him during much of the 1980s and 90s.

However, it was our good fortune to become acquainted with Dr. Dennis Frisbee of Sheridan, Wyoming, who was willing to commute to our campus at least two days a week. Dr. Frisbee's tenure at the Ranch was significant not only because of his medical and psychiatric training but also because, for a number of years, he was the only board certified child psychiatrist available in the area. This specialized training was necessary in order for the Ranch to become nationally accredited by the Joint Commission on Accreditation of Healthcare Organizations.

Dr. Frisbee continued to emphasize the need for staff training and development while demonstrating first-hand the role that a psychiatrist can have in the lives of troubled children. Soon our treatment team was substantially strengthened with the arrival from California of licensed child psychologist Dr. J. Wesley Reilly, who became resident clinical director of all our assessment-treatment programs, working closely with Dr. Frisbee and Dr. Rich in their part-time capacities.

Another major milestone in the evolution of the Ranch came in response to changes in Medicaid funding for the kinds of services we provide. In 1991 the Montana legislature approved residential treatment facilities for Medicaid reimbursement if

Dr. Paul Crellin helped the Ranch develop a "medical model" for treating young people.

they could meet the necessary licensing and accreditation criteria established by the state's Department of Health and Human Services. These demanding criteria meant that in order to qualify we would need to have a full-fledged medical and clinical department that provided around-the-clock medical and clinical coverage under the supervision of a qualified medical director.

A well-known Billings pediatrician, Dr. Paul Crellin, helped us meet these criteria. Dr. Crellin enjoyed the respect of the community for his work with learning-disabled children. His ability to relate to the Ranch team (including medical staff) and the youth in our care helped move us strongly ahead as we continued to make progress in assimilating what we know today as the "medical model" of childcare at Yellowstone Boys and Girls Ranch.

When Dr. Crellin retired, Dr. Rich had left Deaconess Hospital and was happy to accept the position of medical director of Yellowstone Boys and Girls Ranch–a position he still holds.

Together with other professionals like Phil House and Jodi Groot, who you will meet in the next chapter, Joe and others have helped develop the Ranch's on-site and off-site medical and clinical programs.

Today's Ranch is a much different place than it was fifty years ago. Today children come to the Ranch from a dozen states, many of them referred by doctors who have reached the limits of their own abilities and turn to the Ranch to help kids who are in desperate need of intensive care.

Changes in American Culture Bring Changes at Ranch

One of the people who has watched this transformation closely from his unique perspective is Dale Orth. Dale first came to the Ranch in 1957 with his father, Carl Orth, who along with Bob McFarlane guided the Ranch's development in its earliest years.

"We arrived that summer, and I had my sixth birthday on the Ranch," says Dale. "Living on the Ranch was just wonderful. I liked everything about it except the chores."

Following the death of his father, Dale moved off the Ranch with his family. He returned in 1977 after receiving a psychology degree from Eastern Montana College.

"I saw an ad in the paper looking for a counselor to work with emotionally disturbed kids," he says. "There was no mention in the ad of who the employer was. When I called the number and reached the Ranch it was odd. But I had a feeling it was my destiny to be here."

After serving as a counselor, unit supervisor of a boys lodge, assessment coordinator, crisis intervention supervisor, program director, staff trainer, and staff development coordinator, Dale was named senior vice president of administrative services in 1997, the same title he holds today.

"There have been significant changes at the Ranch and in American culture over the last fifty years," says Dale. "And during the past quarter century, there has been greater acceptance socially of the need for counseling for both adults and kids. The challenge for us was to adapt to new mental health techniques while remaining true to our faith and our values.

"The thing that has saved those of us who work at the Ranch over the years is that we have continually recognized the fact that we don't have all the answers. We keep seeking and keep changing what we do.

"The questions we keep asking ourselves are: How do we serve this group of kids best? And what are the best practices with which we can help each child?"

Those of us who have been around as long as Dale has can

look back fondly to the early days when most of the kids who lived at the Ranch seemed to struggle with behavioral problems more than they did with deeper emotional problems. Today, the Ranch is home to many severely troubled young people, many of whom try to physically harm themselves and others. Some are so disturbed that they try to take their own lives.

"In the early days, the Ranch kids were my friends," says Dale. "That would be difficult today. But the same principles hold true. We are trying to care for hurting kids. And the medical facilities and government agencies that refer many of our kids to us today know we do that in a professional, clinical way. They also know we bring a spiritual component to what we do. And for us, that's an important part of the care we give."

The Challenge of Change

As you can see, there has been tremendous change at the Ranch over the years. If I had been able to see into the future back when we were celebrating our twenty-fifth anniversary I am sure I would have been surprised to see the major transitions that were heading our way.

Throughout our periods of change, the one question many of us have continually asked ourselves is: How can we change and improve what we're doing in order to better meet the needs of the kids we serve?

The process of repeatedly asking that question—and the discipline of forcing ourselves to come up with the best possible answers—is what has made us what we are today.

Transformed Lives

**Jenna Kirwan Bertels:
A New Way to Live**

October 6 is a special day Jenna Kirwan will celebrate as long as she lives. It was on October 6, 1997, that Jenna, a teenage runaway with a runaway drug problem, agreed to meet her mom and dad for dinner. After dinner, her parents somehow got her into their car and didn't let her out again until they had driven fourteen hours straight from Seattle to Yellowstone Boys and Girls Ranch.

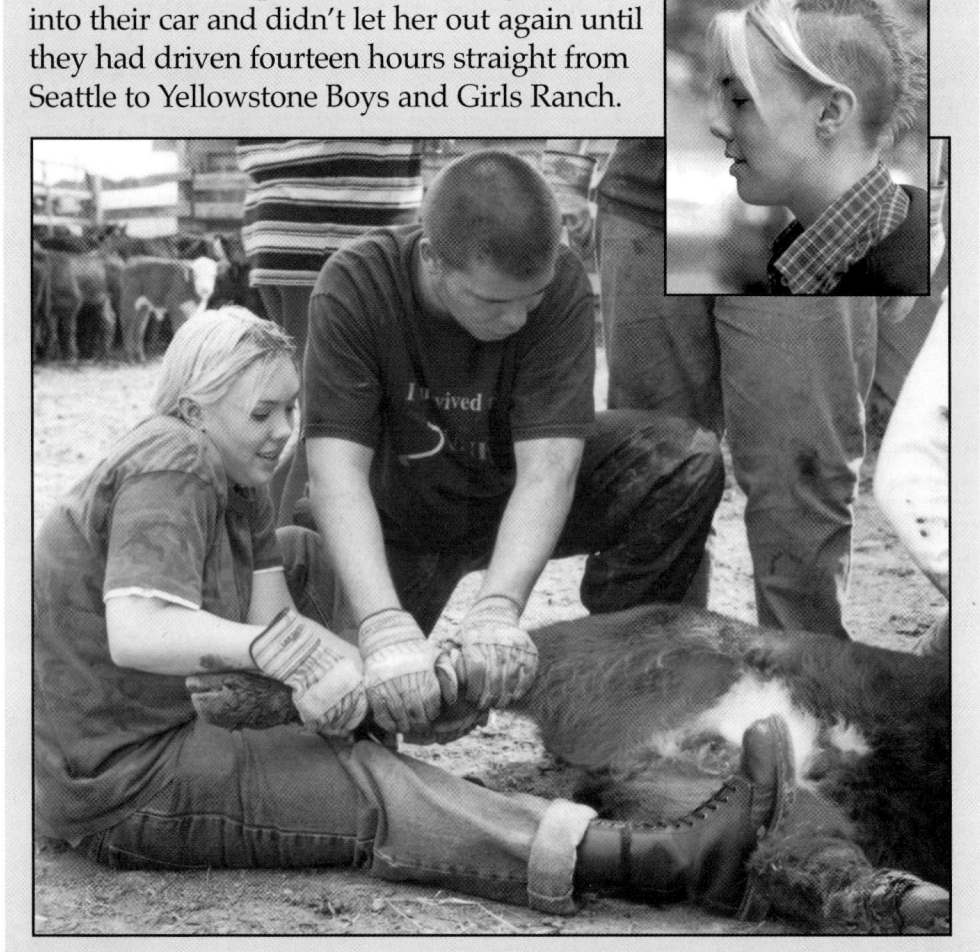

City girl Jenna gets into branding cattle.

It had been a tough few years for Jenna and her family. "The lowest point for me was the day I met her for coffee," says mother Lynn. "We met downtown on her 'turf' near the area where she was living on the street. She came with her sleeping bag on her back and looked dirty and hungry. We hugged, and as she walked away, I could feel my heart breaking for her."

Lynn and her husband, Dick, soon devised an elaborate plan to grab Jenna and fly her to Yellowstone. But once they had her in their car, Jenna became so angry and agitated they decided to drive through the night instead of risking an outburst during a plane flight.

"Jenna had been to several dependency programs, including one she attended after an alcohol-related arrest when she was fourteen," says Lynn. "We took her to Yellowstone because of its reputation and because they really seemed to care."

Jenna, with JoAnne Fessler, on one of her return trips to the Ranch to speak to the kids.

CEO Loren Soft has vivid memories of Jenna's arrival. Looking out his office window, he noticed a car with Washington license plates pull into the parking lot. A couple got out and came into the administration building. As their story unfolded, it became clear that Jenna was brought to the Ranch against her will, and at that moment, was refusing to get out of the car.

JoAnne Fessler, the therapist assigned to the lodge where Jenna would eventually live, was called to come and assist in the admissions process. She arrived and immediately went to the car to visit with Jenna, hoping she would at least open the window to allow a conversation to take place. Finally, the back window of the car came down ever so slightly. There was considerable discussion, although one-sided, as JoAnne did most of the talking.

Soon JoAnne left the car and walked over to the school. She

With husband, Jake.

returned with a young lady from the lodge where Jenna would live. Loren's immediate internal reaction was, "JoAnne, why did you pick that particular young lady to try and talk this girl out of the car?"

However, it was a wise choice. After a few minutes, the window came down a bit further; and, at last, the door opened. Jenna stepped out. She was dressed in full combat gear; boots included, loaded with jewelry on every visible part of her body and sporting a double Mohawk, bleached blonde hairstyle. Loren remembers thinking that the chances of helping this young lady change were slim to none. "Where should we begin? Do we start with the clothes, the jewelry, and the wild hairstyle? Or maybe, we just accept her as she is and help her want to change herself."

"That was the beginning of me being clean," says Jenna, who had grown dependent on a smorgasbord of drugs like speed, methamphetamines, heroin, and cocaine. "And I've been clean ever since."

Her eight months at Yellowstone weren't happy times. "It was the worst time of my life!" she says. "It was awful; but at the same time, it was the best thing that could have happened to me.

"It was while I was at the Ranch that I came to realize I didn't have to live the way I had been living. It suddenly dawned on me that I was so lucky to have an opportunity to try and do something different with my life and connect with my higher power."

After a few weeks at the Ranch, Jenna was smiling more. Her countenance lifted. She began to excel in school and took a special interest in the auto mechanics and welding programs. She was even chosen Student of the Month. Jenna says everyone—from her counselor, to her shop teacher, to the Ranch chaplain, to CEO Loren Soft—expressed concern for her.

Lynn adds, "They did care for her, but they didn't show it in a wishy-washy way. They were strong. They made her work on her issues. They could see she was a very special, unique kid, and they told her that in their interactions with her."

"I had been hiding behind drugs and dark clothing and wild hair," Jenna says. "Once all these things were gone, it was just me. There were no big lights coming from heaven. It was just a process of me seeing that life didn't have to be the way it had been."

Jenna made excellent progress and the time came for her to return home. A few days before her discharge, she came up to Loren in the dining hall with what appeared to be some type of metal sculpture. When he asked her about it, she proudly said, "I made this for my dad. He loves to fish." What she had crafted in welding shop was a free-form base, polished to resemble a lake. On the lake's edge was a fishing pier, and on the pier was a person holding a fishing pole with the line running out to the center of the lake—all made out of metal. She made it for her dad, the same dad who just a few short months before, had placed her in his car and brought her, against her will, to the Ranch.

Loren says, "I was moved to tears as I recalled the amazing transformation of this young lady."

Jenna returned home, and the busy life of helping other children consumed Loren's time. One day Jenna called to say she was enrolling in college and was inquiring about the scholarship program available for youth who have successfully completed treatment at Yellowstone. Jenna met all the requirements and was given the help she requested.

Approximately three years later, an invitation arrived to attend the graduation ceremony for Jenna, who had completed her undergraduate degree in record time. The young lady who had arrived at Yellowstone, having failed in school, gotten involved in Seattle street life, and become totally estranged from her parents, was now going to walk across the stage and receive her college diploma. Truly a miracle and a testimony to the faithful staff at Yellowstone, where the motto, "Giving up is not an option," is lived out every day.

But the story doesn't end there! About a year later Chaplain John Jamison received a call from Lynn, announcing that Jenna was engaged to be married and wanted him to perform the ceremony. "Jenna really wants her Yellowstone 'family' to be represented," Lynn said. "You all are such an important part of what Jenna has become. Will you please come?"

It wasn't hard to say yes to such a request! The Jamisons had a wonderful time observing first-hand the lasting changes that have taken place in Jenna's life. Her father's beaming smile, as he gave her away to her new husband, Jake, brought back memories of the day they arrived at Yellowstone when he had said, with tears streaming down his face, "I just want my daughter back."

Jenna's wedding was a true celebration of a new way of life.

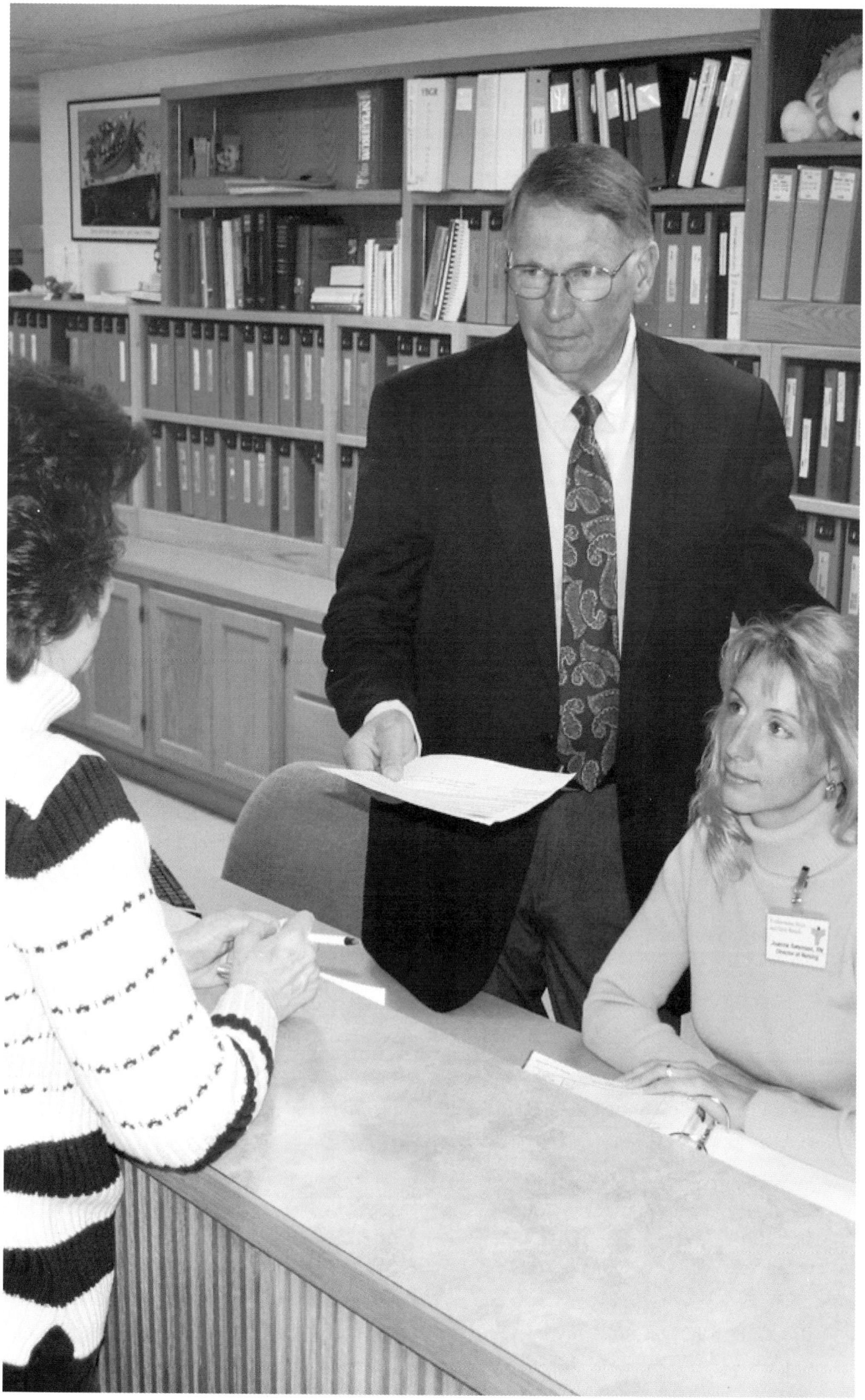

Chapter Eleven

From "Ranch" to "Treatment Center"

Once upon a time, the best experts in medicine, science, and government seemed to believe young people were largely immune from the kinds of mental illness that had been diagnosed in adults over the previous decades.

During the 1970s and 1980s, experts increasingly agreed that young people could experience mental illness too. And soon after, government leaders began passing laws and setting aside public funds to pay for treatment and care.

In a relatively short period of time, these changes in medical practice and government funding caused profound changes in our programs at the Ranch, but not in our core values. In many ways, we were becoming more of a treatment center for seriously emotionally disturbed youth while still trying to maintain the family-oriented atmosphere we'd had since our inception.

We were also receiving more deeply disturbed kids, who were being referred to us from a growing number of social service agencies and private institutions around the country. Often, young people who had proved too difficult to handle at other childcare institutions were sent to the Ranch for the kind of intensive, residential treatment care we provided.

I remember writing about one of these boys in a fund-raising letter, because in those years, the costs involved in upgrading our programs and facilities were growing at a rapid pace. The boy I described was named Danny, and, while his story was unique, it revealed the kinds of problems we were facing more often at the Ranch.

Danny's Story

Danny is an intelligent, active little ten-year-old with big problems. He was abandoned by his parents a few years ago, and now is a very frightened, insecure little boy.

Danny came to our program directly from the Children's Ward at Warm Springs State Mental Hospital. He was institutionalized following an incident in which he stole a gun and held his houseparents at gunpoint for several hours.

Danny decided long ago that the way to protect himself from hostile, unpredictable, and demanding people was to "blow them away." When he came to us, everything imaginable became a gun and the staff his targets. Couches, beds, tables, and cushions became his fortresses as he carefully watched the staff and other children. Every scrap of material and food was hidden away as he prepared to fight for survival once again. No one was to be trusted. Danny had taken care of himself in the past, and was determined not to ever depend on anybody again.

We have come to love Danny with his winning smile and constant flurry of activity. More importantly, he has come to trust his small circle of adults at Orth Lodge. He has traded his "gun" for a whistle and knows that if he blows it we'll be there to protect him.

Now we are trying to prepare Danny to broaden his horizons and become more comfortable with people and activities outside the controlled environments where he feels safe and secure. This prospect still frightens Danny. He wants to stay right where he is, and is afraid that if he makes too much progress he will once again be abandoned.

It takes compassion, care, hard work, and time for young people like Danny to overcome the challenges life has brought them. And in his case, like so many others, the Ranch has been able to play a powerful role in transforming troubled lives.

The Yellowstone Treatment Model

So what's the best way to treat someone like Danny? What are the best methods for addressing and hopefully healing some of the tremendous problems that cripple his ability to live anything like a normal, happy life?

These questions, with which our talented staff team confront themselves on a daily basis, became particularly acute in the 1980s. Generally speaking, until the 80s, the industry's

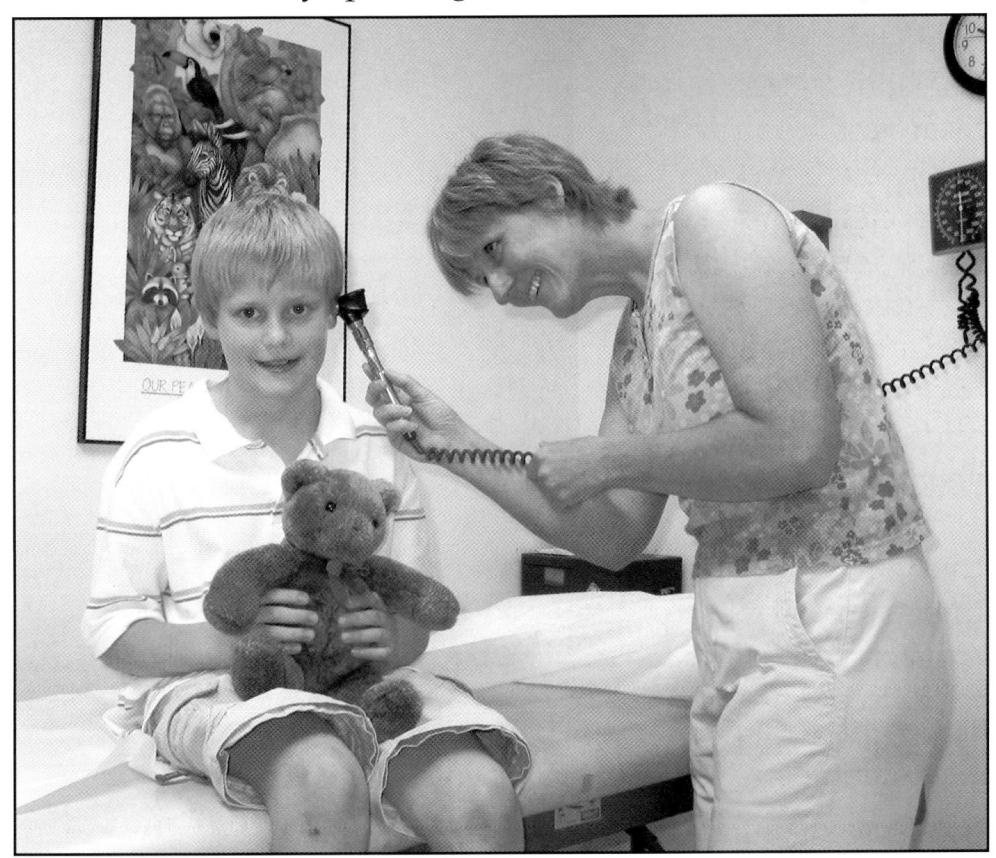

There have been different theories about caring for young people. The Yellowstone model seeks to utilize the best features of various approaches.

approach to working with troubled youth was one of independent specialization.

In very broad terms, these varied approaches came to be seen as fitting into one of the following four "camps."

The psychiatric camp focused largely on the medical aspects of a youth's struggles. Professionally this group was inclined to approach treatment in a medical, clinical manner attributing most disorders to the physiological realm.

The psychological camp spent its time looking primarily at behavioral issues, believing that the child's environment was the reason for his or her problems and that rehabilitation should focus on psychotherapy with a trained counselor.

The educational camp felt that since most of the youth who came to us were several years behind in school, their problems would be largely solved by a successful encounter in the appropriate school setting. After all, history demonstrated that many of society's problems can be solved by making sure each child has a good educational experience from which to approach life's challenges.

The spiritual camp, which was in some ways the basis and inspiration for the founding of Yellowstone, held the basic belief that all truth is God's truth, regardless of whether such truth shows up in the physical, behavioral, educational, or spiritual camps.

Ranch leaders and staff weighed the advantages and disadvantages of these various approaches in their efforts to meet the needs of the increasingly troubled children who were being sent our way. The results of their deliberations could be seen in a new model of care centered on the common conviction that the demand of the hour in childcare was the careful integration of all four disciplines into one comprehensive approach. Working with the problematic adolescent through such an integrated methodology soon became the approach at Yellowstone.

It wasn't long before Yellowstone became recognized across

the nation as a unique, top-rated program with a model of care that has the capacity of addressing the entire physical, emotional, educational, and spiritual needs of youth. Children soon were coming to Yellowstone from all across the United States.

Another big change at the Ranch was our shift from a house-parent model for supervising kids to a treatment model. As more and more severely disturbed young people came to the Ranch, our original approach of having all the kids live in small group homes with assigned houseparents needed to change.

Now our child housing units are more secure, more closely supervised, and more practical for young people who face more difficult struggles than some of the first kids we helped in the 1950s and 1960s.

Some of the houseparents who loved living and working with the kids at close range were disappointed to see the old model disappear, but they realized this was a change that had to be made, in part because some of the kids we worked with acted out in ways that were dangerous to others and to themselves.

These were tough times, as shifts in American culture and health care were causing shifts at the Ranch. Those of us who founded the Ranch in 1957 had appreciated the value of psychology and psychiatry, but had not fully taken advantage of the experts in these fields who were using their training and skills to help troubled kids like Danny.

Now we faced a choice. Were we going to look to the past and refuse to move beyond our earlier methods of childcare? Or were we going to look to the future, and seek ways that we could serve and help kids that incorporated the best in current medical science while staying true to our core values and beliefs?

Thankfully, we decided on the latter course. That decision is a big reason the Ranch has survived, thrived, and continued to help the hundreds of kids who depend on us every year.

Assessing the Situation

Though sincere, our efforts to incorporate the lessons and techniques of mental health into our practices took time to develop. Along the way some critics from the outside made fun of our efforts, mischaracterizing our approach with the following satirical slogan:

Make your beds. Bow your heads. Take your meds.

But before long, we began to make real progress in combining the best techniques of mental health and spiritual counseling. One of the people who played a crucial role in helping us make this transition was Phil House, who loves the word "integration."

Phil came to work with the Ranch as a counselor in 1977, bringing with him a master's degree in counseling. However, he left in 1979, in part because he was frustrated by the attitude of some here who were suspicious about psychology.

After he left, Phil went on to further his education, earning both a master's and a doctorate degree in clinical psychology. He also rounded out his professional experience by working as a family counselor, a counseling instructor, a public school psychologist, and a psychological assistant at a psychiatric hospital. Today he is a licensed professional counselor and licensed clinical psychologist.

He has also been a member of the Montana Sexual Offender Treatment Association, which helps him understand how to deal with both those who are sexual offenders and those who have been the victims of such abuse.

"Dr. Phil" rejoined our team at the Ranch in 1993. Ever since he has helped us integrate the best contemporary psychological practices with the timeless values that have shaped our approach. This dual approach has helped us deal with mental illness and other profound human problems.

For five years Phil was the vice president of the Ranch's

Our "Dr. Phil" (second from left) meets with others in the Ranch's Clinical Services department.

Clinical Services department, where he helped develop the assessment procedures we use to evaluate every young person who is sent to the Ranch.

The Ranch has a wealth of wisdom and practical experience, and it offers a wide range of treatment plans and living arrangements. But what approach will work best for each child? This is a question that can only be answered after a thorough assessment is performed into the specific nature of each patient's problems.

The psychological assessment process we use at the Ranch focuses on four main areas:

1) social-emotional adjustment;
2) cognitive functioning;
3) academic functioning; and
4) vocational/career development.

But as Phil explains, the assessment process the Ranch uses really gets more complicated than that. Our process examines fifteen separate areas, including information gained from parents or guardians, medical evaluations, and assessments that look at a child's behavior during recreation periods, work periods, and during pastoral counseling times.

This "multiaxial assessment" helps Ranch staff pinpoint a child's problems. And the more we know about what's wrong, the more we can do to specifically address those problems.

Down on the Farm

While our clinical facilities resemble some of the nation's best psychiatric treatment centers, the Ranch has other resources that most treatment centers don't, including many acres of farmland and the crops and livestock to go with them. We're still called Yellowstone Boys and Girls Ranch, and that word *ranch* still plays an important part in explaining who we are.

Those of us who founded the Ranch believed in getting kids out of reform schools where they were locked up much of the time and letting them experience life on a working ranch. We were convinced that hard work and contact with Creation could play an important role in their healing.

Today, these ideas have significant credibility among some leaders in the mental health field who believe that places like the Ranch provide a better environment for healing than do the more clinical environments found in many juvenile psychiatric hospitals.

Over the years, farm managers like John Frey, Don Shay, and Carroll Lipp have worked hard to integrate our kids' involvement in our many ranching and farming activities with their individualized counseling regimen and vocational training programs. Today, the man who makes sure farm and Ranch work together is Gary Adams, our director of Farm and Ranch Operations.

Gary joined the Ranch staff in 1989, but his passion for kids and ranching began in his own childhood. "I always loved ranching and farming and when I would see kids who had gotten in trouble, it seemed to me that spending some time working on a ranch could help some of them out. Because of

Gary Adams (left) teaches branding and other skills through the Ranch's Vo-Ag programs.

that, after I graduated from college, it was my dream to start a boys ranch. But when I saw Yellowstone Boys and Girls Ranch was already using ranching to help troubled kids, I decided to join them."

Since Gary came to Yellowstone, he has worked to transform many of the tasks involved in ranching and farming into powerful tools in young people's education and healing.

"We've got four hundred acres of land, and two hundred fifty of those acres are in farm and pasture land," he says. "This is a working farm. And whether young people are branding cattle, building new corrals, fixing machinery that needs to be worked on, using carpentry skills to build new fences, or welding metal for projects around the Ranch, they are having hands-on experiences that tie into what they learn in the classroom."

Gary regularly has interactions with Ranch kids that show

him good things are happening through our vocational-agricultural (vo-ag) programs.

"Kids apply to be a part of work crews that are assigned to do various projects around the Ranch," he says. "In the spring one of the tasks is branding calves. Some of our kids love this, but others find it difficult working with the calves. One young man found it so difficult that he stormed off and sat on a fence. After a while, some of us coaxed him into giving branding another try. Within a few minutes he got more aggressive, and was throwing down calves with ease."

Gary thinks such lessons play an important role in the many services the Ranch offers to kids. "You can call it therapy, or you can call it preparing kids for life," he says. "Whatever you call it, I believe it makes a positive difference in kids' lives."

Making the Case

We believe that the wealth of varied treatment options and programs the Ranch offers make it a positive place for kids to come and work out some of their problems. That's the message we give to the many medical and social agencies that refer kids to us. And many of them agree with us, sending us child after child after child.

But how can we prove that our unique combination of psychological, educational, vocational, and spiritual activities really makes a positive difference in kids' lives? Such proof was always elusive, in part because some kids' problems were so complex and our treatments were so varied. That's why a detailed study conducted by Jodi Groot is so important.

Jodi has worked at the Ranch since 1991, and is a member of the Ranch's psychiatric staff. As part of the research required for her Ph.D. studies, Jodi examined the kinds of impact the Ranch's treatment programs had on kids who came here.

The title of her thesis, which has been submitted to the American Academy of Child and Adolescent Psychology for publication, is "Assessing Change in Behavior and Social

Jodi Groot's research for her doctoral thesis concluded that even severe child behavioral problems could be resolved through the residential programs of the Ranch.

Competence of Severely Emotionally Disturbed Youth in Residential Treatment."

Jodi's study lasted for thirty months. It tracked sixty-three young people who were admitted to the Ranch and had spent at least four months with us. The kids were evaluated at admission and then evaluated again at discharge. The study concluded that most of the behavioral problems kids had when they arrived were resolved by the time they left the Ranch.

Jodi's research is important because there are many troubled kids in the U.S., and decisions are constantly being made about what kind of treatment is best for them.

"One in ten American young people, or as many as six million youth, experience serious emotional disturbances on a daily basis," she says. "And while some research has argued that residential treatment facilities can actually be harmful to kids, my research demonstrated that it was quite successful for most of the young people who come here."

Here's how Jodi stated her conclusions in the paper:

"The services provided and integrated in the residential treatment setting are believed to have had a very positive impact on outcomes for youth in this study," she wrote. "The safety, interdisciplinary care, and therapeutic community provided by a residential treatment setting must be acknowledged."

A Ranch and a Treatment Center

Of course, more research needs to be done, and we will always continue to examine and improve our programs. Still, it is gratifying to see research support what we have long believed: that Yellowstone Boys and Girls Ranch is a great place for kids who are suffering from severe emotional disturbances.

Technically speaking, the Ranch is licensed as both a mental health facility and a residential care facility. Medicaid officials and organizations like the Council on Accreditation have certified the Ranch as a child treatment center. But people who have seen our wealth of programs and resources know that the Ranch is unlike any other treatment center in the country.

In terms of professionalism and patient care, we are a top-notch clinical operation. But in terms of facilities, vo-ag programs, and the commitment of our people, I believe we provide so much more than a typical treatment center ever could provide.

By continually striving to integrate the best professional practices with our deep concern for kids and our unshakable faith in the uniqueness and eternal value of each child, the Ranch has become a place where lives are transformed. And for that I remain deeply grateful.

Transformed Lives

Jim Reed: Learning to Say Good-bye

For half a century, Yellowstone has tried to heal wounded families and reunite children with their parents whenever possible. But in Jim Reed's case, healing would only come through a complete break with a dysfunctional and destructive family.

City boy Jim feeding calves at the Ranch.

Tragedy entered Jim's life at the tender age of three. His mother died suddenly of a heart attack, leaving Jim in the care of a rigid father who was unable to provide any nurturing or emotional support for a lonely little boy. Things went from bad to worse when three months after his mother's death, Jim's father remarried. His stepmother was no more capable of caring for Jim's emotional needs than his dad was. In fact, she only drove a deeper wedge between Jim and his dad as she insisted that any family conflict was Jim's fault.

"I feel that my parents were both psychologically and physically abusive," says Jim. "Everything they said was negative. Everything bad that happened was my fault. No matter how well I did on a test or in sports, their reaction was that I could have done better. Over time I came to believe I couldn't do anything right. I simply gave up."

The physical abuse didn't help either. Jim's dad fashioned a special paddle just for him and used it liberally. Jim remembers that his worst beating came from breaking into his own home on a hot summer afternoon. "During the summer months," Jim says, "my parents would leave for work at 7:30 a.m. They would lock me out of my house with my bike and a little lunch money and tell me to not come back until 4:30 p.m."

During the school year, he could only leave the house to go to school and had to come straight home. As a result, he never made any friends and says he still has a hard time socializing with people, caring about people, and forming friendships. He lived an isolated, dark life.

In front of Grizzly statue at University of Montana.

After years of being beaten down psychologically, emotionally, and physically, Jim gradually sank to the level of his parents' low expectations. As a teenager, he decided to stop following their rules. He began staying out after school and fell in with a group of kids who were adept at getting into trouble.

At the age of fourteen, Jim was sent to Yellowstone under court order. An exceptionally troubled child, he'd been charged with arson, vandalism, theft, and other crimes.

Mike Huggard, therapist in Fortin Lodge at the time, was impressed with Jim's "fight" and determination. "Jim was not happy to be here. He was very oppositional in the beginning. He thought he knew it all and didn't need any help. He had goals for his life, which really surprised me, considering the abuse he had received for so long."

Consistent with Yellowstone's philosophy of reuniting families, Mike made repeated attempts to involve Jim's parents in family therapy. His stepmother refused, and it wasn't long before Mike realized that Jim's dad was unwilling to change any of his behavior toward Jim.

"Jim was not a perfect kid by any means," says Mike, "but when a family is so opposed to a kid's growth and so unwilling to accept any responsibility for the problems, it's not healthy for them to maintain that contact. It's too toxic for the kid. That's why Jim had a lot of courage to step out on his own and make it, despite that lack of family support."

With plenty of encouragement from Mike and others at the Ranch, Jim finally began to believe his life was worth something. He

Jim (right) with Mike Huggard, Therapist.

was able to grasp that not everything that went wrong in his family was his fault.

Jim gradually changed from being an angry boy who trusted no one and completely lacked any self-esteem to a more confident and self-assured young man. Or, as he put it, "I learned to be my own person, to not let others define who I am and how I feel about myself. I gained the ability to detach myself from my parents. I developed self-confidence and self-esteem."

One of Jim's motivations to succeed may have been to prove his parents wrong, but, in his case, it was a positive motivation. Once Jim decided to cooperate with his counselors at the Ranch, he reached his treatment goals rapidly and was able to return to a group home in Oak Park, Illinois, just a few miles from where he grew up.

He graduated from high school and went on to receive a Bachelor of Science in Recreation Management from the University of Montana's College of Forestry and Conservation in May of 2006. At this writing he has several aspirations. He is seriously considering a stint with the Peace Corps or another international organization. He may go on to graduate school, but will eventually work with the National Forest Service or another land management agency.

But what about a family for Jim and the unconditional love, acceptance, and lifetime commitment it can bring?

In the beginning, it was Isabel Lundin, a Ranch staff member who was assigned to Jim's follow-up and transition after he left the Ranch. "I know when I first left the Ranch it was Isabel's job to kind of look after me and make sure I was doing what I was supposed to," says Jim. "But our friendship grew, and now she fills the role of 'mother' for me. We still talk on the phone often. She is someone whom I can call for advice or encouragement."

But Jim also attracted the attention of a businessman in Oak Park who was on the Board of Directors of the group home where Jim lived after leaving Yellowstone. Leonard Slotkowski was quite involved with all the kids at the group home, but he felt there was just something special about Jim. Leonard says, "He was polite and appreciative of the things I did for him. He seemed mature beyond his years. He was obviously intelligent and had goals for his life."

When Jim went off to college, Leonard learned that Jim's family had no intention of providing a place for him during school breaks.

He invited Jim to join him and his extended family for Christmas that first year. "When I got off the phone from telling Jim I'd send him a plane ticket to join me in Chicago, I thought, 'What have I done! He's going to be here for six weeks!'" Leonard's fears were unfounded as the visit went well, and proved to be the beginning of Jim becoming more a part of Leonard's family.

That was a number of years ago. Today Jim calls Leonard "Dad" and Leonard considers Jim his son. Because of Jim's background, it has been a long, slow process of becoming "family." Trust and commitment have grown between them. Jim says, "Leonard has truly taken on the role of a father. He encourages me when I've done something good and chews me out when I mess up." And Leonard adds, "I'm so proud of what Jim has accomplished and want for him what all parents want for their child."

These days, whenever they talk on the phone, they end their conversations with "Love ya." When Jim was home this past Christmas, he cooked a couple of delicious meals from scratch. Leonard jokingly told him, "Hey, if forestry doesn't work out for you, maybe you should become a chef!"

When Jim left Yellowstone he felt, beyond a

Jim "poses" while on a trip to Washington DC with Loren Soft.

doubt, that his life had been transformed. Because of his gratitude, Jim accompanied CEO Loren Soft to Washington, D.C., in 2001 to testify before a Senate Subcommittee on Yellowstone's behalf.

Jim still stays in contact with people at the Ranch. "Every so often, I pass through Billings and stop and say 'Hi' to any lodge staff who were there when I was. I feel it's important because they have a very difficult job, and they may not see the rewards gained by their hard work. If I can go back ten years later and show them the positive results of their work, it may encourage or motivate them to continue."

College graduation May 14, 2006 with Isabel and Leonard.

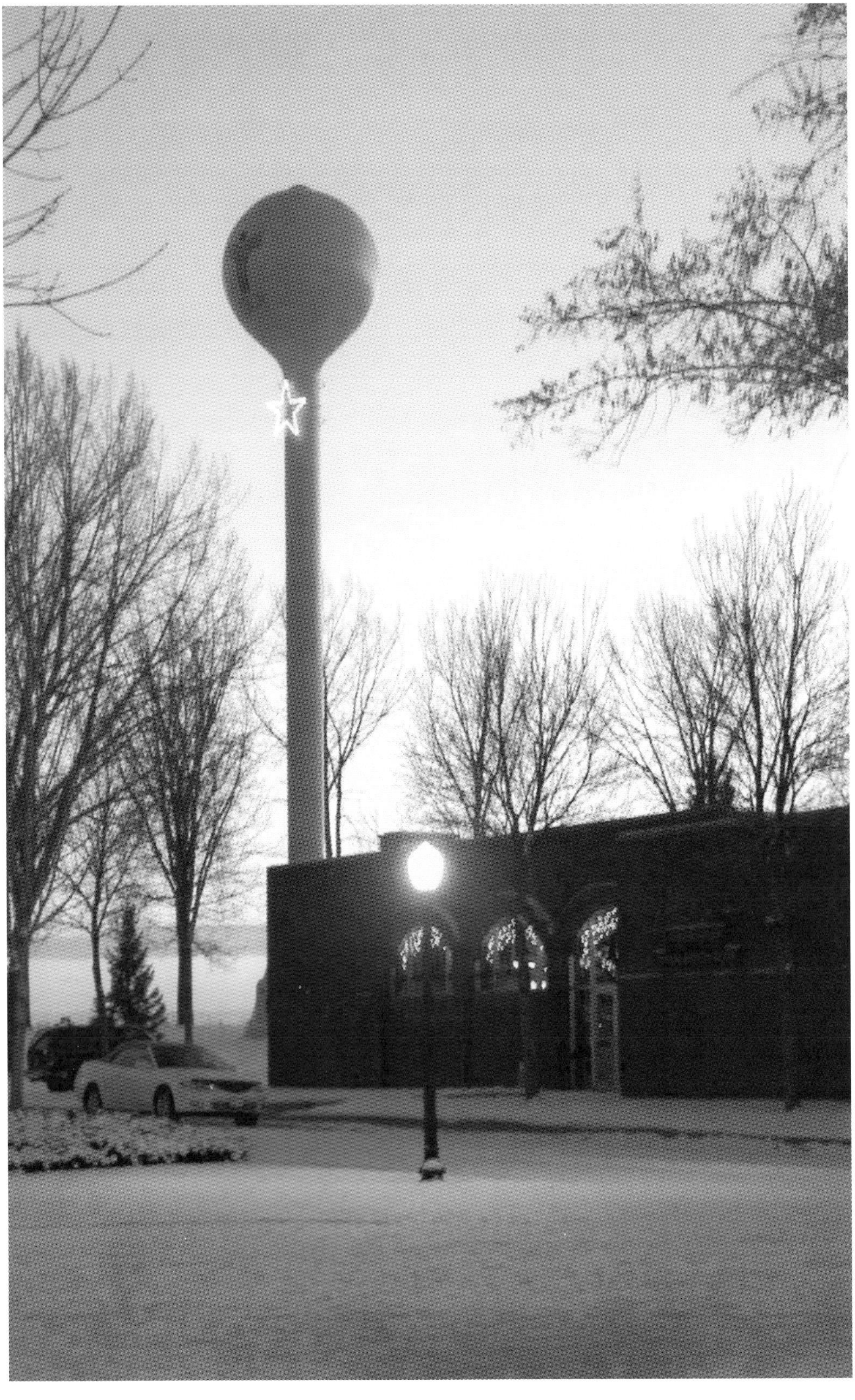

CHAPTER TWELVE

A Guided Tour of Our Campus
(And Some of the People Who Made It Possible)

Fifty years ago when a handful of us first started thinking about creating a ranch for troubled kids, we were moved by the sad sight of young children being locked up in reform schools that often failed to give these children the love, attention, and hope they needed to transform their lives.

There are fewer reform schools in operation today, but many young people spend months in clinical treatment centers that provide them few opportunities to do the things kids enjoy doing, like playing sports, hanging out with other kids, or talking to parent figures who really care for them.

That's why it's always so exciting to see new children arriving at the Ranch and taking a look around our campus. Young people who have been transferred here from austere psychiatric hospitals often feel they have arrived at a paradise on earth. Or, as some of the kids tell us after they have settled in, they feel like they have moved from a warehouse to a community, complete with new friends, a family atmosphere, and more resources and activities than virtually any kind of similar care facility in the country.

In this chapter I will give you a guided tour of our campus.

As I explain our key facilities and what goes on there, I will also introduce you to some of the caring men and women whose gifts to the Ranch made these wonderful facilities possible.

A Wealth of Resources

Entering our campus through the Western-style entrance gate, you can see the **DeHaan Administration Building** on the left. The adjacent building houses our school, the Yellowstone Academy (see chapter 14).

Next to the Academy is the **Nutter Dining Hall**. This building, which is the site of many group activities, is named after a former Montana governor who was an intensely loyal supporter of the Ranch before his tragic death in a 1962 airplane accident.

Across the street from the dining hall is the Franklin and Merle Robbie Chapel, where kids are given opportunities to focus on spiritual issues (see chapter 13).

DeHaan Administration Building

Nutter Dining Hall

We also have specialized treatment and work-related buildings that are used by select students depending on their individual therapeutic or educational needs. These include the Art Barn, vocational buildings for students focusing on farming, ranching, welding, carpentry or construction, as well as our 24-hour medical clinic.

The campus is a full-time residential settlement with a year-round population that's similar to that of a small town. Throughout the campus are nearly a dozen family-style lodges providing safe, secure, and well-supervised housing for various groups of young people based on their sex, age, and specific problems and needs. These lodges have been built with an emphasis on creating a warm, family feeling because we believe kids will be more responsive to treatment if they feel comfortable and relaxed.

But kids aren't the only people who live at the Ranch. There is also housing for a number of our employees, who provide 24-hour support and supervision for the kids. Staff members who live on campus also agree to be a part of our emergency response team that can provide immediate assistance for any behavioral or emotional problems that develop with our kids. Even some of the top Ranch leadership lives on campus, which demonstrates our commitment to around-the-clock, hands-on care.

There is also short-term housing for parents of our young people. We provide this housing because of our conviction that family therapy is an essential part of many young people's treatment, and because many families cannot afford to stay in a hotel while participating in sometimes demanding counseling sessions.

Our campus has a wealth of recreational offerings, including a softball diamond, bicycle trails, landscaped walkways and gazebos, and an equestrian center and challenges ropes course used in our Experiential Therapy programs. Enjoying the resources—and playing a part in their upkeep—is a regular part of life for many of the young people who live on the Ranch.

We love our facilities, and it is a real joy to see kids' eyes light up when they come to realize the wealth of resources that are made available to them here. Our wealth of resources is one of the ways we communicate to kids that we care for them, but these facilities come at a steep price.

Long ago we decided to create a full-service campus. We knew that there was no way the fees we charge would cover the costs of our campus but were determined to go the extra mile and provide our kids with the very best facilities.

Over the past half century all of the money for the various buildings on our campus has come from the contributions of caring donors. In a number of cases we expressed our thanks to these donors by naming the buildings after them.

A Surprising Source of Support

One of the most popular buildings on our campus is the **John H. Uihlein Recreation Center**, which includes an

John H. Uihlein Recreation Center

indoor pool, gym, bowling alley, basketball courts, weight and fitness rooms, and other resources kids love. Most of the kids here don't know who John Uihlein was, or that a substantial portion of his wealth was inherited stock in the Joseph Schlitz Brewing Company in Milwaukee.

After completing military service in WWII, John Uihlein left Milwaukee and used part of his new wealth to buy a beautifully situated cattle ranch on Cedar Creek just south of Ennis, Montana. I met John when he became a calf donor.

I went to visit John frequently and always carried a pair of cowboy boots. I would change into them at the end of John's driveway because of Jack, a big, old hound dog who would always meet me at the front door and attempt to wrap his massive jaws around my ankle.

One time I had forgotten the boots and I simply could not bring myself to face Jack unprotected. So, I headed back to Ennis and bought the cheapest pair of cowboy boots in the store. They were shiny black with sharply pointed toes.

Outfitted in my new boots, I knocked and John came to the door alone. When he opened it and Jack failed to appear, I blurted out, "Where's Jack?" John took one look at my boots and, laughing very hard, he pointed to that big, ugly dog lying on his back over by the wall with all four paws in the air, swollen and obviously hurting! His problem was that the day before he had jumped into a concrete lined irrigation ditch and, struggling for quite some time to get back out, he literally wore the skin off his paws. So - there I stood in my shiny new boots, being laughed at by John, and I would have been safe in my bare feet!

Eventually, John became a member of our Board of Directors, which brought him to our campus on a regular basis. This close-up look at troubled kids and hearing their sad stories substantially increased John's interest. Over the years he gave us many generous gifts. He was also the largest single donor to the rec center's construction cost which is why our Board recognized his generosity by naming it for him.

John died in 1986, and while many people will never know about his unique history or his many contributions to the Ranch, they will at least see his name on our "rec center," which serves not only our own youth but enables us to host athletic events for other schools in the area.

Every Building Has a Story

The Ranch started out small and simple, but today it consists of 400 acres of land and more than thirty buildings. Two of the people who helped the ranch become what it is today were Paul Stock and Phil Fortin.

As soon as the Ranch came into existence in 1957, I began sending out appeal letters requesting funds to help support our work. One of these early appeal letters went to a man who lived in Cody, Wyoming, named Paul Stock, who made his first gift as a memorial in 1958. In 1959 he made more

A Legacy of Caring

memorial gifts and then surprised us by making charitable year-end gifts of Texaco stock.

I made a point of thanking Paul Stock in person and answered the searching questions of a very wise man who had no children of his own, but had the capacity to look way down the road for us. That first Texaco gift was soon followed by generous cash gifts toward future building projects and - increasingly larger year-end gifts of Texaco stock.

Paul kept telling me he thought we needed more land. When the one hundred sixty-acre farm to our east was for sale, Paul said, "I'll pay for it." When another eighty acres north of the Ranch came on the market, Paul again said, "I'll pay for it," thus rounding out our total ownership to four hundred acres. By then we had already built two more new lodges for boys on our expanding campus and we honored Paul by naming one of them the **Paul Stock Lodge**. Today it

Paul Stock Lodge (left) and Fortin Lodge (right).

is the Ranch's intensive care facility for young boys who have significant developmental challenges.

Paul Stock died in 1972 and proved his abiding interest in our child-care work with a final gift through his will of 30,000 shares of Texaco stock, which established our Endowment Fund.

Paul had also introduced me to a friend of his named Phil Fortin, a successful Billings businessman. Paul was a casual kind of guy who shot from the hip, but Mr. Fortin was much more analytical. That's why he turned me down the first time I asked him to help support the Ranch. In future visits I provided him with more detailed information about our work, and he happily supported us.

I went back to see Mr. Fortin when we were trying to build a cannery on the Ranch so that we could preserve fruit and vegetables to use throughout the year. The cannery was the first new building we had built on the Ranch. I had already lined up a number of the elements we needed. Local companies donated lumber and cement block. A local construction firm donated labor. And we found the cannery equipment in Bozeman, where it had been part of a U.S. government program during World War II.

But even with all the donated goods we still needed money to get the cannery going. So I organized my case, carefully summarizing the need and the benefits, and presented this to Mr. Fortin in his office. After I made my case I saw him reach under the edge of his desk. I didn't know what he was doing, but soon his secretary came in. She had responded to a hidden buzzer. Mr. Fortin told her to write the Ranch a large check, and our cannery was on the way to being completed.

That was just the beginning. Before he died in 1983, Mr. Fortin became one of our largest benefactors. Early on, the Fortins began making annual Christmas gifts that would enable each of our youth to visit a local retail store for a shopping trip. In the beginning these gifts covered $15 worth of clothes for each of the boys. By the time these gifts ended nearly thirty years later, they were covering $50 worth of purchases for every boy and girl who lived at the Ranch.

Whether the Fortins gave donations that were used for buildings or for Christmas gifts, we always made it a point to prepare detailed reports, complete with photographs, to show them where their money had gone. We still take photos of our kids enjoying Christmas shopping excursions, which are now funded by other donors.

We showed our gratitude to the Fortins by naming a lodge in their honor. Today **Fortin Lodge** is a secure facility divided into two residential units. Fortin West Lodge houses up to eight adolescent boys with developmental challenges, while Fortin East Lodge houses nine younger troubled boys.

Other Lodges and the People They Honor

Walking around the Ranch campus today provides a quick survey of our history and a brief introduction to some of the many people who invested in our work over the years.

The most important building to each of the young people we serve is the residential lodge that becomes their home

McVay Lodge

here. Our approach is to house our Ranch residents in comfortable lodges that balance the needs of individualized residential treatment with a low-key family feel. This is why lodges are the most numerous buildings on our campus, and each lodge bears the name of a valued donor.

McVay Lodge is named after John McVay. During his youth John wanted to be a pastor. And even though his career took a different path, John remained a man of faith who cared deeply about kids.

In the 1960s John frequently gave us calves from his own ranch outside Lewistown, Montana. Then in 1969 he saw this urgent headline in our *Wrangler* newsletter: BOYS RANCH CROWDED AND WAITING LIST GROWS. As John read about the growing number of youngsters who were waiting to be accommodated at the Ranch, he made a considerable challenge grant offer that inspired other donors to participate in the construction costs of a new lodge.

By doing so, John provided the impetus to raise the money for construction and then matched that amount as endowment to ensure it could be taken care of in the future.

Today McVay Lodge is a residential unit where ten teenage boys who have problems with learning or personality disorders are learning to transition to life in the world outside the Ranch.

King Lodge is named in recognition of an endowment challenge grant offered by the Carl B. & Florence E. King Foundation. Mrs. King was especially concerned about the increase in younger boys being referred to the Ranch and wanted to see a specially designed "little boy lodge" added to our campus. This need also had strong appeal to our donor family because they responded to the challenge generously and King Lodge was completed in record time.

King Lodge was initially designed as a multilevel structure that met the housing needs of little boys being referred to us thirty years ago. However, experience has taught us that our

King Lodge

treatment plan for deeply disturbed little boys can be much better served with a floor plan which accommodates them all on a single level. So a totally new Little Boy Lodge has just recently been completed on our East Campus.

Leuthold Lodge is named for John and Grace Leuthold, both of whom served on the Ranch's Board of Directors. We asked Grace to serve on our board in 1957 because she was a member of the Montana Child Welfare Advisory Board. She knew about helping hurting children, and her knowledge and wisdom helped us greatly. She and John also participated in many Ranch events, such as open houses and Christmas programs.

Leuthold Lodge

The Leutholds were well aware of our need for buildings and funds, and one day they let me know they were going to

make a significant donation that would serve as an endowment challenge in order to spur other donors to help finance a new boys lodge. Today, Leuthold Lodge provides a safe and nurturing atmosphere for boys with significant learning disabilities. The ages of these boys vary widely, but their IQs are in the 80-85 range.

Grace Leuthold died at the age of ninety in 2003, and John passed away two years later at the age of ninety-eight. But their memory lives on at the Ranch they loved and supported so deeply.

Here are brief profiles of some of the other key donors who helped the Ranch provide the facilities needed to care for kids:

Shumaker Lodge, a lodge for girls ages twelve to eighteen, is named after Mr. and Mrs. Jake Shumaker, who were ranchers near Ismay, Montana. Jake served as an area trustee for the Ranch, gathering livestock donations from friends and neighbors and contributing many calves of their own for the benefit of children at Yellowstone.

As Jake began considering retirement, he sought advice from the Ranch about estate planning. The sale of his ranch funded a Yellowstone gift annuity that helped both the Shumakers and the Ranch. Today Shumaker Lodge provides residential care for girls who require less supervision than some of our other girls. As a result, our girls really feel like they have accomplished something once they transition into this lodge.

Shumaker Lodge

Mary Brekkeflat Lodge and Scott Medical Clinic

The Mary Brekkeflat Lodge and **Scott Medical Clinic** are located on our East Campus in the building originally known as our Assessment-Treatment Center. The growing need for an added dimension of assessment of new arrivals dates back several years to our alarming experience with Kip, the young lad who had witnessed the murder-suicide of his mother and stepfather.

Construction was finally started on this much needed facility in 1980 with a start-up grant from the Carl B. & Florence E. King Foundation, which required a two-for-one match to cover construction costs. This match came from a series of major grants from the Kresge Foundation in Detroit, the Ruth and Vernon Taylor Foundation in Denver, the Steele-Reese Foundation in New York and the Fortin Foundation right here in Billings, as well as big hearted responses to several appeals to our faithful donor family. The assessment center was designed as a secure co-ed facility with a boys bedroom wing and a girls bedroom wing, plus classrooms and a dining area with food prepared in our central kitchen on the main campus.

The Endowment Fund for this building, equal to its construction cost, came as a result of some far sighted estate planning by Mary Brekkeflat's husband, Sigurd Brekkeflat, who had acquired the famous Kootenai Lodge on Swan Lake near Big Fork, Montana. The Kootenai Lodge dates back to Montana's booming copper era of the nineteenth century.

Sigurd created an estate plan which enabled the eventual sale proceeds of the Kootenai Lodge to provide a very substantial income to him for life and finance the endowment of the Assessment-Treatment Center, which we then officially named the Mary Brekkeflat Lodge in his wife's memory.

The state-of-the-art Scott Medical Clinic is housed on the ground floor of the "Mary B," as we call it on campus, and was financed entirely through a generous grant from Tom and Joan Scott, of Billings.

The Mary B provides safe and secure facilities for critical-needs youth between the ages of eleven and eighteen who represent a danger to themselves or to others. Girls live in Brekkeflat North while boys live in Brekkeflat South.

Jessie Grant Lodge is a less restrictive, residential unit for girls ages eleven to eighteen. It was built with funds given by

Jessie Grant Lodge

our donor family with substantial gifts from Margaret Hamilton of Tubac, Arizona and James Taylor of Bozeman, Montana. Both of these folks were frequent challenge donors to campus expansion projects over many years.

An Endowment Fund, equal to the cost of construction, came from Mr. Charles Grant of Outlook, Montana, honoring his wife, Jessie. The Grants were Montana pioneers whose ranching history goes all the way back to the homestead days.

Alvina Kramlich Lodge

The Alvina Kramlich Lodge is named after Alvina Kramlich, whose own childhood experiences made her particularly sensitive to the needs of kids at the Ranch. One of nine children, Alvina was orphaned at age four. She and her siblings were separated and put up for adoption, a process she described as being "picked over like a litter of kittens."

In time, Alvina found her way in the world, and when she acquired significant financial resources, she worked with the Yellowstone Foundation to design an estate plan that helped the Ranch while challenging others to give as well. Now the girls lodge built in her name provides a place to heal for girls who are also experiencing difficult childhoods.

Kramlich Lodge is a residential treatment unit that offers a more relaxed atmosphere than some of the other lodges. Youth in this lodge are undergoing treatment that will help them make the transition to life on the "outside," and the in-house kitchen has provided many tasty feasts cooked by the girls.

Dorothy's Lodge, one the latest additions to the east side of our campus, is now home to up to eight active and very challenging boys, ages six to twelve. This lodge is our effort to address the sad fact that the Ranch is receiving increasing numbers of very young boys who have experienced deep emotional scars. Although there is a lot of hope when you get a boy at a young age, there is much sadness that there are so many at this age who need the help the Ranch can provide.

The lodge gets its name from a group of women who have given their time, talent, and resources to help the youngest and most vulnerable of our youth have a chance to know that someone cares for them.

Among them is Dorothy Hollatz, who worked in our business office for forty-seven years. After her passing in 2004, we discovered she had quietly established a trust that helped build the lodge. As *The Billings Gazette* reported,

Dorothy's Lodge

Hollatz helped hone YBGR's fund-raising techniques and did a little of her own….More than half of the money for the building came from Hollatz and Dorothy Marie Lewis. The other Dorothys are associated with the Ranch and will help with the future endowment for the building but are remaining anonymous for now….The lodge has room for eight boys to live in a structured environment that provides diagnosis, medicine, behavior modification, access to schooling and other services. There is an emphasis on integrating services in a homelike-environment instead of institutional-style care.

Bigger Buildings Serve Broader Ranch Needs

Although a room of your own goes a long way toward meeting the needs of our kids, there are other buildings on campus that play large roles in Ranch life.

We mentioned the DeHaan Administration Building at the beginning of this chapter. This facility is named in honor of Henry and Mae DeHaan. One of the largest land owners in Gallatin County and long-time successful farmers in the Gallatin Valley, the DeHaans made significant gifts to the Ranch for current needs as well as investing significantly in Yellowstone's future. These endowment gifts continue helping the Ranch years after the initial donations were made.

The Casper Education Center (which is actually a part of Yellowstone Academy) was a key addition to the school and the auditorium is now used for campus wide get-togethers, concerts, and graduations.

The center bears the Casper name because it was largely endowed by Alvy Casper, a long-time friend of Yellowstone, in memory of his wife, Kathleen. As with many other major donors, Alvy challenged others to match his gifts. By the time Alvy died in 1991, the Caspers were major contributors to the Ranch Endowment.

Casper Education Center

Heptner Education Center

The Heptner Education Center is named for Leona and Jeanette Heptner, two sisters who spent their working years teaching rural school near Gillette, Wyoming, and loving children. These classrooms provide additional teaching space for many day-school students who are bused daily to Yellowstone from other school districts that aren't equipped to handle these students' unique educational needs.

In 1992, the Heptners made a challenge grant to build an addition to the Ranch's original school building. In 2001 they donated the funds to build the Heptner Education Center, complete with four additional classrooms. Each of them also left substantial gifts through their wills to the Ranch Endowment Fund.

A Growing Campus to Meet Growing Needs

The campus of Yellowstone Boys and Girls Ranch is undergoing continual growth and development to better serve our growing population of boys and girls.

The biggest structure on the entire campus is the 160-foot wide by 260-foot long **Bill and Anita Jones Equestrian Center**, which was dedicated in 2003. The center is where specially trained workers use horses to help young people

Bill and Anita Jones Equestrian Center

confront some of their deepest challenges (see chapter 14).

Some of our buildings are a part of our continuing effort to improve our vocational education offerings for our youth.

The Kramlich Vo-Tech Building houses a welding shop where both boys and girls learn this marketable skill. Our Ranch welders find numerous opportunities to use their skills to help our cattle operations. Currently we are in the midst of a multi-year upgrade of the feedlot used for our small herd. The project includes replacing aging and weakened wooden fences and corrals with long-lasting steel pipe fencing.

The Broken Spoke is a bicycle shop where boys and girls learn to repair bikes that have been donated to the Ranch. The experience they gain here not only helps other Ranch residents have workable bikes but it gives these students skills that will help them when they leave us to enter the workforce.

Students enrolled in classes at the Kramlich Vo-Tech Building use their skills throughout the Ranch.

Another major addition to our vocational programs is the **Poetzl Horticultural Center**, a major greenhouse project that

Poetzl Horticultural Center

has been coordinated by "retired" Ranch employee Bob McFarlane, who was our "employee number one" in 1957. Bob supervised the reconstruction of the greenhouse, which was donated to the Ranch by its owner, Russell Gordy. Bob and a crew of Ranch kids and volunteers carefully took it apart and transported it to the Ranch. We dedicated the greenhouse in 2005, as was reported in *The Billings Gazette*:

> On Sunday, donors and others toured the 13,000-square-foot greenhouse that will provide employment for at-risk youth and a place to learn about horticulture for middle and high school students through Yellowstone Academy....The horticulture center will provide a place to work for those involved with the Living Independently Fostering Employment program (LIFE), which helps young people learn job skills. The Ranch may also team up with Special K Ranch (about

40 miles away), which provides life and work experiences for people with developmental disabilities, to grow plants for local nurseries, according to Pat Friesen, director of the greenhouse. The Horticulture Center, along with Dorothy's Lodge, is a testament to the power of generosity and how it can be transformed into something tangible.... "Wherever you see great work," Jim Soft (Foundation president) said, "somebody has sacrificed."

Many Ways to Give

There are a number of buildings at the Ranch which are not named for the donors who made them possible. These donors preferred to treat their support of the Ranch as a private matter, and we honor their preferences.

And many people have helped the Ranch in other important ways, such as a group of caring members from St. Joseph's Catholic Church in Harlowton. Some women from the church spent months making quilts for the more than one hundred boys and girls who live at the Ranch. They have continued this labor of love so that each young person who arrives at Yellowstone receives a quilt.

As church member Anne Anderson told *The Billings Gazette*, "This is one of those God stories." The women prayed as they created the quilts, and Anderson says she hopes the children will receive not only physical but also spiritual warmth from the gifts.

It seems that no matter where one looks on the Ranch today one finds ample evidence of people's concern for troubled kids and their willingness to express that concern in tangible ways. Such generosity has made it possible for us to offer the range of resources and facilities we do.

Yellowstone's Campus:
A Beautiful Place to Heal

Transformed Lives

Debbie Champion:
"I Want to Give Back"

When Debbie Champion applied for a job at Yellowstone, she asked right away if it would be a problem that she had been at the Ranch as a youth in treatment a number of years earlier. She didn't want to waste anyone's time if it wasn't appropriate to apply. The answer she got was, "No. It's definitely not a problem. In fact, it might help you."

By the age of fourteen, Debbie had a pattern of being truant from school for weeks at a time. When the truancy officers finally caught up with her, they were puzzled. She wasn't a rebellious kid. Why was she cutting school so much? Further investigation revealed she was extremely depressed and suicidal. When they realized what she had been dealing with at home, they weren't at all surprised. What fourteen-year-old wouldn't be depressed by the burden of being forced to accept adult responsibilities that were way beyond her?

Debbie arrived at Yellowstone a fragile, hurting, suicidal young lady.

She put up a tough façade in the beginning. Sure she had missed a lot of school, but she said it was no big deal. When asked about her family life, she lied and claimed her parents were wonderful. She'd say she had no idea why she was sent to the Ranch.

Gradually, Debbie began to let down her guard. All the lies and covering up began to fall away. Debbie had endured so much heartache in her short life, but in time her overly confident shell crumbled. She finally felt she was in a safe place where she could talk about the burdens she was carrying. Loving, caring people would listen and not blame her for everything that had gone wrong.

Debbie's parents had divorced around the time she was six or seven years old. Before long her mom had taken up with a man who had just been released from prison and who shared her fondness for

Debbie (left) with Andrea, one of the girls at the Ranch. Debbie gets satisfaction from investing in the lives of kids who have severe issues.

drugs. Soon they were so enmeshed in their lifestyle, they'd go off and leave Debbie and her two sisters alone for days at a time. Debbie and her older sister would take turns staying home from school to care for their younger sister.

When Mom and her boyfriend were home, they would irrationally blame Debbie for everything. Debbie says, "To this day I don't understand why, but I became the brunt of my mother's wrath. She had me believing all the bad things in her life were my fault. She'd tell me the divorce was my fault; her abusive boyfriend was my fault; her anger was my fault. People at school were getting suspicious, but I lied to protect my mom. I thought a bad home was better than no home at all. And I really believed I was a bad kid."

Safety and security were the major factors that allowed Debbie to finally deal with her issues in treatment. "When I realized I wasn't going to be kicked out of the Ranch after a month, I started to let down. The staff in Shumaker Lodge helped me to recognize that it was not my responsibility to take care of my mom and my little sister. Once I started to believe that all the problems in my family were not my fault, I could begin to learn to love and protect myself."

When Debbie's depression began to subside, she found she had a strong will to survive and make the most of a bad situation. Thankfully, being required to attend school at the Ranch helped her see the importance of an education and helped her believe she could make it in school. After leaving the Ranch, Debbie was living on her own by the time she turned eighteen, but stayed in school and graduated from high school while fully supporting herself.

She also worked full time while putting herself through college, which led her to seek a job at the Ranch while still in school. Debbie had always dreamed of somehow being able to give back to those who had helped her so much. In her childhood, Debbie was inappropriately forced to be a caregiver. Now she has come back to be a caregiver in a healthy way, armed with a psychology degree and life experience that speaks volumes to the children she's helping.

Debbie says, "The kids ask me very personal questions, and I answer them honestly. When they ask if I ever get depressed I tell them I still struggle. There are days I just want to stay in bed and cry, and I'm tempted by all the negative thoughts I used to give in to. The difference is I'm able to analyze it and say, 'Okay, Debbie, it's time to get out of bed. It's unfortunate that bad things happened to you, but are you going to use it as an excuse to not do anything with your life at all?'"

"I tell the kids I work with, 'Battles don't go away; they just get easier to conquer.'"

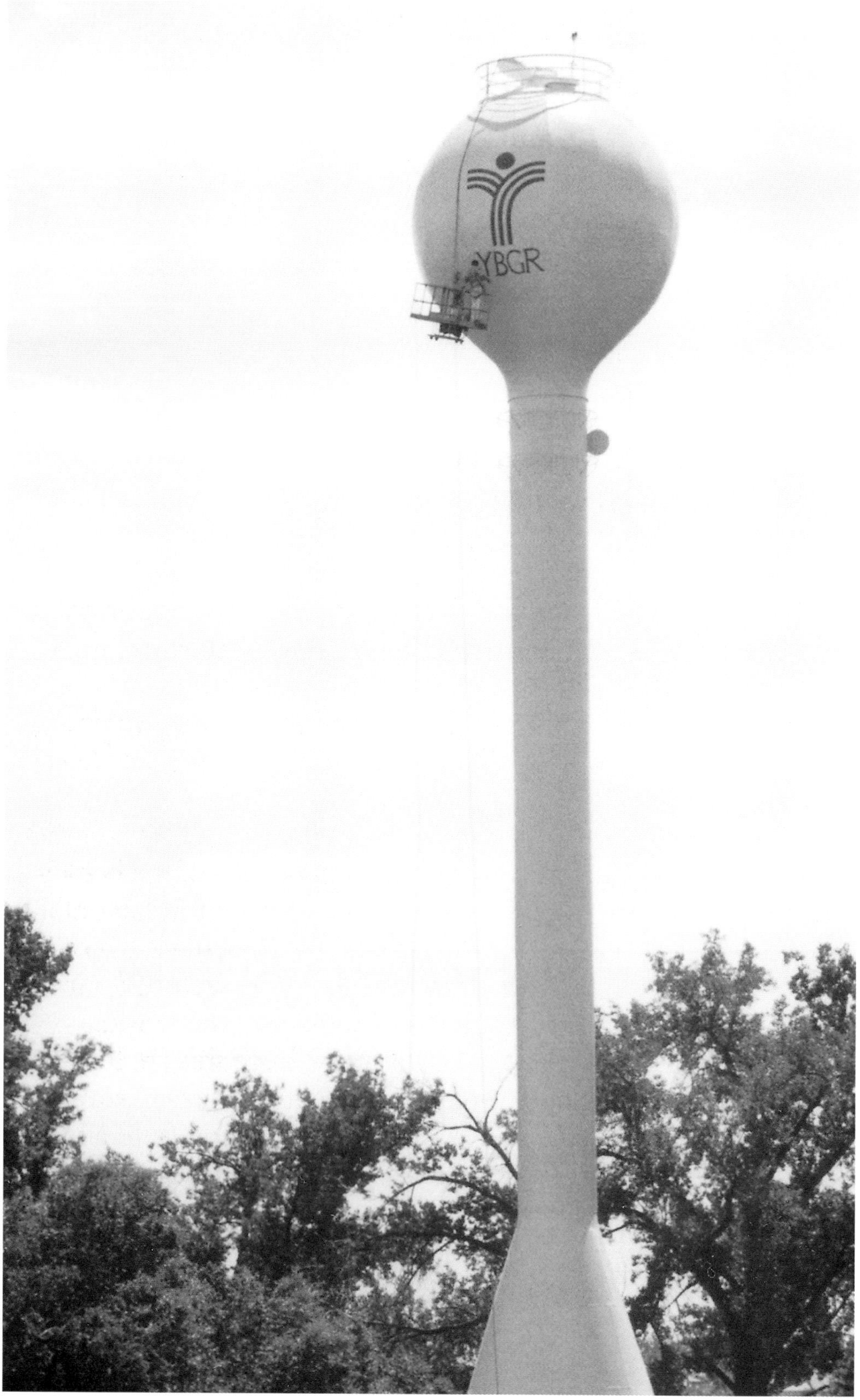
YBGR

CHAPTER THIRTEEN

Changes at the Top

I've always believed that people are the most important factor in helping companies excel at what they do. In recent years this belief has received resounding support from Jim Collins, author of the bestselling business manual, *Good to Great: Why Some Companies Make the Leap…and Others Don't*.

Published in 2001, *Good to Great* has become a trusted guide for many corporate leaders and managers. One of the book's recurring themes—and a concept that has been fundamental to the success of Yellowstone Boys and Girls Ranch—is the conviction that bringing skilled and passionate people to your management team makes all the difference in the world.

As the previous chapters of this book have shown, the evolution of the Ranch over the past fifty years has been extraordinary. Over that time we have made the transition from a humble, family-style ranch for troubled boys to a professionally esteemed hospital-grade facility for severely emotionally disturbed children.

None of us involved in founding the Ranch or in guiding it during its early years could have ever foreseen all the major changes we would undergo in our first half century. But there's one thing we did know: if we brought the right people to the Ranch and enabled them to excel at what they do best, we would be able to handle pretty much anything that came our way.

Today, the wisdom of this approach can be seen in every department of the Ranch, as people we hired years or sometimes decades ago have emerged as the new leaders for the Ranch as it enters its second half-century.

A Change in Leadership

Bob McFarlane, with his multiple talents and varied skills, was the right "pioneer" to manage the Ranch and its restless family of boys in our early beginnings. And as substantial support began to emerge from our rural ranching population, we were excited to witness the emergence of an impressive group of the most successful ranchers who were willing to accept local leadership as area trustees. These trustees contacted scores of their neighbors, who over the years gave the Ranch hundreds of calves, thousands of bushels of grain, as well as gifts of ranch land and mineral rights.

Bob McFarlane volunteered to become the trustees' coordinating leader if someone surfaced to take over his role as Ranch superintendent. In time, Loren Soft was ready to assume that role. The Area Trustee Program grew so quickly that Bob was asking for someone to help him. His answer came in the person of Irwin Eleson, an experienced ranch hand from Crawford, Nebraska, who had joined our staff in 1964.

Irwin is a can-do mechanic with years of varied experience including work as a carpenter, an electrician, a plumber, and an expert welder. Best of all, he understands livestock and has a gift of making friends wherever he goes.

We put Irwin behind the wheel of a new pickup truck donated by Keith Chevrolet in Chester, Montana, and in no time he was recruiting additional area trustees and finding new calf donors by the score. He loved to visit with people and

A Legacy of Caring

Bob McFarlane (left) and Irwin Eleson (right) have seen many changes at the Ranch during their decades of service.

was constantly invited to spend the night with friends new and old who shared their successes and their dreams with him. Many of Irwin's friends also shared their land, their resources, or other gifts with the Ranch over the years.

After formally retiring in 1994 at the age of seventy-three, Irwin immediately came back to work at the Ranch on a half-time basis. Today he is still fixing things, hauling livestock, and making friends for the Ranch. Like Bob McFarlane before him, Irwin–now well into his eighties–continues to give a major portion of his time to helping hurting children.

A New Executive Director

Loren was first hired as a summer worker in 1963 to help with our ranching and athletic programs. Then right after he graduated from Eastern Montana College (now Montana State University-Billings), Loren was hired as principal/teacher in our Ranch grade school, which included four teachers at the time. He quickly began to serve Superintendent Bob McFarlane in other ways around the Ranch. When Bob moved on in 1969 to his role with our area trustees, Loren was ready to assume additional responsibilities.

It's difficult to summarize a lifetime of service in a few brief pages of a book, but I think history will tell that one of the most significant things Loren did during his many years with us was to guide us through the turbulent years of the 1980s and 1990s when both the Ranch and the whole growing field of child counseling and psychiatric care were undergoing tremendous change.

As part of his leadership during these decades, Loren helped us forge the public-private partnerships between the Ranch and various local, state, and federal government agencies. Such partnerships helped us expand our variety of programs and offer them to an ever-greater range of needy children throughout the country.

In 1985, I announced that it was time for me to "pass the baton" of the title and duties of executive director to a younger man of the next generation. I had devoted twenty-eight years of my life to carrying the load of executive director, with all of the management and campus development duties that entailed. In addition, I was also serving as the president of our newly formed Yellowstone Boys and Girls Ranch Foundation, which included continuing duties in fund-raising. I passed the executive director baton to Loren Soft, who was ready to receive it, was well qualified to carry on our work, and was committed to core values that had guided the Ranch from its founding.

"Loren is committed to the highest quality of childcare and is known and respected nationally in this very special field of human services," I wrote in the *Wrangler*. "Loren now stands ready to continue and improve the work of Yellowstone Boys and Girls Ranch which a few of us started more than a quarter of a century ago."

Loren accepted the title and the challenge, and said I had served as role model for him in the areas of consistency, authenticity, unselfishness, and tirelessness. Loren did a tremendous job of developing new services, recruiting new skilled staff, and strengthening our reputation as one of the finest treatment programs for emotionally disturbed children in the nation.

More than a Son

The Ranch flourished under Loren Soft's able leadership, and he got a well-deserved promotion to Ranch CEO. In the meantime, I was still somewhat involved in the solicitation of large gifts from interested individuals and family foundations. I was also working with other organizations helping them solve their fund-raising problems.

By 1988 I was seventy years old. I had heart bypass surgery in late 1987. I wanted a more relaxed schedule than the pace I had kept for the many years I drove an average of 30,000 miles a year throughout the highways and byways of Montana, Wyoming, and other states in an effort to raise the funds we needed to stay in business. I felt like I needed a lighter load, and I wanted to get out of the way so others could take a greater role in leadership.

Another major change in my life happened in August 1988

Father and son: Franklin and Wes Robbie

when Merle, my beloved wife of forty-seven years, died of cancer. The cancer had been discovered that January, and the doctors did everything they could to slow its advance, but, ultimately, there was little anyone could do.

Merle had been beside me every step of the way during the first three decades of the Ranch, and she had helped me work through many of the tough decisions and crises that I endured during those years.

Merle's life was celebrated at a beautiful memorial service where our son, Wes, represented the family with a very touching tribute to her.

I formally retired in 1989 and was named an advisor to the Ranch Foundation. I still enjoy calling on Ranch friends today. Thankfully, there was a trusted associate to whom I could hand the responsibilities for overseeing the work of the Foundation as its second president. This was my son, Wes, who had worked alongside me since 1968 in his position of assistant to the executive director.

Wes was an able leader who, after helping lift the Ranch's fund-raising burden from my shoulders, would take the Yellowstone Foundation to a new level of professionalism and efficiency. Wes implemented many positive changes that are still in effect today. He retired from the Foundation at the end of 2001 after thirty-three years of work with the Ranch. He now serves as vice president for a nonprofit organization called the International Deaf Education Association, which works with hundreds of deaf children on the island of Bohol in the Philippines.

Building an Endowment

After Loren Soft began working at the Ranch in 1963, we became acquainted with his younger brother, Jim, who eventually would follow Wes as president of the Yellowstone Foundation. Jim was an excellent basketball player who received a full scholarship to Eastern Montana College and worked at the Ranch with our athletic programs during the summers. Those of us who got to know Jim enjoyed attending his games during the school year and working alongside him during the summer.

After graduating with a business degree, Jim worked with a Billings brokerage firm. Then he returned to basketball but with a difference, joining Campus Crusade for Christ's semi-pro Athletes in Action team, which traveled throughout the country.

In 1972, after two years of traveling, Jim was ready to devote himself to a professional opportunity that challenged him and utilized his many gifts. I felt Jim would be a wonderful addition to our Foundation, and believed he could play an important role in the future development of the Ranch. Jim agreed to join us, and he rapidly convinced all of us that he had been the right choice for this pivotal position.

The Ranch needed to focus more on long-term—or deferred—giving that could be invested in an endowment to help us become less vulnerable to inevitable financial ups and downs. I knew this was vital to our long-term growth and survival, and Jim was the man who helped us move in this direction through a variety of helpful tools that enable people to plan how they will give.

Planned giving essentially involves devising creative ways to help people preserve their wealth, reduce their taxes, and eventually, distribute their resources through tax-sheltered investments that provide for both their families and for worthy charities like Yellowstone Boys and Girls Ranch.

However, since human service charities, like Yellowstone, do not enjoy a natural constituency (in the manner that churches have parishioners, hospitals have patients, and schools have alumni), we were not sure our small donor family had the potential to put in place an endowment large enough to help secure the future.

This question, plus the question of whether or not the Ranch could successfully meet the complex estate and financial planning needs of charitably minded ranchers and farmers, was put to the test early on when Mrs. M. D. Blankenship asked Jim how Yellowstone could solve her twin problems of capital gains tax and estate tax.

Mrs. Blankenship was seventy-five years old at the time and her failing health confronted her with the problem of how to divest herself of a thousand animal-unit cow ranch consisting of twenty-one thousand acres which she and her late husband had built up since the early 50s.

The Blankenships had become acquainted with the Ranch by being among our first calf donors in 1958, so Mrs. B. explained her problem to Bob McFarlane and Irwin Eleson. They then introduced Mrs. B. to Jim Soft.

Jim went to work with Mrs. B.'s attorney (in Montana) and her accountant (in Texas), and together they solved the "twin" tax problems and provided a very comfortable income for Mrs. B. and family through a Yellowstone charitable trust.

This large transaction even necessitated a special revenue ruling from IRS in Washington, D.C., and required more of Irwin Eleson's talents. During the months the Ranch, as trustee, was searching for a qualified buyer, Irwin was overseeing a 2,500-ton hay operation!

The Blankenship Trust represented our first major living planned gift. It established us as a credible organization among local financial, accounting, and legal professionals who were looking for someone knowledgeable about how to use charitable trusts and charitable annuities to solve difficult donor problems.

Our reputation for establishing the first charitable trust and gift annuity program in Montana quickly spread beyond our state's borders as satisfied donors moved to retirement communities and shared their "win-win" experiences with their new neighbors.

The Creation of the Yellowstone Foundation

The Yellowstone Boys and Girls Ranch Foundation was formed as an independent nonprofit organization in 1984. Many charities separate their fund-raising functions from their program activities. In addition to managing endowment, trust and annuity funds, the Foundation also carries out the fundraising activities of the Ranch. The Ranch oversees everything involved in our work with children. Each organization has its own offices, slate of officers, and board members.

Jim enjoys telling donors about our reasons for creating the Foundation and the Endowment Fund.

"Roots may be invisible, but they are essential to the life of a tree," Jim explains. "But what happens when the tree structure grows much larger than the root system that supports it?" The answer is obvious and not pretty: parts of the tree die off. This simple metaphor has helped many people see the importance of creating a strong support system for the work of the Ranch.

Today the Yellowstone Boys and Girls Ranch Foundation helps the Ranch by raising funds to construct new buildings, renovate older structures, and supplement key programs that might not be funded without its help. The Foundation currently serves in a fiduciary capacity for many donor friends, managing nearly 100 charitable trusts and more than 250 charitable annuity contracts.

These planned giving tools provide immediate current income plus tax savings for donor clients and future gifts to the Ranch Foundation.

The Foundation also helps many people who do not choose

to donate exclusively to the Ranch, having distributed over $2 million to other charities in the last decade alone.

In a little over two decades, the Foundation has built a sizable Endowment Fund. Looking to the future, our goal is to see the fund grow so that it can help ensure the continued financial viability of Yellowstone Boys and Girls Ranch.

Providing Spiritual Leadership

Another fine example of how the Ranch has been able to get the right people on the team is John Jamison, who joined us nearly forty years ago and has served as our full-time chaplain for nearly twenty years.

John was a student at Colorado State University in the late 1960s. One day he was talking to a group of students about his desire to start a ranch for troubled kids after he graduated. One of the students who happened to hear him that day was my daughter Kathy, who arranged for me to meet with John and other interested students.

"If you really want to get some worthwhile experience, find a boys ranch whose style of operation you like and apply for a job," I told them. "In a couple of years you will really know if that's what you

John Jamison has always had a strong love for the great outdoors.

want to give the rest of your life to."

Then, in the summer of 1969, John Jamison, who had just received his forestry degree, knocked on our door at the Ranch.

Chaplain John Jamison (above) directs the spiritual care for Ranch young people like Abby.

We put him to work immediately, and over the next few years he used his knowledge to help us organize camping trips, scouting programs, and wilderness treks for our kids. John also ran campus maintenance work crews, coached baseball, became an alternate lodge parent, managed boy crews in garden harvesting, and tutored slow learners in math and science. He also developed and managed our on-campus fire department, which was important since we were so far away from Billings services.

This hectic schedule would have been more than enough for anyone, but there was one other item John added to his long list of tasks whenever he could. He loved to volunteer in our Ranch chapel programs. His interest in kids' spiritual development led him to pursue a theological education, and he was ordained as a chaplain through the Christian and Missionary Alliance denomination. He supplemented this education later on with a certification in Clinical Pastoral Care, which enables him to provide pastoral care services for people in times of crisis and loss—things our kids here at the Ranch know all too well.

Over the years John, along with his wife Carolyn, have become trusted friends, spiritual teachers, and parent figures to thousands of troubled young people who have come to the Ranch for care.

The young people who come to the Ranch come from a variety of religious—and non-religious—traditions. That's why our Pastoral Care programs, which are funded by private donations—not government money, are ecumenical and open to all.

For some of our kids, Christian faith is an important part of who they are, and we try to develop that. For others who don't believe in God, we try to cultivate an awareness of a "Higher Power" much like the 12-Step programs that evolved from Alcoholics Anonymous. And for our Jewish kids, we try to help them develop a deeper religious identity as Jews.

Abby grew up on a kibbutz in Israel located north of Jerusalem. Her mother brought Abby to Chicago for medical treatment, but while there she developed emotional problems. When her mother received a recommendation to send Abby to the Ranch, she almost didn't let her come here because of our emphasis on faith as an important part of healing and recovery.

Over time, Abby's mom came to see that a deeper sense of Jewish identity would help Abby deal with some of the many problems she faced. For months, Chaplain Jamison met weekly with Abby to discuss the lives of people in the Hebrew Bible, or what we know as the Old Testament. We also had Abby meet with a Jewish teacher who is on staff at Yellowstone Academy.

By the time she left us, Abby had a renewed sense of her own self-worth and God's love for her. She read Psalm 23 during one of our weekly chapel services just prior to leaving the Ranch. Her mom sat in the back of the sanctuary, nodding her head in hearty approval of the progress her daughter had made.

For those of us who work at the Ranch, our commitment to serving kids comes from a sense of gratitude for all the things we have been given in our life and a sense of responsibility for using these gifts wisely. When we communicate these important messages to our kids and see them lived out on a daily basis, we know that a significant part of our mission here has been accomplished.

I never knew John would become a successful chaplain when he applied for a job back in 1969, but we could all tell that John was the kind of person we wanted on our team. And he has proven us right time and time again.

A Long-Term Commitment

Stability and commitment have been an essential part of Ranch operations in the past half-century. As a result, the Ranch has gone through few senior leadership changes. This has enabled us to remain focused on the urgent task of helping troubled young people.

In June 2004 our coworkers and friends celebrated one of our transitions at a dinner honoring Loren Soft, who was passing the baton of Ranch leadership to his successor, Ry Sorensen. In his farewell speech, Loren commented on the long-term dedication that so many of our employees and leaders have made.

"Our organization has been blessed with a significant number of individuals who have long tenures as employees. A recent Ranch annual report listed current employees who had been with the Ranch for five years or more. There were a total of 107 people, some of whom had been with us for more than thirty years."

We have honored employees who served ten years or more by listing them in an appendix at the back of this book. Ry deserves special attention because he served many important roles in his more than twenty-five years of service, including thirteen years as Ranch president and chief operating officer.

A Life Invested in Others

Ry first came to the Ranch in 1980 when he and his wife, Kathi, worked as houseparents at King Lodge. He brought with him a wealth of expertise and credentials, and Ry's own life experience increased his deep personal commitment to the Ranch's work and philosophy.

Growing up in South Dakota during the 1950s, Ry never heard people use the term "dysfunctional family," but that is what he grew up in. The family experienced both alcoholism and the kind of religious faith that favored judgmentalism over love and grace.

As a teen, Ry became involved in substance abuse issues of his own. After he ran away from home, he wound up in jail. His grandfather was the only family member who ever visited him there. Later, expelled from high school for recurring behavior problems, Ry enlisted in the Navy, thinking that would be an easier life. He may have been misinformed about what serving in the Navy would be like but he's glad he signed up anyway.

"The Navy saved my life," he says. "I reported to a Chief Petty Officer Schmidt, and this man took an interest in me and extended me grace. In time, I experienced success in the Navy that I had never realized before in my life."

The fact that this officer helped Ry was one of the reasons Ry later decided to devote his life to helping others at the Ranch. His own firsthand experience with the transforming power of grace motivates him to make grace available to today's troubled kids.

"Being here at Yellowstone is all about investing in people," said Ry. "This became more important to me after I met the Lord. I realized there had been an investment made in me by Someone I had no knowledge of. And the Ranch is just an extension of that grace.

"We use all the latest professional approaches here, but the stuff that really allows those approaches to make a difference in kids' lives is our willingness to come alongside them, extend them grace, and allow change to take place in their lives. That's what people did in my life, and now that's what we're trying to do in their lives."

Leading the Ranch Into the Future

Unfortunately, we were not able to enjoy Ry's leadership as long as we would have liked. Ry served as Ranch CEO for nearly two years before he had to resign due to recurring health problems from injuries he had received while serving with the U.S. Navy in Vietnam.

His resignation saddened us all, but Glenn McFarlane, Dale Orth and Joe Rich who have been with us for many years are working together to keep us moving forward. Dale and Joe you have already heard about and the McFarlane name should sound very familiar.

Glenn McFarlane grew up on the Ranch and called many of our Ranch boys his friends. After a college degree in business administration and considerable experience in banking, finance, and marketing, Glenn joined the Yellowstone staff in 1990. He was instrumental in navigating the Ranch through the complexities of Medicaid funding and setting up our finance department. Today, as the Ranch's Chief Financial Officer, Glenn carefully balances the needs of our kids with the funds available to care for a "family" much bigger than yours and mine!

These gentlemen will guide the Ranch until we complete a national search for a new CEO. I won't have as big a role in this decision as I did in our earlier years, but I'm confident that we will choose the right person to take the Ranch into its second half-century. And frankly, I can't wait to see what we can accomplish in the years ahead.

Glenn McFarlane exemplifies the Ranch motto daily in dealing with staff and kids.

Transformed Lives

Tony Torres:
Healing Body, Heart, and Family

When thirteen-year-old Tony Torres came to Yellowstone Boys and Girls Ranch, he was struggling with burdens that could have crushed most other teenagers.

"When I came to the Ranch, I was lost and confused," he says. "I had family problems, physical problems, depression, and feelings of abandonment."

In Tony's case, his negative feelings were more than legitimate. His mother had always struggled to care for him, but she abandoned him after he experienced kidney failure and required regular medical care.

Mark Jaskot was a supervisor at Leuthold Lodge where Tony stayed. Mark remembers the staff discussing whether the Ranch should admit a youngster with as many challenges as Tony had.

In the end, they decided they shouldn't limit their ability to care for kids with unique needs.

"We never hesitated to admit him because of the extra time and attention his health issues would

Tony playing Mustang basketball at the Ranch.

require," says Mark. "I didn't think we should hold back giving him the help he needed just because of his physical problems."

Tony's arrival challenged Ranch personnel to go the extra mile to care for him, but they tackled the problem with enthusiasm. Staff adjustments were made so that Tony could be taken to a Billings hospital three days a week for his needed dialysis treatments.

Even though Tony faced an understandable struggle with illness and depression when he arrived at the Ranch, in time he displayed an unquenchable zeal for life and a commitment to meeting his problems head-on.

Tony (right) showing some of his Vo-Ag class work. One of his favorite classes was Vo-Ag with Mr. Klempel.

"My mother abandoned me when I went into kidney failure before I came to the Ranch," says Tony. "But the people here didn't abandon me. They cared for me."

Once he was showered with loving care, Tony started to emerge from his darkness and despair. Today, the people who worked with him remember Tony's smile, his courage, his sense of humor, and his positive attitude.

"What a great kid," says Lisa Frazier, director of Recreational Therapy. "When we went on an overnight camping trip, I think it surprised Tony that I cared enough to provide the special food he needed."

Lisa also remembers how much Tony loved playing basketball with the Ranch's basketball team, the Mustangs. While there may have been some risks to letting Tony play, Lisa thought he could manage his illness and counted on him to let the coaches know when he was too tired.

While dialysis and recreational therapy helped Tony's body and mind, the Ranch's Pastoral Care Program provided an atmosphere for Tony to grow spiritually. "I'd been thinking a lot about the things I was learning at Chapel," says Tony. "One day when I got back from dialysis, I asked Jason, my pastoral care counselor, how I could have a relationship with Jesus. My life really changed after that."

His favorite Bible verse was Joshua 1:9: "Have I not commanded you? Be strong and courageous. Do not be terrified; do not be discouraged, for the Lord Your God will be with you wherever you go."

This verse is familiar to many, but for Tony it was the key to a new level of living. One sign of his spiritual growth was the fact that Tony regularly prayed for the mother who had abandoned him. Instead of returning rejection for rejection, he overcame rejection with love.

Another sign of Tony's faith was his continuing prayer for a new kidney. Tony was encouraged by verses from the prophet Jeremiah. "For I know the plans I have for you," declares the Lord, "plans to prosper you and not to harm you, plans to give you hope and a future. Then you will call upon me, and come and pray to me, and I will listen to you." (Jeremiah 29:11, 12)

Tony's newfound desire to get well was complicated by the fact that, when he arrived at Yellowstone, he was not even eligible to be on a transplant list for a new kidney. He was so fragile, both emotionally and physically, he was not considered a good candidate for a transplant. But, in due time, his earnest prayer would be answered.

Tony wanted to participate fully in life even if he wasn't feeling well. He became a positive role model for other Yellowstone kids. He had a way of getting others involved in activities and often encouraged those who felt down. He also contributed to the broader Billings community, reading an excerpt of Martin Luther King, Jr.'s "I Have A Dream" speech at a local Martin Luther King Day program.

Tony's role in this program helped awaken a sense of pride in his own cultural heritage. He studied and learned as much as he could about his Black and Hispanic heritage and invited others to learn about their own cultures and backgrounds. "God loves diversity," said Tony. "He ought to, He made each one of us!"

After a little more than a year at the Ranch, everyone agreed that Tony was in good enough shape to leave. It was at this time that Linda Luckett, his aunt from California, came to the Ranch to visit Tony on his birthday. She invited Tony to live with her, and he gladly accepted the offer. "God gave me a new family," he says.

When Tony was seventeen he received the kidney transplant he had been waiting and praying for so long. Today, Tony is finishing high school and is on his school's honor roll. Basketball is still his favorite pastime, and now he has the energy to play almost daily with his friends.

Most of his fellow students have no idea about the horrors he has endured, but he never forgets how far he has come. "Without the Ranch and my Aunt Linda, I think I would be dead," he says.

Thinking back on his time at the Ranch, Tony is thankful, both to the staff and to God. "It makes me feel good to think about Yellowstone Boys and Girls Ranch," he says. "I found myself while I was at Yellowstone, and I learned that I was valued, both in God's eyes and by the staff. They never give up on anyone!"

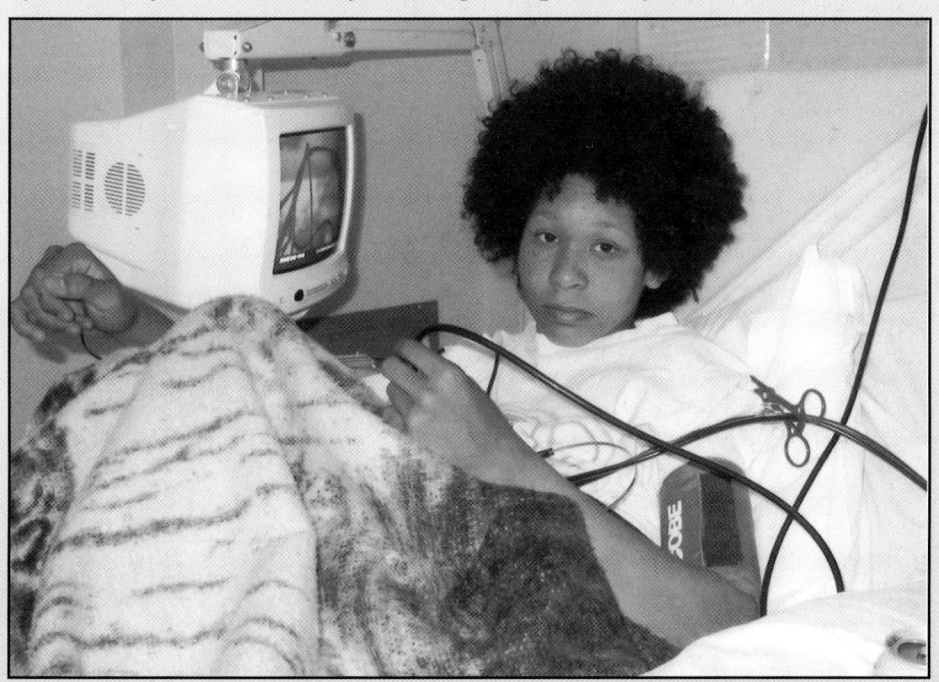

Tony undergoing dialysis at Deaconess Hospital in Billings.

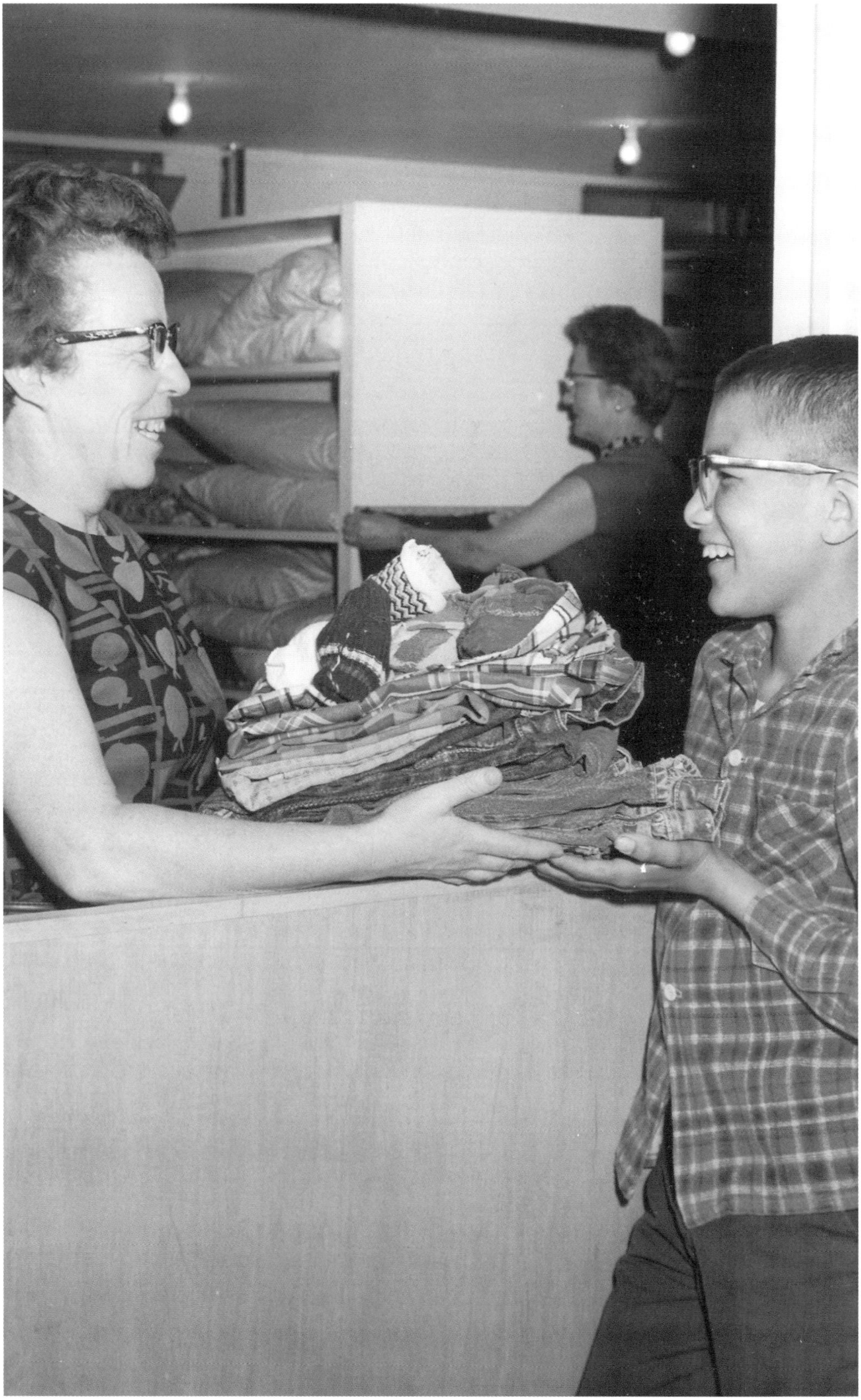

CHAPTER FOURTEEN

No More Kid Stuff

Jess is a charming, winsome seventeen-year-old with clear, blue eyes, an easy smile, and exciting plans for his future. But there's another side to Jess that's darker and not as attractive. This side comes out when Jess's feelings of anger and alienation cause him to lash out and push away those who try to befriend him.

You would be angry, too, if you had experienced the things Jess has. He was molested by a trusted youth worker at his family's church when he was twelve. Then his beloved grandfather died, leaving Jess feeling alone and adrift.

Over the next few years he slipped into drug use, alcohol abuse, and abysmal grades. When he ran away from home, his parents finally realized how bad things were and decided to send him to Yellowstone Boys and Girls Ranch for intensive care.

After two long, hard years of struggling with feelings of hopelessness and victimization, Jess is now taking charge of his life, stepping into leadership positions among the other youth at the Ranch, and making plans for his life after he graduates from high school.

Even his faith in God, which was severely damaged by the abuse he suffered at church, is on the mend. "We're working on our relationship," says Jess with a smile.

Clarissa is one of the many young women who are being cared for at the Ranch. Put up for adoption when she was six months old and raped by a companion of her mother's when she was only four, Clarissa rarely received nurturing and guidance from the adults in her life. Instead, those who should have cared for her taught her how to smoke pot, take LSD, drown her sorrows in alcohol, or inhale glue and paint fumes.

The most dramatic of Clarissa's many desperate cries for help happened the time she locked herself in her mom's pick-

Young people like Clarissa, walking here with her mother, receive help and healing at the Ranch.

up truck with a can of spray paint and a cigarette lighter. After filling the cabin with fumes, she set the fumes ablaze, causing an explosion that almost killed her.

"I didn't see any point in being here on earth," said Clarissa, who was brought to us after failing to respond to the kinds of treatment offered in a foster care program and a group home. "Whether I was here or not, it didn't seem like anyone noticed."

Today Clarissa's sense of self-esteem is recovering from the darkness of the past. And during a recent family counseling session, she even experienced a major breakthrough with her mom. "It was the first time when my mom left that I didn't want her to go," says Clarissa.

The more than six hundred boys and girls who are currently being cared for on a daily basis through the Ranch's various treatment programs suffer from a variety of significant problems.

Some are sad, angry, irritable, and easily upset. Others suffer from a deep depression and a sense of despair about life. Some experience feelings of worthlessness so profound that they have little desire to live or to even get out of bed. Some have withdrawn from life, experiencing a loss of interest in normal activities and perhaps compensating by engaging in risky behavior with sex, drugs, or alcohol.

Some of the kids we work with express their frustrations about life by developing an unhealthy preoccupation with their own deaths and imagining how much better life might be in heaven. In some circles, kids who think about heaven might be regarded as saintly, but we know to watch such kids very carefully, knowing that some of them might be tempted to speed their way to the afterlife by putting an end to this life.

Many of the kids we work with have been ignored, ostracized, or picked on by other kids prior to coming to the Ranch. And some of the adults in their lives have labeled them as "troubled," "at-risk," "on the edge," or "fringe." The psychiatric community has its own terminology for kids like Jess and

Clarissa. The clinical term for such kids is SED, which stands for Seriously Emotionally Disturbed.

But, here at the Ranch, we just call them "kids," and we do whatever we can to help them recover from the pains they have suffered, reassemble the fractured pieces of their lives into a cohesive whole, and help them develop a game plan for their lives that provides both hope and practical living for the future.

We work with each young person who comes to the Ranch to develop an Individual Treatment Plan that is designed to address his or her unique needs and challenges. This chapter will explain a couple of our programs that have been the most successful.

A Unique School for Unique Students

In addition to all the other problems they face, young people who come to the Ranch often struggle with academic challenges as well. Some of them under-perform academically. Others have fallen behind other students their age—some by as little as a quarter, and others by entire grades.

In order to help the youth get their educational process—and the rest of their lives—back on track, we have developed one of the most unusual educational programs in the United States. The Yellowstone Academy is our on campus school for students in grades kindergarten through the twelfth grade.

One thing that's unusual is the fact that the Academy is a combined public-private school. It offers grades K-8 as a public school that is accredited by the Montana Office of Public Instruction. And it offers grades 9-12 as a private school accredited by the Northwest Association of Schools and Colleges.

But perhaps the most unusual thing about the Academy is that it is the sole school in Montana School District 58, which was created by an act of the Montana State Legislature in 1965 to address the unique educational needs of the youth living at the Ranch. To our knowledge, School District 58 is the only four hundred-acre private not-for-profit elementary public

Jessica found the support and challenge she needed to achieve at Yellowstone Academy.

school district in the United States. This distinction provides avenues for state and federal funding for special needs youth and ensures that all credits earned by the students are fully transferable to any other public school in the United States.

Today we educate more than a hundred Ranch kids at the Academy. In addition, seventy young people from surrounding areas attend the Academy as day-school students. These students, who have a variety of learning or behavioral difficulties, attend the Academy because their own schools have determined that they will have a better chance of succeeding at the Academy than they would in their home schools.

In recent years a dozen students from these other districts have graduated from Yellowstone Academy. During the same time, more than two hundred students have returned to their own schools. In these cases, the training they received from the Academy staff helped them overcome problems that had interfered with their ability to receive an education in their previous schools.

In addition, the Ranch works in partnership with surrounding schools by providing a range of mental health counseling and therapy programs for students and parents.

We didn't know the Ranch would become a pioneer in educating SED kids when we founded our school nearly half a century ago. But by caring for our kids and applying ourselves to their unique challenges, we have developed a number of educational programs that have attracted attention throughout the region and the country.

Behind the Walls of Yellowstone Academy

From the outside, the Academy looks much like any other school. Its has walls made of red bricks, windows decorated with children's art, and wide sidewalks that at times are overflowing with energetic students.

But inside, one can see what really makes this school unique.

For one thing, classes are small. Most of our classes have ten to twelve students, which is far fewer than the average public school class size. Another thing that's unique about the classrooms is that each room has at least two staff present at all times. This includes a full-time teacher and another staff, either a teacher's aid or a childcare professional. This combination results in a staff-to-pupil ratio of one-to-five that is not seen in other school settings.

And, unlike many other schools which take the summer off, the Academy operates year-round, fitting five academic quarters into the calendar year so that students who have fallen behind can catch up more quickly.

The reason for these unique approaches to education can be found in the statistical profile of the Academy's student population. More than 80 percent of our students are classified as Special Education students. And of these kids, 80 percent are SED.

Ann Henson has been a teacher at the Academy for nearly twenty years, so she is very familiar with the deep dysfunction of the typical Academy student.

"One thing about our students is that they are very sensitive," says Ann. "Something relatively simple—like a comment someone made at breakfast—can upset them. And our goal is to help them reestablish their balance, or it can go downhill from there and result in emotional or physical outbursts."

On most days, the majority of students are relatively calm. But in rare cases kids act out their inner turmoil. When they do, the Academy staff members are prepared to address the situation. In addition, the school is equipped with an emergency alert system that lights up in hallways and rooms throughout the school, making the entire staff aware that there is a problem. All the school's sixty-five staff members are trained in counseling techniques. But if this gentle approach doesn't

In her 20 years at Yellowstone Academy, Ann Henson has taught reading and so much more.

work, staff can call on their training in therapeutic crisis intervention techniques that are designed to contain an out-of-control young person without causing injury.

The Academy's in-house psychiatric doctors and nurses may also be called in to assess whether problems may have been complicated by a student's problems with medications.

Most Academy students are completely unaware of the extensive system of safeguards and precautions that are in place to keep the school functioning. Rather, they simply feel more safe and secure here than they have in other schools. And in those rare cases when problems erupt, these problems are isolated and dealt with, allowing the rest of our students and teachers to go on with their schooling.

Teachable Moments

Ann Henson is a teacher who as a paraplegic teaches classes from her wheelchair. "We call crises our windows of opportunity," she says.

For Ann and the other teachers at the Academy, crisis situations are seen as golden opportunities to connect with kids and address their problems.

"I am not intimidated by what goes on around here, which is just my personality," she says. "I have a great deal of compassion for these kids. And part of that comes from my own experiences in growing up and dealing with difficult things. As a result, I am very empathetic with them.

"The whole point of everything we do here, including the small class sizes, is to develop relationships with these kids and help them work through their traumas and their treatment issues so they can learn, improve their coping skills, adjust to whatever it is they need to adjust to, and reenter their homes, schools, and communities functioning as well as they can."

As you might expect, graduation day is a happy time at the Academy.

"We've had kids come here in handcuffs, and leave with

their arms around their parents and their teachers," says Ron Hatcher, who served as the Academy's superintendent for more than a decade.

Ed Zabrocki worked in public schools for decades before joining the Academy as its superintendent in 2001. Although the work can be more demanding, the rewards can also be more dramatic.

"I like the situation here because you're dealing directly with kids," he says. "There's a lot less interference from different groups pushing a particular agenda. Instead, it's just about helping the kids."

Ed Zabrocki came to Yellowstone Academy after a career in public education. "Here it's just about helping the kids," he says.

Not Just Horsing Around

Not all of the Ranch's educational activities happen within the walls of the Academy. In fact, many of our programs work together to help kids develop the skills they need to survive after they leave us.

People are fascinated by horses. Perhaps it is their strength, their beauty, or their unique ability to bond with humans that makes horses so intriguing. In recent years a number of books and movies have shown how horses can play an important role in helping humans address their problems.

For example, one difficult horse was a central character in Robert Redford's film The Horse Whisperer, based on the novel by Nicholas Evans. In the film, thirteen-year-old Grace Maclean loses her leg when a truck strikes her and her horse Pilgrim. In addition to the physical injury, both the girl and the horse suffer in other ways that leave them fearful of human contact. Grace's mother takes her daughter and the horse to a ranch in Montana where a horse whisperer named Tom Booker (Redford) tries to heal both the child and the animal.

Programs that use horses to help people recover are often called equine therapy, and the Ranch has been involved in such programs for years. But even before such programs became popular, we realized that amazing things could happen when horses and kids were brought together in the right kinds of ways.

"It's hard to explain what happens, but we have found significant breakthroughs with kids when working with animals," says Loren Soft, the former Ranch CEO who has long believed that horses can play an important role in helping severely emotionally disturbed kids.

Some at the Ranch even quote the late British leader, Sir Winston Churchill, who said, "There is something about the outside of a horse that is good for the inside of a man."

In recent years there has been growing interest in Equine Assisted Psychotherapy. An organization known as EAGALA (Equine Assisted Growth and Learning Association) was founded in 1999 to help the burgeoning field establish training and credentialing procedures for therapists.

Leslie Mathews, who joined the Ranch in 2000, is a longtime member of EAGALA, but she continues to be amazed by the therapeutic breakthroughs that can happen when kids work with horses.

"Kids and horses are similar in many ways," says Mathews, who has been riding since she was two years old and now directs the Ranch's Equine Therapy program. "Both are very expressive. And both will shut down when they feel they are dealing with conflicting signals about what to do. A lot of times it is easier for kids to see these kinds of tensions in a horse than it is to see it in themselves."

Mathews spends her mornings teaching horsemanship classes to Ranch residents as part of their vocational education training. But, in the afternoons, Mathews teams up with Ranch therapists to focus on equine therapy.

"The afternoon sessions aren't about horsemanship or rid-

Equine therapist Leslie Mathews and horse Gracie help Meghan learn important life lessons that can't be learned in traditional classrooms.

ing," she says. "They're about helping kids deal with things they're not dealing with in regular therapy sessions. And the horses help them do this."

An article in *The Billings Gazette* explored the Ranch's Equine Assisted Psychotherapy Program and provided some hints about why it works so well:

> In an exercise called Life's Little Obstacles, participants try to move a horse to get it over a jump. The rules make the task tough because they cannot touch the horse, or use halters or lead ropes.
>
> Because they react to people's body language, the animals offer immediate feedback on how people communicate nonverbally. Participants also learn that, to change the horse's reaction, they must often change their own behavior.
>
> Mathews says she looks for teachable moments even during horsemanship sessions.
>
> "We had a young girl give us one of these teachable moments a few weeks ago," she says. "Her horse scared her, so she jumped off, threw her helmet on the ground, and stormed off.
>
> "We approached the girl and asked her, 'Where is your horse and what is he doing right now?' Thinking about this reminded her that she had to think of some one other than herself.
>
> " 'Oh, my gosh,' said the girl. 'I have to go back and take care of my horse.' "
>
> Within a few moments, the girl had picked up her helmet, put it on, and climbed back up on her horse.
>
> "This girl's way of reacting to situations in her life that frustrated her was to walk away," says Mathews. "That's what she did to her horse, too. But after we talked to her, she was able to reconnect with the horse and finish the activity she was doing with him. This

simple event turned into a success for her.

"My main objective out there is not to teach riding," says Mathews. "My main objective is to teach kids to relate to one another, to learn to be safe in their choices, to learn about themselves, and to have some fun at the same time."

In 2003 the Ranch invited the public to a dedication service for its new 41,000 square-foot equestrian facility, which is named the Bill and Anita Jones Equestrian Center in honor of a couple that has supported the Ranch in many ways over the years.

In addition to housing equine programs for Ranch kids, the Center also serves the surrounding community by providing a venue for barrel racing, dog shows, and other events that attract visitors from throughout the region. The Center also enables the Ranch to partner with organizations like Eagle Mount, a local group that provides riding and other recreational activities for disabled children and adults.

Serving and Growing

The development of Yellowstone Academy and the Ranch's Equine Assisted Psychotherapy Program illustrate our commitment to helping kids in any way we can. And our willingness to "go the extra mile" by recruiting private donors to underwrite the costs of these and other programs is one of the main reasons the Ranch offers programs and facilities to kids that they could not experience anywhere else.

We knew we were making a serious commitment years ago when we agreed to help troubled kids. And programs like these are part of why we achieve a level of success with these kids that other institutions find amazing.

We were talking earlier in this chapter about movies featuring horses, but there is one more horse movie we haven't mentioned that I think summarizes much about the Ranch philosophy. That movie is the heartwarming box office success called *Seabiscuit*.

The star of the movie was an aging and unexceptional horse named Seabiscuit who rose to fame during the Depression years—a time when many Americans needed a hero to believe in, or at least a diversion that could momentarily take their minds off their financial problems.

But the movie also focused on the horse's jockey, a feisty man named Red Pollard who had his own hard-luck story. Red had been abandoned by his parents during the Depression. He suffered from a disorder called reactive attachment disorder, though no one would have ever called it that decades ago.

There's a powerful line of dialogue in the movie that was applied to both Seabiscuit and Red Pollard: "You don't throw a whole life away just because it's banged up a bit."

That's how we feel about the kids who come to stay with us at the Ranch.

Transformed Lives

Ella Brower:
"I'd Like to Be the Face of Yellowstone Boys and Girls Ranch"

Ella came to her counselor about a week before leaving Yellowstone and said, "I'd like to be the face of Yellowstone Boys and Girls Ranch." She wasn't sure exactly what she meant by that; but she did know that her life had changed dramatically because of the loving care she had received here, and she wanted to tell the world about it.

Ella explains, "When I first came to Yellowstone, I was all shut up inside, like I was living in a cave. I didn't care about myself, and I wouldn't come out for anyone."

Ella is a beautiful native Inuit (Eskimo) whose parents' alcohol and drug abuses had led to unspeakable neglect and abuse toward Ella from the time she was an infant.

When Ella was removed from her home at age eleven, she was suffering from depression, posttraumatic stress, and reactive attachment disorder.

Reactive attachment disorder prevents a child from being able to form meaningful relationships with others. Children who suffer from this dis-

Ella says she felt like she was "living in a cave" when she first came to Yellowstone.

order often seem very personable and friendly at first. But when a significant connection begins to develop (such as an "attachment" to a foster parent), the child recoils from the relationship out of fear that it won't last and often lashes out in hurtful ways (the "reactive" phase).

Because of Ella's multiple problems, she had failed in four foster home placements and been hospitalized seven times within eighteen months. Residential treatment at Yellowstone was a last hope for Ella.

It took a long time for Ella to begin to trust anyone enough to share her thoughts and feelings honestly. Beth, a counselor in the Brekkeflat Intensive Unit, remembers, "When she first came, Ella was extremely sad and quiet and felt truly unloved. She was afraid to go to sleep without someone close by, so I would sit in her doorway and talk until she fell asleep."

Finally, Ella began to talk. She'd say things like, "Why should I go on living? Why did I have to suffer through so much abuse? Why did God let me live?" She couldn't understand how God could love her and yet let her suffer so.

Beth says the most remarkable thing she observed about Ella's progress was how she finally made peace with God and allowed Him to help her work through her problems.

At first, whenever there was any conflict with staff or peers, she would retreat back into her "cave" and refuse to communicate. She slowly learned that conflict isn't bad; that talking about things helps people understand and accept one another. Ella had never been allowed to speak up for herself, and the frustration had come out in hurting herself and others. Now, she doesn't feel the need to lash out because she's learning how to articulate her needs in acceptable ways.

Ella's feelings of self-esteem grew through Recreational Therapy at the Uihlein Center. Nate Nunberg, a recreational therapist, remembers Ella participating in every intramural activity offered. "At first she was so quiet and shy," he says. "As she got involved at the UC, she became much more outspoken and interested in building relationships with staff and peers." Ella, a natural athlete, was especially proud of the fact that she could play flag football as well as the boys!

Horsemanship was also a highlight for Ella. "I will never, never forget the horses!" she says. Ella had never been on a horse before coming to Yellowstone.

Ella's ease with horses was evident as she rode at the dedication of the new Equestrian center.

She happened to be at the Ranch when the new Equestrian Center was built and dedicated. Equine Therapist Leslie Mathews worked with a number of the youth, developing a synchronized routine for them to perform with their horses at the dedication ceremonies. Leslie recalls, "When I told Ella she'd be at the front carrying a flag, she was fearful about the responsibility it entailed. But when I said, 'You can ride one-handed. You don't need to hold on to the saddle horn anymore,' it made her very proud." Ella did a beautiful job, exhibiting how she had grown and matured in many ways.

Ella spent her last few months at the Ranch working part-time for Karen Tetrault, receptionist at the administration building. Karen says they talked a lot about family and Ella's native culture. She missed her grandma, especially the muktuk (raw whale blubber) she would make. Another delicacy she missed was salmon. When Karen asked how the Inuit prepare salmon, Ella replied, "Oh, you don't want to cook it. That ruins it!"

They also talked a lot about clothes. Or, as Karen says, "Ella talked. I mostly listened." The transformation was amazing. Ella grew from an introverted, sullen girl who didn't care at all about her appearance, into a bubbly, normal fourteen-year-old who loved clothes and make-up.

Ella also loves people now and isn't afraid to tell them. She now has a permanent foster family in Alaska that loves her and say they will always be there for her. Ella has an intense love for her native people and dreams of serving them in the medical field one day—in Alaska, of course.

Ella's life is not perfect, and she is still working on the hurts and scars that brought her to Yellowstone. But Ella's foster parents, Yael and Jeremy, say Ella is very bright, capable and teachable. They encourage her to dream big.

"I think the main goal of Yellowstone is to help kids have a normal life," says Ella. "They want us to have a loving family and to have our dreams come true."

Ella told her story in pictures and video before returning to Alaska. Ella's happy smile and gratitude have been used in several ways to tell others about Yellowstone Boys and Girls Ranch. She got her wish and has become "the face of Yellowstone!"

Filming for a promotional video before leaving treatment.

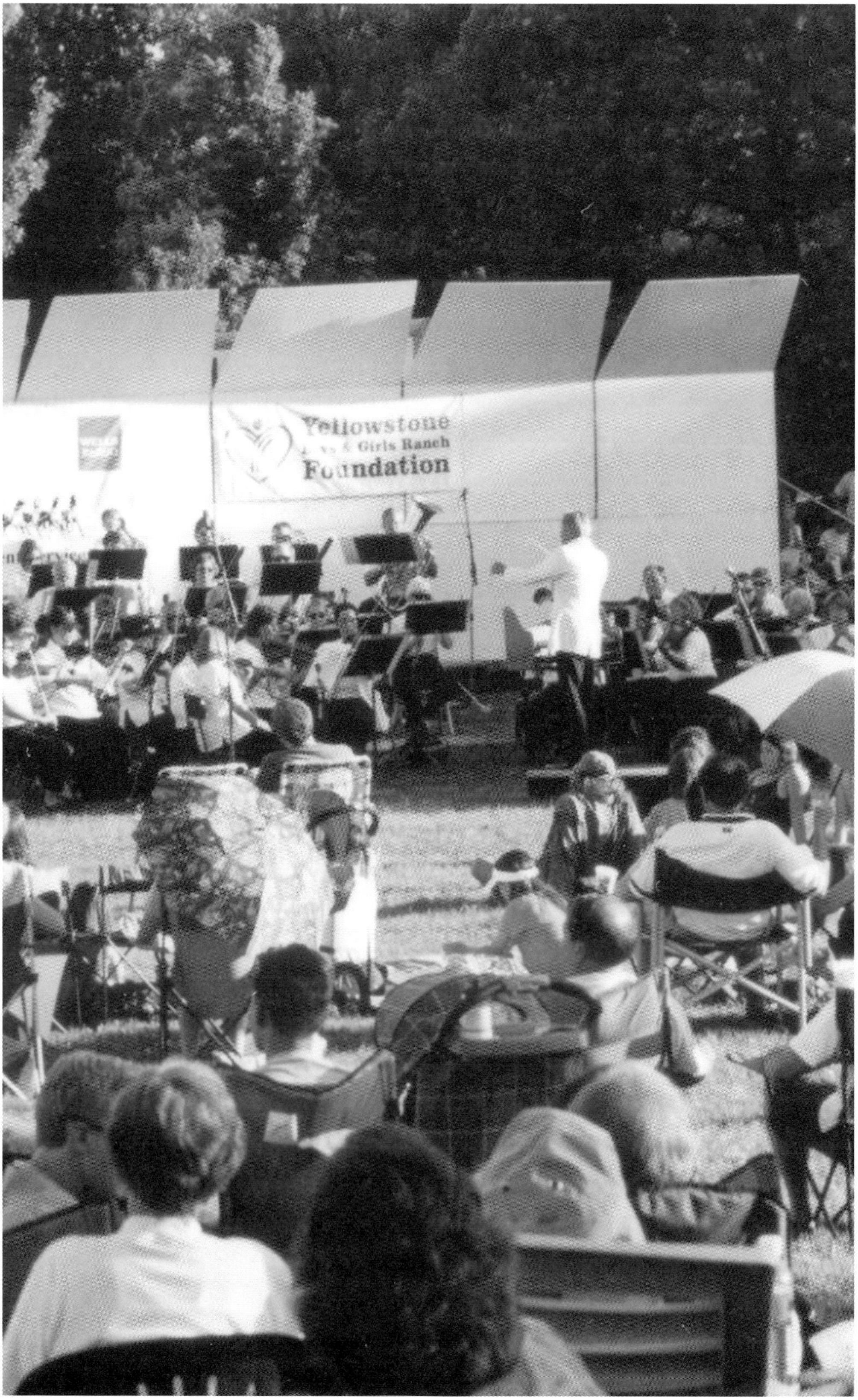
Yellowstone
& Girls Ranch
Foundation

CHAPTER FIFTEEN

Giving Back to the Community

It was a warm June evening as I packed up lawn chairs and blankets and headed to Billings' Pioneer Park for an evening of fun and relaxation with my family. But we weren't the only ones going to the park that summer evening. Another seven thousand people had the same idea: enjoying one of the city's most popular events, the annual Symphony in the Park concert featuring the Billings Symphony Orchestra and Chorale.

Everyone picked out grassy spots on a hillside facing the concert stage, bought snacks and drinks from one of the many local vendors, and settled in to enjoy an evening of orchestral compositions, patriotic music, and community spirit.

For me and other workers from Yellowstone Boys and Girls Ranch, the Symphony in the Park is more than a nice evening that combines musical and natural beauty. The Ranch and the Foundation have been major sponsors of the annual event for more than a decade.

There are many worthwhile projects we could support. So why, year after year, do we lend our support to the Symphony in the Park? The answer is simple. Those of us who work with the Ranch see ourselves as a part of the greater Billings community. Over the years, this community has played a crucial role in our ongoing existence and success. For us, supporting this annual concert is a way to demonstrate our appreciation and commitment in tangible ways that all can see and enjoy.

Our support of the Symphony in the Park isn't the only way we try to give something back to the community that has given so much to us over the past fifty years.

A Christmas Gift for the Community

Ranch chaplains do so much more than talk to kids about religion. They help many of us at the Ranch express our core values through our varied activities and programs. In the 1980s Chaplain Tom Carey came up with such a good idea, we have been using it ever since. Tom suggested finding out if the kids would be interested in organizing a Ranch Christmas celebra-

Christmas celebrations have been an important part of Ranch life for many years.

tion that would help them understand the meaning of giving.

"Christmas is a tough time for many of our kids," says Chaplain John Jamison, who now carries on the tradition started by Chaplain Carey. "For those who can't be reunited with their families over the holidays, it is often a season of grieving, sadness, and even depression.

"One of our goals here at the Ranch is to engage our kids in something bigger than themselves. We don't do that just because it makes people feel good. Rather, we try to do things for others because that is a basic part of our values. And over the years this has become an ever-bigger part of our overall therapeutic approach."

One boy had good things to say about the celebration. "It's time for us to go beyond just having pity parties for ourselves all the time. We need to think about how we can help someone else who has it even tougher in life than we do."

Counting the Ways

The Christmas celebration got some of us thinking. Were there other ways we could get our kids to look beyond themselves and their problems and have a positive impact on the world? Out of these discussions came the creation of the Ranch's Community Service Program that now involves all our kids in various activities that reach out to the surrounding community.

Every year, lodge leaders establish service goals for their kids and determine which projects could have the greatest impact. In one recent year, kids in our twelve Ranch lodges invested 2,438 hours in dozens of projects that benefited the community.

The complete list of projects fills six single-spaced pages. But here's a brief summary of some of the things they've done:
• Sorted and hung donated clothes for Family Services, Inc., a local agency that serves poor and needy residents
• Served at the annual "Souper Bowl" celebration sponsored

by the Montana Rescue Mission, and also baked cookies and made sandwiches for the Mission, which works with adults who deal with substance abuse problems and other issues
• Picked up trash, performed cleaning duties, painted picnic tables, and provided gardening and landscaping help for ZooMontana
• Served dinner to the elderly with the local Council on Aging
• Exercised animals and cleaned

Ranch youth volunteer to help with local projects like constructing Habitat for Humanity houses (top) and visting residents of area nursing homes.

animal kennels operated by Help for Homeless Pets and the Billings Animal Shelter
• Made greeting cards, hosted a birthday party, visited residents, and gave other help to the Evergreen Nursing Home
• Sorted food donations received by the Billings Post Office for its annual community food drive
• Played many hours of Bingo with residents of the

Ranch youth also help area residents with household chores such as painting (top) and assist in maintenance at the Beartooth Nature Center.

St. John's Lutheran Home for the elderly
- Cleaned parks and roadsides for the University of Montana-Western and the cities of Billings and Dillon
- Painted a building at Grace Bible Church, which welcomes Ranch kids to its services and youth programs
- Created props and provided other backstage assistance for the Billings Studio Theater
- Created public service announcements about drug and alcohol abuse that were broadcast on local radio stations

Every year we think of new things we can do to help the community, and local organizations provide us with lists of tasks they need done. Together, the lodge leaders divide up the tasks and get their kids ready for work.

Over the years, the Community Service Program has become a fundamental aspect of Ranch life, and counselors try to use kids' experiences in the community to help them be less self-absorbed and more connected to the outside world.

The community service projects have even become a source of healthy competition between the various lodges, with each group of kids trying to devote more time to outside work than the other groups.

In 2004, the girls who live in the Mary Brekkeflat Lodge and Jessie Grant Lodge spent 470 hours on community service projects, earning them the Ranch's Community Service Award for the year.

The award was nice, but even better was the sense of accomplishment and self-esteem the girls gained from serving others.

Community Based Services: Expanding Beyond Residential Treatment

During the 1990s it became obvious to those of us in therapeutic childcare services that a national policy agenda in mental health care for children, youth, and families was building toward "community-based systems of care." A system (or continuum) of care is an array of services matched to the severity of the needs of children and youth. They may include in-home services, foster care, group homes, independent living, school based mental health programs, and case management.

In the mid-1990s, Loren Soft could see the momentum building and commented that "someday we will serve more children off-campus than on." He enlisted the help of Chief Operating Officer Ry Sorensen, and David Groot, who joined the Ranch as a counselor in 1990 and served as the vice president of Community Programs. They put together a gifted team of people, already part of our program, to develop services within communities that would hopefully prevent at-risk children from having to enter residential treatment.

"These programs have grown significantly over the last decade," says David Groot. "We are able to take the knowledge and skills we have developed at the Ranch and offer them to hurting people in their home areas. This is very gratifying and it's a concrete way for us to extend the mission and vision of Yellowstone beyond the main campus."

Through off-campus offices in Billings, Livingston, and Lewistown, our CBS staff provides support, counseling, mentoring, and other valuable services to well over a thousand children, youth, and families each year in several communities throughout Montana. On any given day more than five hundred youth are being served in these mental health programs.

At times the services are high-level mental health interventions such as intervening with suicidal adolescents and getting them placed in a psychiatric hospital. Often the services are as simple as helping a youth with homework, playing basketball at the YMCA, or going to youth group to help the young person become positively involved in the life of the community.

The services we offer to the community have evolved over the years, but here are some of the major ways we help those outside the Ranch improve the quality of their lives:

1) Youth Case Management

Yellowstone is responsible for coordinating the care of seriously emotionally disturbed (SED) youth for a ten-county region. Shawn Byrne is the director of this program. Shawn notes that along with facilitating treatment teams and planning care, the twenty case managers are responsible for coordinating what may be several different social service agencies involved in treating SED youth who still live in their home community.

"Case managers spend a lot of time coaching, guiding, and motivating youth and families," Shawn says, "The unique aspect of our case management program is that we invest in caring relationships with families. They know that we want them to get the services they need in order to live healthy, satisfying lives."

2) School Based Mental Health Programs

We currently have teams of therapists and behavioral specialists working in twelve public schools. Each of these teams works with twelve to sixteen students with serious emotional problems. Stacy York directs this program. Stacy comments that a school superintendent said to her, "I don't know how we served these students without you."

Along with crisis intervention and consulting with teachers, our school programs provide a refuge for kids who struggle socially and academically. Sometimes the stress of school for these students is relieved by something as seemingly simple as a brief walk around the playground, or having their hair fixed, or playing a board game with an adult who cares.

3) Therapeutic Family Living

This service provides counselors and therapists who work with children and their families in their own homes to help them address problems that plague their lives.

Not all children with problems struggle with issues that are complex enough to warrant their being placed at the Ranch.

The solution is to take the care offered at the Ranch and make it more widely available to families in their own homes. Not only does the Therapeutic Family Living program help us care for people who do not come to the Ranch, but it allows our counselors to deal with family issues that may be contributing to the difficulties the child is having.

Amy is a concerned mother who expressed her appreciation for the help offered to her son, David. "David would not have had a change of heart if it were not for his treatment manager and youth and family support worker," she told us. "They showed him compassion, gentleness, and concern. I don't feel David would have made this change without these people in his life."

4) *Therapeutic Foster Care*

The Ranch also provides foster care through licensed, trained, and carefully screened treatment families who have agreed to provide care, counseling, and other services to children who have special needs that are best cared for in a warm and friendly family setting.

The Ranch carefully matches children with selected treatment families, and then assigns a treatment manager to the family to monitor the children's progress.

Brenda Quillen, director of Therapeutic Foster Care states that "therapeutic foster care not only provides much-needed help for the children it serves, but it also brings a special kind of gratification to those families who feel called to carry out this kind of intense and emotionally demanding work." Brenda has created a community of foster parents who rely on one another to help troubled kids.

Don and Becky Bergland have served as foster parents for many years. They have been Montana's Foster Parents of the Year. Don Bergland notes that they work with Yellowstone because of the organization's commitment to the spiritual development of children as well as the physical and psychological. Becky tells stories of children they have served and says that foster parenting is about planting seeds.

Yellowstone's foster families express a common theme about the rewards of working with children in their homes.

"We feel so blessed to have had this time with our foster child," said Carla, one of our therapeutic foster parents.

5) *The LIFE Program*

LIFE stands for Living Independently and Fostering Employment. And that's exactly what this unique program does.

The LIFE Program helps troubled kids who have received some kind of therapeutic care make the transition to independent living and financial survival. Youth are matched with trained Life Coaches who help them develop an individually tailored living plan that takes their problems into consideration while stretching them in ways that prepare them for life and work in the real world.

Another aspect of the LIFE program is its emphasis on peer support, which connects young people in transition to those who have already made significant progress in life.

"The program gave me a home of my own and a fresh start in life," said David, one young man who overcame significant personal problems and is now thriving on his own.

6) *Community Homes*

While some young people need the kinds of intensive care the Ranch's residential programs offer, others do better with more moderately structured environments. The Ranch's three Community Homes provide warm, supportive, and helpful family environments that focus on helping young people develop the character, academic abilities, social skills, and coping abilities that will enable them to grow to the point where they no longer require formal supervision.

These Community Homes, which are located in Billings and

Lewistown, are supervised by workers who serve as the young people's counselors, guides, and foster parents. Through their close and constant care, they help young people make the needed adjustments to move beyond highly supervised living to successful lives of work and service to others in the larger community.

All together, the Ranch's various Community Based Services offer hope and healing to children, youth, and families throughout Montana who might not otherwise be able to take advantage of these kinds of help.

These Community Based Services have grown significantly over the last decade, and one of the major reasons for their success is due to the hard work and expertise of David Groot.

"This is very gratifying, and it's a concrete way for us to extend the mission and vision of Yellowstone beyond the main campus," says David.

David Groot spent many hours on the road supervising the work of our off-campus facilities for families throughout the state.

A Philosophy of Service

Many business leaders talk about customer service these days, and that's because they realize that customers can easily take their business elsewhere if one store or company treats them badly.

But there's something deeper behind the Ranch's philosophy of community service. For us this "something deeper" extends all the way to our core values and beliefs. Whether it's community service activities Ranch kids perform or the therapeutic Community Based Services our workers provide, the same philosophy of service to the community underlies our work.

One of the biblical stories that has been important to many of us at the Ranch over the years is Jesus' parable of the Good Samaritan. In the story Jesus points out that many people passed by the man who had been robbed and beaten up, but the Samaritan stopped and cared for the injured man.

"Which of these do you think was a neighbor to the man who fell into the hands of robbers?" asked Jesus, who told those who heard him, "Go and do likewise."

One of the reasons we care so deeply about kids is that we believe they are God's children. They may have been abused and beaten up in life, but that doesn't remove the essential element in all of them that cries out for respect and love.

And it's because of this belief in the essential dignity of all the kids we serve that we require them to serve others. For us, purpose and meaning in life are based on something more than mere personal gratification. True purpose and meaning come through service to others, and when we can teach our kids to understand this important truth and practice it in their daily lives, they are already well on the way to recovery.

Transformed Lives

Fred Wittman:
"If I can make it, you can!"

"Fred represents the best Yellowstone Boys and Girls Ranch has to offer, in terms of partnering with the community to help a young man succeed, who, otherwise, would have had very little hope of succeeding," says Chaplain John Jamison. He remembers, with a smile, the "behavioral nightmare" Fred was in chapel as a little boy living in King Lodge.

Fred and his mom, Joan, agree that without the Ranch, he would probably be in prison, a mental institution, or dead. Instead, Fred graduated from high school at Yellowstone Academy in June of 2006 and, armed with the tools for survival gained at Yellowstone, has an excellent chance of leading a productive, independent life.

Traumatic events in Fred's young life brought out rage in him that his mother couldn't control. Setting fires, chasing people with knives, and trying to harm himself as a five and six-year-old,

Fred the "mascot" telling part of the Christmas story when in King Lodge.

were the frightening realities of their family life. Joan says, "Fred had complicated feelings inside that he wasn't capable of expressing verbally. So, he lashed out at himself and others."

Consequently, Fred was placed at Yellowstone in King Lodge, which was the little boy lodge at the time. "He made an instant impression," says Tracy Preston, who was a counselor in an older boy lodge, "not because of his aggressiveness, but because he was so cute!" Fred was a little, tiny guy who immediately became a mascot for the older kids. "They took him under their wing," she says. "They always included him, made sure they said 'hi,' and made him feel accepted."

Tammy Baldry, who was a night counselor in King remembers working with Fred. Fred had endured merciless teasing because of his size and Tammy could relate. "I have a son who is small for his age, so I know how hurtful teasing can be when you are so young," she says. "But, if he knew you respected him, Fred would go out of his way to please you."

Fred learned a lot from his time at Yellowstone as a little guy. "I learned that friends are there to help you and to understand," Fred says. "Also, that poem you hear about 'sticks and stones' is very wrong. Words do hurt!"

After a time in King Lodge, his treatment team agreed it was time for Fred to return home. "Things were okay for awhile," says Joan, "but more upheaval in our personal lives caused Fred to regress."

The next several years were punctuated with hospitalizations, other out-of-home placements, and another stay at King Lodge. Lots of mental health issues had to be identified and treated. One stable factor for Fred and his mom was the commitment by Yellowstone staff to work with the public school, behavioral specialists, and medical professionals in the community to keep Fred safe and in school.

Fred has done much of his schooling at Yellowstone Academy, including taking most of his high school classes through the Day Treatment Program. Fred's mom says, "Tracy Preston has been his teacher for the last three years and has exhibited enormous perseverance with Fred." Tracy is humbled by her gratitude, but says, "Fred and Joan did all the work. I was just there to give support. You can hand someone all the tools in the world, but they won't be successful if they're not willing to do the work."

Tammy, who now teaches at the Academy, too, enjoys seeing Fred in the halls. "I can see why Fred has been more successful here than in public school," she says. "Small class size, less peer pressure, more control over students' interactions, and close relationships with teachers all help these borderline kids 'make it' in school."

"To long-term kids like Fred, the Ranch is like another family," says Joan. "They offer so much more than just a therapeutic environment. They offer the personal aspect, too. The Ranch has helped fill an emptiness in Fred's life. They've helped him learn social skills, what is acceptable behavior, and helped to round him out as an individual."

Fred adds, "I experienced a lot of rejection at other schools. It was very hard. Coming back to day school here felt like coming home. I've learned to trust people at the Ranch because they have gone through the same things I have."

Everyone agrees that Fred is a much different person than he was when he arrived at Yellowstone ten years ago. Tracy says, "Fred is very sensitive to others' feelings. He's an incredibly well-mannered, polite young man. I wouldn't have said that four or five years ago."

Chaplain Jamison adds, "Fred has grown into someone who likes people and likes to help people." In music class recently, another youth was having trouble understanding a drum beat. "I helped him

Fred and Chaplain Jamison enjoy a moment together in the midst of a busy school day.

with that," says Fred, "and it gave me a thrill to be there for him." Fred also goes out of his way to open doors for the women and girls at the Ranch.

Fred has emotional challenges he'll have to manage his whole life. Yellowstone's goal is to help Fred, and many others like him, lead fulfilling lives outside an institution and as productive members of society.

That statement sounds rather cold and clinical. But, combined with the warm, loving atmosphere which always seeks the good of the child and family, Yellowstone has an exceptional track record with children most others would give up on. "I'm extremely proud of Fred," his mom says. "It took a lot of courage for Fred to be willing to dig deep and deal with his issues. The family atmosphere at Yellowstone is what brought Fred to the point of wanting to work so hard."

Fred's life story represents a bridge, of sorts, from Yellowstone's first half-century to its next half-century and beyond. He has a lengthy history with the Ranch much like many of its early residents, but he has also been the recipient of almost all the expanded programs and services Yellowstone offers today.

Fred has a hopeful future, due in large part to Yellowstone's convictions that every life is precious, every life is worth fighting for, and "It sure makes a difference when you know somebody cares."

Fred's Yellowstone Academy graduation photo.

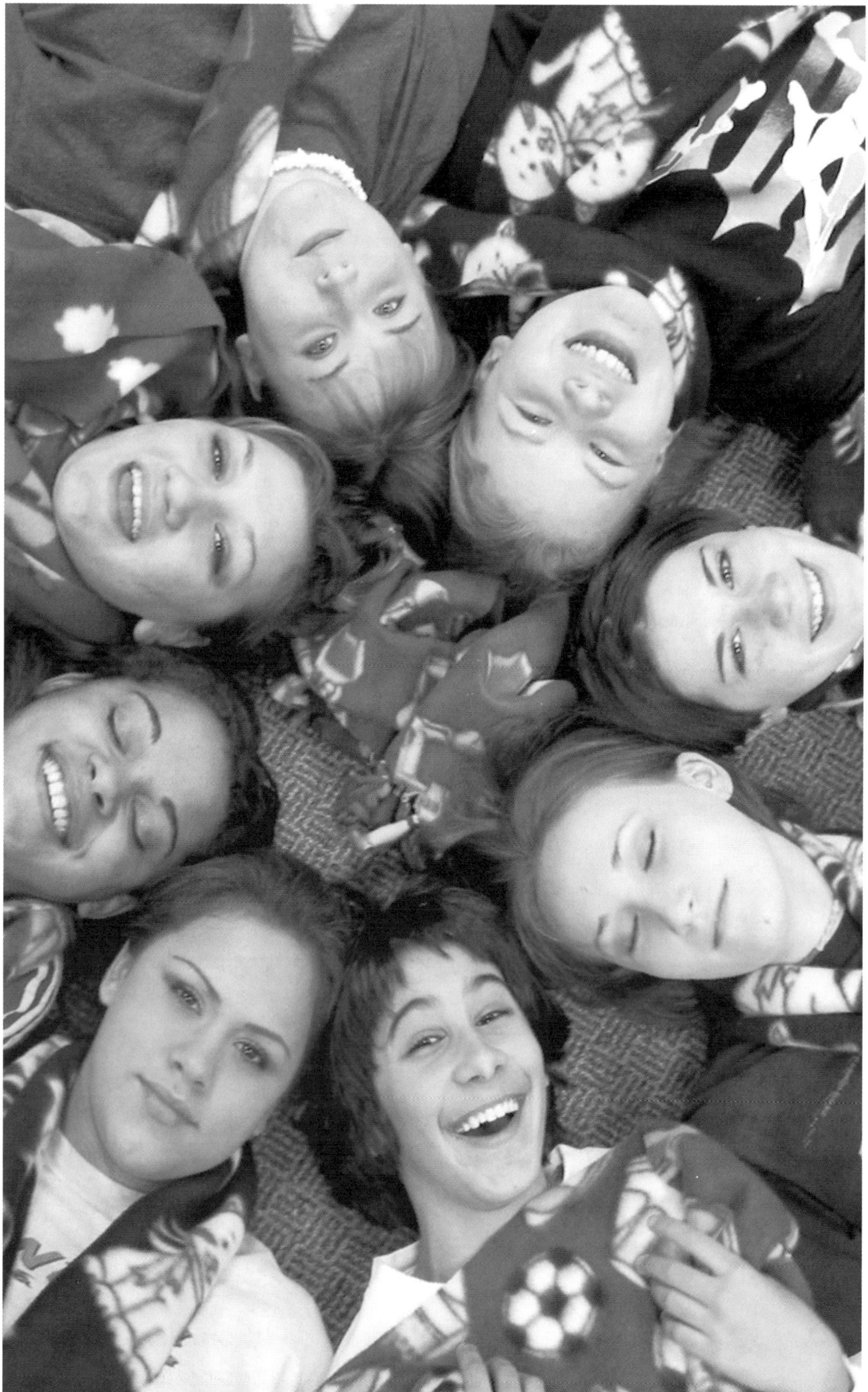

CHAPTER SIXTEEN

A Legacy of Caring

When I drive out to Yellowstone Boys and Girls Ranch today, there are times when I have to pinch myself to make sure I am not dreaming. As I drive in through the Ranch's big front gate and look around me, I can't believe how the dream some of us had more than half a century ago has grown into a major, modern facility that provides specialized care to hundreds of emotionally troubled young people.

Things have changed a lot at the Ranch over the past fifty years, but the reason we exist has not changed, as I can see when I read some of the anguished letters that distraught parents send to the Ranch.

Urgent Letters to the Ranch

For example, one mother poured out her heart to us about her daughter, providing sobering detail about the many problems that had made normal daily life impossible for one loving family:

> She has 2-3 temper tantrums daily, one lasting five hours with her screaming and kicking the floor. She has

torn up books, broken and thrown household items, etched foul language into furniture, and tried to scratch, kick, bite, and punch her family members when she is in a rage. She also bangs her head on the floor.

At the beginning of each school year she tries to make friends, but by the end of the year she has alienated them all. During her major pity parties she talks of dying, choking herself to death, and running away.

My husband and I love our daughter very much. She is a very talented and beautiful girl. We have tried different medications and therapies over the years, to no avail. She needs help, and we believe she needs the structure and program the Ranch offers.

Enduring Value

Sometimes I am shocked and saddened when I realize how broken and damaged some of the young people are that we help. And frankly, some people don't understand why we put so much energy into so many "lost causes."

I have heard numerous Ranch leaders explain why we do what we do by talking about dollar bills.

If you will look into your wallet or purse, you can probably find a few different bills in different denominations: $1, $5, $10, $20, and so on. And if you look carefully at these bills, you will see that not many of them are in perfect or pristine shape. But that doesn't mean you throw them out, because they still have value.

Even if you took one of those bills out of your wallet or purse and crumpled it up into a tiny ball, dropped it into a mud puddle and stomped on it with all your weight, that bill would still have value once you plucked it up out of the mud, dried it out, and straightened it up.

In essence, that is the key to why we do what we do. The young people who come to the Ranch are not in perfect or pristine shape. Some have been damaged and torn. Others have been hurt so badly that their pain and suffering have disfigured their lives.

But we still believe these young people and their families have inherent value, and because of that value, they deserve all the dignity, respect, caring, and compassion we can offer them. In our eyes, the fact that the young people here have serious problems doesn't decrease their value. They are still precious, and we will do everything we can to help them.

If we are successful, other people will be able to see the same value in them that we do. Even better, these young people will be able to see this value in themselves, which is sometimes the hardest challenge of all.

Frantic Phone Calls

Other parents who are too frantic to write and mail a letter will phone the Ranch, where they reach Director of Admissions Rishay Watson.

When frantic parents or worried social workers call the Ranch, they usually reach Rishay Watson.

"When the phone rings, you never know who will be on the other end of the line, or what they are struggling with," says Rishay. "But the one thing that brings about most of the urgent calls is something I refer to as a 'trip-wire event.'

"In many cases, problems have been developing for years. But when parents finally pick up the phone and call us, it is because something has happened that frightened them. It might be a case of their child engaging in self-abuse or self-harm. Or it might be an assault on parents or siblings in the home. Or it might be a case of a child running away from home.

"Whatever the cause is, when parents call here, they're in chaos. So my first task is to help get through that chaos and see if there's anything we can do to help. And in many cases, these children arrive here in as little as forty-eight hours."

When Rishay isn't on the phone, she and other Ranch intake workers are helping families with the logistics of their travel to Billings.

"We spend a fair amount of time at the airport and seeing that families' needs are being taken care of," she says. "When people are in chaos, they don't think clearly. So some families arrive in Billings without any transportation, or hotel reservations, or even any luggage. We help them get whatever it is they need."

The job of responding to frantic parents' urgent phone calls isn't an easy one, and Rishay never knows what she will be doing from one day to the next. But even though the demands are great, so are the rewards.

"After we begin working with the young people, we get a different kind of phone call from parents. Now instead of calling out of desperation, they are calling out of a sense of gratefulness and thanking us for saving their children's lives.

"And in many cases, the parents are relaxed and relieved for the first time in years. I can recall parents saying that the night after they entrusted their children to the Ranch was the first time in years they'd had a good night's sleep without worrying about what would go wrong. One parent even told me: 'This is the first time in years that we have not been held hostage by the emotional outbursts of our child.'"

The Family Factor

Parents who entrust their children to us believe that doing so will be best for the children. But over time as we work with the children to develop an individualized treatment program of therapy and care, it is our goal to bring parents back into the picture as soon as possible. Individualized treatment includes individual therapy, recreational therapy, musical therapy, pet therapy, chemical dependency treatment, and family therapy.

When the young people, their parents, and their therapists are ready, parents are invited back to the Ranch for an important process we call on-site family therapy. During this process parents participate in a number of therapy sessions involving Ranch counselors and their children. Some of these parents even join our "family" for the week by taking advantage of on-campus housing that we make available to them.

In some cases, parents

The Challenges Ropes Course helps young people and their families learn to trust each other.

and children work together on our Challenges Ropes Course, which requires that they work together to complete a series of exercises and physical tasks. In the process of working on these tasks, parents and children have been able to develop the kinds of trust that may have been lacking in their relationship before.

"Much can be accomplished in a short time as family members are forced to communicate, depend on one another, defer to each other's strengths, and take risks in developing trust," says Anne Helsby, a Ranch therapist who often uses the ropes course during family therapy.

In time, some of the families who were writing us desperate letters or making frantic phone calls are sending us messages of thanks. Here's a letter we received from one mom after we helped make it possible for her son Matt to experience some significant transformations in his life:

> I will keep the staff and children at the Ranch in my prayers. Your staff gave my son hope and gave me continued trust that God really is in control. Eternal impact is made on the children through the counselors, teachers, and staff at YBGR, and I thank you for that. My family has been changed by the communication and cooperation skills you demonstrated for us.

From Helpless to Helping

When a young girl or boy first comes to the Ranch, we assess their needs and prescribe an individualized treatment plan designed to address their unique problems. And, in the vast majority of cases, the treatment we provide allows young people to return to their communities, their families, and their schools without the problems they had when they first came to us.

Everyone who works at the Ranch has his or her own favorite stories about kids who turned a significant corner at the Ranch. Recently I talked to some of our frontline counselors who do the heaviest work with Ranch residents.

Lyle Seavy, vice president of Strategic Planning, remembers a teenager who was involved in a brutal assault that left his victim almost dead. After serving time in jail the young man was sent to the Ranch where a lengthy process of intensive counseling got at the root of his buried resentment and rage.

"They brought him to our residential program, where we pieced this young man back together again," says Lyle. "This was some of the best psychotherapy I've ever seen in my life. This young man is now in college."

Max Soft, director of Residential Services, recalls a young man with significant development problems who was removed from his home and sent to the Ranch. When he first arrived he showed his displeasure by standing on his head in a corner of his room.

"You've heard about people who have two strikes against them," says Max. "But this young man had effectively struck out before he ever got to the plate. We worked with him, and today he lives on his own and works at the local Dairy Queen, which is a big deal for him. He's a meaningful part of society. And he gives me a big smile every time I see him."

Helping kids achieve this kind of progress is accomplishment enough, but there's actually something more we would like to see some of our graduates accomplish. In addition to helping them, we would like to see them become helpers themselves.

One of the young men who graduated from the Ranch had a tough time after he left us. When one of our counselors saw him about a decade later, he was sleeping under a bridge and living on handouts. But something he had learned during his chemical dependency treatment eventually came back to him. He cleaned himself up, enrolled in school, and today he is helping others by serving as a pastor.

But one of our favorite recent success stories is Debbie Champion. A counselor in one of our girls' lodges, Debbie understands the girls here at the Ranch very well because she used to be one of them.

"I came from a background like a lot of these girls," says Debbie, who grew up in an abusive situation featuring unstable living arrangements and divorced parents who used plenty of drugs.

"I needed a place where I could feel safe and secure, which I got here," says Debbie. "This helped ease me into what I needed to do. And I can honestly say I don't think I would be where I am today if it weren't for the help I got at the Ranch."

Debbie Champion (left) has enjoyed moving from being helped at the Ranch to helping.

Looking Forward

The Ranch has made many big changes over the past half century, and there are probably more big changes in our future. Thankfully, we have had wise men and women helping us as employees, executives, and board members.

Wayne Hirsch is a regional president with US Bank who

served on the Ranch's Board of Directors from 1997 to 2005. During that time, Wayne helped guide us through some of the many decisions we made about the kinds of programs and treatment we would offer.

"The Ranch is nothing like the bank business," said Wayne recently. "In the banking business, if a new product or service doesn't succeed you cancel it, and it's no big deal. But when you're in the business of caring for kids there's nothing simple, nothing static. Things are changing all the time."

For example, professional definitions of mental illness change regularly, as do the medical community's understandings of what kinds of treatment would be best to treat various illnesses. "State legislatures and insurance companies are also involved," says Wayne, "meaning that you can never be sure about who will pay for these services."

Such uncertainty would be enough to make most bankers seek a more predictable business than therapy for troubled kids. But Wayne isn't a bottom-line-only kind of guy.

"I have a real soft spot in my heart for young people, especially the young people who may be struggling to make it in our society," he says. "And I believe that as long as there are kids like these, there will be a need for a place like Yellowstone and the kind of caring the Ranch provides. At least I hope there will be."

Ranch board member Wayne Hirsch says that no matter how much things change, the Ranch will be here to help troubled kids.

A Final Glance Back

I hope so, too. And this hope rises in me every time I leave the Ranch and look up at the writing on the back side of our big front gate: IT SURE MAKES A DIFFERENCE WHEN YOU KNOW SOMEBODY CARES.

The motto fits us as well today as it did fifty years ago when we first created it.

As I look back over the past half century I can't help feeling that there has been divine guidance in my life and in the history of the Ranch. Life is made of a series of small steps and decisions that, over time, reveal a direction. Little did I realize when I accepted the call to that little community church almost lost in the expansive wheat fields of north central Montana that it was step one in God's master plan for the rest of my life.

After getting me to Montana, God then used the YFC Rallies to acquaint me with the geography of this vast area...and, finally, He used a tender young "delinquent" named Denver to open my eyes and my heart to the unmet needs of troubled children.

Then He sent me on a lifetime search for people of compassion who would share the dream and help make it happen.

The prophet Jeremiah knew a thing or two about divine plans, and he tried to explain some of his insights to the people of Israel. Speaking for God, Jeremiah told the people: *"I know the plans I have for you, plans to prosper you and not harm you, plans to give you hope and a future."* (Jeremiah 29:11) I want you to know this verse is shared with every child who comes to the Ranch, for we believe each and every one of these young people should be able to experience love and hope!

Looking back now from the perspective of my late-eighties, I can say I have become increasingly aware of the fact that I have been the beneficiary of such divine planning. So has the Ranch. And so have the thousands of boys and girls who have come to us for help over the last five decades.

And I am confident that the story doesn't end here. Rather, it continues on into the future, and will include many more good and wonderful things which are simply too amazing for us to imagine now.

What does the future hold for Yellowstone Boys and Girls Ranch?

We are poised for growth, as are the wheat fields surrounding the Knees community of Montana, where the vision for the Ranch was born more than half a century ago.

APPENDIX 1:

Our Board Members

Yellowstone Boys and Girls Ranch Board Members

Charter Board Members
Forrest Crum
Frank Flynn
Ted Keating
Grace Leuthold
Bill MacKay
W. L. "Les" Shryock
Norm Warsinske

Board Members
(Past & Present)

D. Scott Asay	John Eastman	Pedro Hernandez
Claudia Baker	James P. Eschler	William Hritsco
John Bohlinger	Michael Follett	Wayne Hirsch
John Bradford	Zara Frank	Mark Johnson
Nancy Brown	Gerald Franz	Royal C. Johnson
William T. Carlisle	Kenneth S. Frazier	Gini Jones
Con Christiansen	Gerald M. Gaston	Gale A. Lair
John Cote	Ernest Goppert, Jr.	John Leuthold
Greg Cross	Harry Gottwals	Judy Martz
Austin Darkenwald	Louis Hall	Marilynn Miller

Terrill "Terry" Moore
Tom Nelson
Wayne Nelson
Glenn Nolte
Leo O'Brien
Paul Odegaard
Linda Oge
Howard Porter
Richard Rawlings
Phillip Rostad

Jerry Schutz
Lynette Scott
William Serrette
Dan Singer
Richard Smith
James B. Spring
Ingvaard Svarre
Bob Svoboda
William G. Thomas
Loren Thompson

William Toner
John H. Uihlein
Eva Van Arsdale
Warren Vaughn
Norm Warsinske
John Williams
Langdon Williams
Cal Winslow

Yellowstone Boys and Girls Ranch Foundation Board Members
(Past & Present)

Craig Anderson
Butch Bratsky
Nick Cladis
Greg Dorow
John W. Dowler
Lou Hall
Terry Haven
Lee Jockers
Mark Johnson

Royal C. Johnson
Doug Lair
John Leuthold
Rick Leuthold
Joe Loendorf
Michael G. Matz
Terrill "Terry" Moore
Aidan Myhre
Tom Nelson

Paul Odegaard
Linda Overstreet
Lynn J. Perey
Lee Scherer
W. L. "Les" Shryock
Daniel Singer
Mac Stevens

Pioneer Youth Home (Dillon, MT) Board Members

Patricia Blade
Norman Frankland
Lynn Giles

Sheila Giltrap
William A. Hritsco
Donna Jones

Karl Ohs
Mardell Scott

APPENDIX 2:

Our Longtime Employees

Yellowstone Boys and Girls Ranch and Yellowstone Boys and Girls Ranch Foundation are fortunate to have employees whose commitment to helping kids has spanned a decade or more. The employees listed below (in alphabetical order) have all worked for Yellowstone a minimum of ten years—some of them for more than forty!

Bud Adams was the Ranch plant manager from 1968 to early 1980.

Gary Adams is YBGR's director of farm and ranch operations and Yellowstone Foundation's field representative. He was hired in 1989.

Gertrude Albert worked as a secretary/typist from 1969 to 1980.

Karen Andre is Yellowstone Foundation's bookkeeper and receptionist. Karen started her career in December of 1970 in the direct mail department, gradually assuming responsibility for other direct mail clients. Karen began assisting in the accounting department, and with the coming of the computer age, accepted all bookkeeping duties at the Foundation.

David L. Armstrong retired January of 2006 as youth case manager program supervisor at Community Based Services. He came to Yellowstone in August of 1995 and was a counselor in Shumaker Lodge and clinical case manager.

Robert (Bob) Armstrong came to YBGR as King Lodge unit manager on October 31, 1986. He was promoted to the human resource manager position in February of 1988. He worked in human resources and safety management until leaving July 17, 2002.

Kathryn Bailey has held numerous positions in her 25 years at Yellowstone. She is currently a night counselor at Shumaker Lodge.

Carl Barry Barthuly is a special education teacher and beginning in August of 1981 has been a teacher in almost all class situations at Yellowstone: computers, title math, reach, self-contained, and interim principal.

Jeannie Cantrell has been clerk for School District 58 since 2004. From 1978 to 2004, she was a paraeducator at Yellowstone.

Catherine Collins is a registered nurse. She has worked at Yellowstone since November of 1990.

Dorothy Cooley was a teacher from 1962 to 1976.

Tammy Dennis is an accountant at YBGR. She was first hired August of 1994 as an accounts payable clerk and currently has the position of payroll manager.

John Eastman is vice president of development at Yellowstone Boys and Girls Ranch Foundation. He has been director of social services at YBGR and was YBGR board of directors president. He was employed at the Ranch from 1972 to 1976 and at the Foundation from 1993 to present.

Trisha Eik worked for Yellowstone Boys and Girls Ranch from 1984 through 1996 as a secretary before being promoted to director of admissions.

Irwin J. Eleson is semi-retired, still working half-time at the Ranch in farm maintenance support and doing some fund-raising. He came to YBR in January of 1964 to work in the farm and livestock program. He traveled Montana and Wyoming as Yellowstone's field representative.

Linda Ericson is a retired R.N. who worked in the YBGR clinic and as a group home nurse the last few years of her career. She was at Yellowstone from September of 1990 to June of 2005.

Teresa Fischer has worked at Yellowstone since 1987 as the assistant food service director

Gary and Karen Flohr were houseparents in King Lodge, childcare supervisors and East Campus groundskeepers. After leaving YBGR in 1981, Gary returned as VP of support services, worked in the aftercare department/marketing and is currently director of marketing.

Lisa Frazier is the recreation services supervisor and recreational therapist for the Uihlein Center. Lisa came to YBGR in January of 1982 as an intern in therapeutic recreation. In 1989 she became a certified therapeutic recreation specialist, continuing her employment in the UC.

Polly Frey is currently retired after nearly 30 years at Yellowstone. Polly worked in the mailing and memorial departments and was Franklin Robbie's secretary for many years. She also had an enjoyable time with the bell choir.

Roger Gearhart was personnel director from 1975 to 1985.

Kari and Jan Gibson were program staff and served as houseparents from 1973 to 1983.

Steve Gillett is a therapist at Lewistown, Montana's Community Home. Previously he was a therapist at King Lodge and from 1991 to 2001 enjoyed great camping trips and outdoor activities on and around the campus.

Mark Goodell joined YBGR in June of 1984. He started at Leuthold (on-line counselor) after which he moved to Fortin (on-line counselor/school tech) and then to McVay as a unit leader.

Duane Grams worked at the Ranch 1975-1990. He was a childcare worker and worked in the Uihlein Center as a recreation specialist.

James A. Gran has been a mechanic at Yellowstone Boys & Girls Ranch since April of 1987.

Jeff R. Gray came to Yellowstone Boys Ranch in 1976 as a recreation specialist for 13 years, then became the PE/health teacher and is presently employed at Yellowstone Academy as a special education teacher.

David Groot joined Yellowstone in 1990. He started as the primary therapist in Fortin West and became a therapist in the psychiatric intensive care unit. In 1993 he was a clinical supervisor for one-half of the campus. In 1997 David was the first director of community programs, becoming vice president of community programs in 2000. Since then he has supervised the development of therapeutic family care (in-home services), youth and family support, and the LIFE program.

Jodi Groot started working for YBGR in 1990. She was hired as a primary therapist in the Paul Stock intensive care unit. While teaching nursing at Montana State University, she supervised the placement of student nurses at the Ranch. She served as an on-call therapist from 1994-2000. In 2000 she joined the Ranch full-time as a psychiatric clinical nurse specialist and completed her Ph.D. in psychiatric nursing in 2004.

Joyce Grubaugh was Yellowstone Boys and Girls Ranch's cook from October 1989 to October of 1999.

David Halcomb currently directs the chemical dependency program at YBGR. Previously he served as an on-line counselor in the Mary Brekkeflat unit, assistant unit manger in Fortin West and unit manager of Leuthold and Fortin East and West Lodges. David has worked at YBGR since January of 1992.

Mike Hammer is currently a lead counselor at McVay lodge. He and his wife, Denise Stumbo Hammer, came to Yellowstone in 1979 to be teaching parents at Paul Stock lodge. Mike expanded the bike program to include the six-day 360-mile Yellowstone Park trip while he was a recreation specialist.

Dan and Sharon Hansen worked from 1969 to 1984 as houseparents. Dan served as program director, chaplain, and superintendent. Sharon worked in the clothing room and helped Dan with the Chapel.

Rick Harbin was a child care worker from 1977 to 1990.

Doug and Ann Hartley worked at the Ranch from 1969 to 1983. They served as houseparents, worked in the clothing room and Doug became the Ranch groundskeeper.

Ron Hatcher was a houseparent from 1961-1964, a P.E. teacher and then director of education from 1990 to 2003. He was also director of aftercare from 1993 to 1997.

Lourie Helmer, LCPC currently is program therapist in Bozeman, Montana, with YBGR CBS/SBS. Beginning in March of 1994 Lourie has been a counselor at Jesse Grant and Shumaker, education tech at Yellowstone Academy, and therapist in McVay Lodge.

Beverly Henman is Yellowstone's baker. Since 1989 she has also been cook's helper and dining hall supervisor.

Gladys Henry retired as Yellowstone Foundation's direct mail supervisor in July of 2001 after 40 years! In addition to supervising other employees and boys from the Ranch who helped get the mail out, she consulted with other youth organizations, helping them set up their direct mail departments. She remembers being the donut girl for many years too.

Ann Henson is a Title 1 reading teacher. She has been a self-contained classroom teacher from August 1987 to present.

Gary Hickle, CPA is Yellowstone Foundation's vice president of finance. He was employed in October of 1986 as director of accounting.

Kathryn Robbie Hickle has done part-time clerical work at the Foundation from her early childhood through college. Through the 90s she worked during the Christmas seasons. Kathy became director of communications in August of 2001.

Linda J. Hinkle retired in 1993. She helped compile the beginning donor files from 1958-1959 and came back to administer the memorial department and serve as secretary for the livestock program at Yellowstone in 1963.

Pearl L. Hoines-Stoner is a counselor CIV. Since 1990, Pearl has worked nights at King and Dorothy's Lodge (little boys lodge) and filled in for other lodges.

Dorothy Hollatz came to Yellowstone in 1959 and worked faithfully for 40 and a half years! Starting in the mailing department, she helped recruit thousands of donor friends, managed the memorial department for several years and eventually moved to the planned giving department where she was assistant to the VP of development for the last 28 years of her career. At her death on May 14, 2004, she surprised us by leaving Yellowstone a significant bequest through her estate.

Jeanine Holt-Seavy, as director of human resources, is responsible for personnel administration and employee relations' activities. Jeanine began her career in 1981 as a residential treatment counselor, unit manager and director of human resources. After going to an agency in Minnesota as their HR director, she returned to YBGR in March of 2000.

Betty Orth Honaker supported her husband, Carl Orth, was housemother and encourager, cooked, canned, and ironed hundreds of shirts and pants. Upon Carl's death she worked in the town office. Betty was employed at Yellowstone from August 1957 through June 1974.

Phil House, Psy.D. directs the psychology department and provides psychological services for YBGR as a clinical psychologist and Yellowstone Academy as a school psychologist. He began working at YBGR in 1977 in what was known as the Youth Assessment Center and then he became the YBGR clinical director. After three years at YBGR, he moved to other settings of service outside of YBGR before returning in 1993.

Ken Jackson worked at the Ranch from 1972 to 1989. He worked with the wilderness program, was an alternate houseparent, caseworker, director of admissions, and therapist.

Carolyn Jamison has been at Yellowstone since 1971. Currently she is a pastoral counselor. She has also held the positions of teacher, school counselor and vocational counselor at YBGR.

John Jamison is currently the chaplain and director of pastoral care services. Prior to accepting that position in 1989, he was actively involved in many aspects of youth care at the Ranch including wilderness camping, work crews, athletics, and direct care. John was first employed in 1969. In 1972 he married his co-worker, Carolyn, and they help encourage the youth and staff in their spiritual growth and development.

Mark Jaskot is the unit leader at Leuthold Lodge. He first came to Yellowstone as a counselor at Paul Stock West in 1985.

Chuck Jorgenson started at the Ranch in 1985 as a carpenter. He then served as assistant director of plant operations and currently is Yellowstone's director of plant operations.

Robert Kuhr currently holds the title of director of training and development. Other positions he has held are counselor, shift supervisor, clinical consultant for crisis intervention, experiential coordinator, and trainer. Employed at the Ranch 1982-1985 and 1989-present.

Robyn Kuhr is Yellowstone's director of therapeutic services. Beginning in 1985, Robyn was a counselor at Leuthold Lodge, unit leader of King Lodge, primary therapist in Brekkeflat and director of intensive programs.

Carrol V. Lipp was employed at YBGR from August 1973 through February of 1994. He worked in the farm, livestock and maintenance departments.

Isabel Lundin directs the marketing and professional relations department at Yellowstone Boys and Girls Ranch. Isabel came to YBGR in 1992, first as director of marketing, then VP of corporate development and now VP of professional relations.

Taylor Mayer came to Yellowstone December 6, 1993. He has held the positions of on-line counselor, primary therapist, and psychological assistant. He currently works in psychological assessment and consultation.

Glenn McFarlane currently is the Ranch's chief financial officer. He came to Yellowstone in 1990 as director of marketing and has also held the position of finance director.

Tom McKinney, the Ranch's controller, is a certified public accountant and a Fellow of the Healthcare Financial Management Association. He is a member of the Montana Society of CPA's and a past chairman of the Not-for-Profit committee.

Roberta Michel was hired in 1995. She started as a counselor and later was program manager in Dennis Wear Community Home. She became unit leader at Kramlich Lodge and currently is unit leader in Jessie Grant Lodge.

Greg Miller is a primary therapist at YBGR. Starting in 1979, he held positions of head teaching parent in Fortin East Lodge, program director, program director specialist (quality assurance and utilization review), and lead clinical staff at Transition Group Home.

Lynn O. Oldenburg was employed at Yellowstone 1982-1985 and 1987-1998 as a therapist, case manager, and did psychological testing.

Dale Orth currently is vice president of administrative services. He was first employed at Yellowstone in March of 1977.

Linda Patenaude began as a relief on-line counselor in 1992. She received her master's degree in social work in 1998 and has been a therapist for the past seven years.

Joan Patton was employed by the Ranch in August of 1991 as executive secretary and office manager. She is now administrative assistant for human resources.

Gary Pearson came to Yellowstone in October of 1991 as a counselor. He is currently night supervisor.

Deb Perrigo is a licensed addiction counselor. Previously she was on-line staff case manager at Community Based Services. She has worked at Yellowstone since 1993.

Jo Ann Rea was employed in 1989 as a staff nurse in the clinic where she became a registered nurse clinician in psychiatric nursing. In 1998 she became intake coordinator until she retired in 2001.

Helen Remington has been employed at Yellowstone Boys and Girls Ranch since September of 1977. She was the dining hall supervisor and currently is director of food services.

Wes Robbie's history with Yellowstone dates back to the very beginning. He rode in the car with his dad, Franklin, as he was looking for the property on which to put Yellowstone Boys Ranch. In high school he worked as janitor at the business office, worked a couple of summers at the Ranch and then became assistant to the executive director after college graduation. He then became vice president of administration of the YBGR Foundation and served for twelve years as Foundation president.

Ken and Kris Rose worked at the Ranch from 1970 to 1984. Ken served as physical education director. Kris worked in both the school and the administration building.

Marge Rufus began part-time in Christmas of 1964 preparing and taking bank deposits. Shortly after, she worked full time in bookkeeping, and retired December 31, 1986,

Les and Penny Scammon started as houseparents in Fortin West beginning in 1970 and then moved to the Maryott unit as houseparents and Ranch manager from 1972 to 1976. After a fourteen-year absence, Les returned to Yellowstone and managed the farm program from 1990 to 1995.

Randy L. Scammon was employed at Yellowstone from 1993 through 2005. Positions he held were teaching assistant at Yellowstone Academy, relief counselor in lodges, counselor at King Group Home and assistant program manager at King Community Home.

Jim Scheetz has worked at the Ranch in maintenance as a carpenter since April of 1992.

David Schwarm is director of continuous quality improvement & HIPAA compliance officer. David started at what was then YTC in 1992 as a staff nurse. He later assumed the quality assessment and accreditation responsibilities for the Ranch. During his tenure he has also held positions of clinic manager and director of medical records.

Tom Schwartz worked for Yellowstone Boys and Girls Ranch from October 1986 through November of 1998 as emergency night supervisor, direct care staff.

Lyle Seavy is vice president of strategic planning at YBGR. He was a night counselor, counselor, unit manager and night emergency coordinator 1982-1985; associate director, then director of residential services; clinical supervisor and VP of residential services 1994-2006.

Don Shay served as farm manager from 1967 to 1986.

Lois Shorten worked in the clothing room and helped with housekeeping from 1961-1977.

Alberta Smith worked in the clothing room from 1965 to 1978. She then moved to the kitchen where she was responsible for all the baking until 1989.

Marge Smith was employed at Yellowstone from 1969 through 1980. She initially worked in the laundry then moved to the administration building where she became office manager.

Mark and Myra Smith worked at the Ranch from 1971 to 1981. They were alternate houseparents, worked in the office, served on program staff, and supervised the arts and crafts program.

Ron Snelling served as an alternate houseparent, worked in the fire department and in program staff from 1973 to1986.

James Snyder is Yellowstone Academy's principal. He first came to Yellowstone as a special education teacher in December of 1995.

James C. Soft came to Yellowstone Boys and Girls Ranch in July of 1972 first as a development officer, then director of development, and executive vice president before becoming the Foundation's president.

Janice Soft retired from YBGR in 2004. During her years at Yellowstone she was a clerk at Yellowstone Academy, town runner, relief houseparent, and chapel organist from 1970 to 1971.

Loren Soft retired as YBGR's CEO in 2004. Loren's career at Yellowstone began in 1963 as a summer employee. Through the years he was a relief houseparent, teacher and school principal, and Ranch superintendent and executive director. Currently he is a consultant with Yellowstone Resource Center.

Ry Sorensen's career at Yellowstone began in 1980, when he and his wife, Kathi, became houseparents in King Lodge. In 1981 Ry became director of social services, serving YBGR until 1987. In 1991, he and Kathi returned to YBGR, he as director of operations and she in the business department. Kathi left YBGR in 1994. Ry was selected to replace Loren Soft as CEO in 2004. He served in the CEO position until 2006, when he resigned and left YBGR as the result of injuries received in combat with the U.S. Navy in Vietnam.

George Staley supervised the maintenance department from 1970 until 1986.

Carla Stadtmiller is Yellowstone Foundation's executive secretary. She administers the memorial program and is assistant to the VP of development. Carla came to Yellowstone in 1991 at first working in the direct mail department.

Richard Streeter currently is director of intensive residential programs and school board chair for School District #58. After coming to YBGR in October of 1992, he has held the positions of night counselor, counselor, assistant unit manager, unit leader, and intensive treatment coordinator.

Frieda Sukut was Yellowstone Boys and Girls Ranch's cook from 1991 to 2001.

Peggy Swalley is program manager, King Community Group Home. She has held this position since coming to Yellowstone, March 9, 1987. Peggy and her husband, Kevin, were live-in managers at King for seven years. King is now staffed 24 hours with no live-ins.

Karen Tetrault started December 23, 1991, as the town runner, worked in intake and then became Yellowstone's receptionist, the position she currently holds.

Brice Turk was employed at Yellowstone from August of 1986 through November of 1997. During that time he was a counselor and then unit manager for Paul Stock East, and Fortin East and West.

Diane Unruh was Yellowstone Boys and Girls Ranch's clinical receptionist from April 1992 through September of 2002.

Loren Van Roekel has been a youth case worker since 2000. He and his wife started as houseparents at McVay in 1980. He has also been assessment unit staff, community homes program director, and unit manager of Level VI program.

Sally Venard is director of YBGR community homes. She has held positions of counselor, assistant unit leader, program manager, and lead program manager since July of 1988.

Sandy Venneman began working for Yellowstone in the memorial department as temporary Christmas help in October of 1978. She retired in December of 2005 as direct mail supervisor.

Kimberly "Kim" Wagner came to YBGR in July of 1990 and worked in the McVay Lodge classroom as a teaching assistant. On Fridays she was a counselor in Mary B Lodge and also was a relief counselor for 11 years.

Teresa Wagner is currently a youth case manager. She began working at Yellowstone as a lodge counselor in August of 1991. Since that time she has also been a clinical case manager and worked in intake/admissions.

Terri (Cleary) Walters was employed at Yellowstone from 1985 through 1997 first as a clinical assistant and then as unit manager at Mary "B" Lodge (sexuality treatment center).

Larry and Doris Ward were responsible for food service including butchering and canning 1961-1984. Larry taught hunter safety for many years and took boys on hunting trips.

Renee Warner was hired in 1978 to work one-on-one with a little six-year-old boy. After taking time out for a church mission, she returned to Leuthold, transferred to Shumaker and then worked in the sexual offenders unit. She has worked as a counselor with boys and girls for 28 years, currently in McVay Lodge.

Rishay Watson is director of admissions. Beginning in 1993, she has been a counselor in Shumaker and Fortin, case manager and intake and referral supervisor.

Frieda S. Wells retired December 31, 1986 from the Foundation. From the fall of 1961 she had been the bookkeeper and also was part time office staff for several years.

Anna Wessell began working for YBGR in 1988 as a night counselor for Jessie Grant Lodge. She later worked as an evening counselor in both Jessie Grant and Shumaker Lodges until 1998 when she moved into her current position as plant operations assistant in the maintenance department.

Margaret (Maggie) Whitley first came to YBGR in October of 1990 as a counselor in McVay Lodge and worked full-time at Dennis Wear Group

Home. After her children were born, she worked relief in many different locations. Her current position is relief counselor.

Jerry Williams is a professional relations representative in Yellowstone's Marketing department. Originally hired in February of 1989, he has been a counselor, assistant unit manager, unit manager, and director of residential programs at YBGR.

Jodi Willis began as a childcare counselor in 1991, was a unit manager in Shumaker Lodge and is now plant operations assistant.

Steve Willis is currently a counselor at King Lodge. He came to Yellowstone in 1991 and began working in the little boys unit, at that time, King Lodge. He was also a relief counselor before taking his current position.

Wendell Wilson, assisted by his wife Anne, served as chaplain from 1970 to 1980.

Linda (Byerly Walton) York was employed at Yellowstone from November 1972 through August 1991. She was a cook, alternate houseparent, office worker, secretary to the CEO and office manager. "These years at the Ranch were the best of my life!" she said.

Grant Young started work as a clinical assistant trainee at Fortin East in 1987 and is now a lead night counselor. He has also worked at Brekkeflat and King Community Home.

APPENDIX 3:

Our Supporters

Yellowstone Boys and Girls Ranch Foundation Visionaries

Yellowstone's Visionary Members through precise financial and estate planning help assure there will always be resources at the Foundation for the benefit of needy children. With gratitude, we recognize these donors who through their charitable planned gifts are building a secure future for Yellowstone's boys and girls.

(As of May 2006)

Benefactors

Mincy W. Blankenship
Sigurd Brekkeflat
Alvy Casper
Henry & Mae DeHaan
Clarence Gebhardt
Ernest J. Goppert, Sr.
Charles F. Grow
Hazel S. Guider
Berl & Kay Hamilton
Willard Harris
Jeanette Heptner

Leona Heptner
Willa Huckins
Jean B. Jacobs
Otho & Margaret Jager
Matt & Mabel Koskela
Art & Alvina Kramlich
Clyde & Jeanine Pederson
Paul Stock
Miles White
Paul & Donitza Williams
S/W Trust

Leaders

Kenneth C. Carpenter
George & Marie Christie
John & Lucy Cochrane
Jack & Evelyn Davidson
Ray & Thena Dewey
James & Virginia Ewing
Bill & Anita Jones
Benora LaMar
Reginald & Margaret Langdon
Mary Jane Martin
Winifred Packer
Tim & Anita Petterson
Herbert Poetzl
Sidney Price
George & Florence Scales
Payton J. Shumaker
Frankie Stinchfield
Edith Tash
The Vanderhoofs
Dorothy Zettel

Builders

Richard & Karen Albrecht
Ray & Arlene Anderson
Robert M. Anderson
Charlie & Bunny Aumell
Donna Bausch
Embree S. Bird
Erna Blehm
Billie Jean Bloxham
John & Bette Bohlinger
Paul & Martha Boss
Merlin & Myrtle Bouchard
Ruth Bowen
Dorothy Bracken
Henry & Betty Bratsky
Gwendolyn Brem
Elmer Britten
Steve & Kelly Bruggeman
Karl & Lilyan Bryan
Harry & Opal Buchanan
James & Eleanor Burton
Mary Jo Carlson
Tom & Eleanor Conway
William R. Covert
Charles & Margaret Creon
Ralph Crisman
Charles Crow
Everett & Wanda Crumley
William L. Davey
Stanley R. Davison
William H. Dawe
Harry & Bea Dawson
Mila Divers
Earl & Fay Doney
Virginia Dunn
Hart & Jean Eastman
Rosemary Ebert
Wayne & Marcia Edsall
Betty Fjeld
Alvinia W. Fossum
Jack & Irene Framke
Percy & Adrienne Frazier
Esther Frost
Lester Gladowski
Robert Gotz
Jessie Grant
Charles & Elizabeth Green
Helene Gumina
Elizabeth Hawley

Floretta Hickle
Fred Hoff
Jean Hofferber
Dale & Jane Hoffman
Dorothy Hollatz
Byron C. Holliday
Ernest Hruska
Donald & Ella Huston
Bill Jamieson
Garnet & Jeannine Keefer
Dean & Betty Keil
Frank & Louise Klingle
Mert & Patty Klitzke
Verene Kvigne
Arthur C. Lammerding
Ethel Land
Axel Larsen
Peter & Donna Larson
Joe & Betty Lee
Bob & Elsa Lenhardt
Ed & Muriel Lenhardt
Dorothy Marie Lewis
George D. Lewis
Robert Little
Mathilda Maier
William Maier
Otto & Yvonne Mansfield
Morna A. Marshall
Henry May
Mary R. McCormick
Shirley McCune
Sylvia Mick
Emily Mollander

Freda B. Naff
Monte & Susan Naff
Jerry & Karol Newgard
Peter & Mildred Olegar
Martin H. Oleson
June Pierce
Hubert A. Plymale
Thelma Price
Ben & Ferne Redant
Lee Revear
Ardel & Ila Ronning
Peter & Jennie Schaper
Louie & Greta Seibel
Opal R. Shoemaker
Les & Barbara Shryock
Victor & Jeanette Simpson
Helen Sloan
Verna L. Smith
Magnus Swanson
Ann Taylor
Mary J. Thieme
Virginia Thompson
Lena Thorpe
Bill & Donna Todd
John Holt Uihlein
Sam Waldenberg
Margaret Wallace
Shirleen Weese
Viola Wetterstrom
Georgia Whipps
Harry & Rose Witt
Ray & Betty Woodward
Robert & Winona Wynia

Friends

Hazel Alden
Marian Bernet
Phillip Bond
Bill & Virginia Boone
Reanette Cook
Kathleen P. Cosgriff
Henry & B.J. Dahl
Eunice Dowd
Elaine R. Edelberg
George E. Emmons
R. E. Fisher
Emma Gentry
Alice R. Harbaugh
Edward & Frances Hargis
Arthur Hoefer
Edith C. Hughes
James Hurst
Ronald C. Jacobs
Lee & Nancy Jockers
James D. King
Margaret Krshka
Edward & Mildred Larsen
Donald L. Leonhardt
James R. Linton
Charley Nell Llewellyn

N. Louise Marshall
Hazel McCurdy
Elaine Mehlhose
C. Patrick Minette
John & Mazie Nicholson
Imogene Olson
Lester & Fern Olson
E. O. Overland
Ronald N. Paul
Alma S. Petersen
Elaine Peterson
Bernice Robinson
Verna I. Rudman
Cordelia Sauerbier
David Schlinker
Loretta C. Schultz
John Shaw
Earl D. Shelton
George & Louise Snell
Robert & Laura Steele
Ray & Mabel Stoner
Merlyn Taborsky
Arva Dorothy Taylor
Elmer Tweeten
Frances Zipperian

A BENEFACTOR is an individual or husband and wife who have made over one million dollars in irrevocable gifts through their estate plan.
A LEADER is an individual or husband and wife who have made over five hundred thousand dollars in irrevocable gifts through their estate plan.
A BUILDER is an individual or husband and wife who have made over one hundred thousand dollars in irrevocable gifts through their estate plan.
A FRIEND is an individual or husband and wife who have made over fifty thousand dollars in irrevocable gifts through their estate plan.

Yellowstone Boys and Girls Ranch Family Tree

A child, like a leaf on a tree, needs nurturing. Alone, it will wither and fade. Yellowstone Boys and Girls Ranch has nurtured hundreds of neglected, abused and troubled children since 1957. Yellowstone's Family Tree was created in 1990 to honor our family of friends who have given cash or livestock gifts for Yellowstone's boys and girls. It is our privilege to name them here.

Boulders

Charlie & Bunny Aumell
Charles M. Bair Family Trust
Fred Bowen
Burlington Resources Foundation
Paul & Patty Carlson
Ralph Crisman
Everett Crumley
Faith Chapel
Lewis P. Gallagher Family Foundation
Bonnie R. & Leonard A. Hamilton
Fay K. Harwood
Leona S. & Jeanette L. Heptner
Eva (Mickey) M. Adams Hoff
The Hoffmans - Dale, Jane, Rusty, Annie
Gertrude Kamps Foundation
Gilbert V. Kelling, Jr.
J. W. Kieckhefer Foundation
Mrs. Ethel Land
Lair Family
Leonhardt Foundation
Lauren P. Miller
Margaret T. Morris Foundation
M. J. Murdock Trust
Brad & Elizabeth Nassif Family
Danny Oliver
Homer & Mildred Scott Foundation
Tom & Joan Scott
Frank J. Schultz
Steele-Reese Foundation
Shirley M. Steinlicht
Walt Story
Maude Strand
Esther Tax
Ruth & Vernon Taylor Foundation
Dennis & Phyllis Washington Foundation
Langdon & Joyce Williams

Acorns

Bill & Michele Abney
Billings Breakfast Exchange Club
The Billings Gazette
Mr. & Mrs. Everett Breigenzer
Greg Bucell
Harry & Opal Buchanan
Paul & Pattie Coolidge
Corporate Air
Frances Erickson
Gordon Galarneau
Helen Doornbos Hull
Grace Jones Richardson Trust
John Leuthold - Grace Leuthold
Laila Lindberg
Mr. & Mrs. Steve Lindholm
George & Hertha Lund
MDU Resources Foundation
Joe F. & Roberta Napier Foundation
Family of Gilman Ordway
Frank J. Schultz
Opal Shoemaker
Richard & Sharongae Smith
Art Story
Dean & Connie Studer
Esther M. Stufft
Clara Svarre
Ruth & Vernon Taylor
US Bank
Blanche Vavra
The Webers
Wells Fargo Private Client Services
Jerome & Chris Young

Leaves

Bill & Michele Abney
Leonard & Pauline Ackerman
Irma Adams
Stephanie M. Alexander
American Fork Ranch
American Foundation
C. Perry & Anne Anderson
Mr. & Mrs. Craig Anderson
Mr. & Mrs. Gene Anderson
Marcia & Buck Anderson
Geo. M. & Dott I. Armstrong
Artcraft Printers
Hugo Asbeck
Charlie & Bunny Aumell (In Memory of Veva Rainey)
David Baird
Dr. Gertrude Baker
Bar Double T Ranch
BARSI LLC
John Baldwin
Robert Ballou
Thomas J. Ballou
Gary Baltrusch
James Bama
Mr. & Mrs. Bill Barber
Frank & Bettie Barber
Joe & Maggie Barrett
William Barrett
William H. Bell
Edwin & Joanne Beery
Russell Berg
Andy & Janelle Bergum
Billings Breakfast Exchange Club
The Billings Gazette
Embree Bird
Dan Blackford Family

A Legacy of Caring

Erna Blehm
John & Bette Bohlinger
Bonner Foundation
Gordon Borcherding
Beatrice Borkowski
Paul & Martha Boss
Bud & Carol Boyce
Dorothy Bracken
Wallace & Marilyn Bradley
Mr. & Mrs. Everett Breigenzer
Stuart & Patricia Bray
John & Neva Brill
Brock Livestock
Mr. & Mrs. Robert Brotherton
Mr. & Mrs. Bill Brown, Jr.
Dennis & Evonne Brown
George C. Brungard
Greg Bucell
Ruhlon & Pat Buhler
Christian Bunning
Burlington Northern Santa Fe Foundation
Burlington Resources
John & Jennette Burnett
Burtell Family
James & Eleanor Burton
Cassie Cady
Jacob Caffyn
Jacob & Clara Caffyn
Jacob W. Caffyn by Clara L. Caffyn
Doug & Shelley Cahill
Eleonore T. Campbell
Robert Candee
Mr. & Mrs. Vincent Carey
Mary Carrier
Glenda Rose Carroll
Castle Mountain Ranch
Pearl L. Cawlfield
Checkerboard Cattle Co.
John B. Chamberlin

Vern & Cherilyn Cheff
Cherry Creek Ranch, Inc.
Phillip J. Chevallier
Ken & Elaine Chilcote
Richard & Judy Childress
Flossie & Fred Chisholm
Janet Christensen
Alton Christiansen
Circle S of Montana
John & Myrna Clawson
Noreen Clayton
C/M Ranch
John C. & Lucy M. Cochrane
Thomas & Flora Coghlan
Rod Cole
Tom & Marquieta Colgan
The John D. Conners Family
Dorothy Conrady
Paul & Pattie Coolidge
Jack Cooper
Corporate Air
William & Barbara Cowan
Dr. & Mrs. Paul Crellin
Charles & Margaret Creon
Robert K. Crial
Greg & Corrine Cross
Charles T. Crow
Everett Crumley
Mr. & Mrs. Henry J. Dahl
Dahl Corporation
T. J. (Tom) Daly
Charles P. Damon
Evelyn & John Davidson
Jack Davies
Mark Davies
Alice K. Davis
Deluxe Check Printers Foundation
Ethel J. Dennis
Ray & Thena Dewey
Vera Dexter

Mark Diehl
Richard & Julie Diehl
Philip & Holly Difani
Howard & Joanna Dixon
Jock & Jamie Doggett
DON
Bill & Dorothy Donald
Mary E. Donahue
Francis Donegon
Earl T. Doney
Richard & Phyllis Donn
John Dooling
Daniel E. Doty
David & Wendy Douglas
John & Suzanne Dowler
Robert & Helen Driscoll
DuFresne Foundation
Virginia T. Dunn
Ann Dupont
Kendall & Linda Dupuis
Tim & Eva Dwyer
Tim Sr. & Marjorie Dwyer
John F. Eastman
John & Patricia Eastman
Rod & Sandi Eaton
Mr. & Mrs. Robert Ebeling
Elaine R. Edelberg
Roy & Margaret Eissinger
Bernice Ellinghouse
Chet & Geri Ellingson
Kathryn M. Elliot
Robert & Esther Elliott
Donald Elmer
Everett Elmer
Harold H. Emch, Jr.
Cecil Emery
Lillian Engle
Gustave Erickson
J. R. Erickson
Kermit "Bud" Erickson

Steve & Jane Erickson
Michael J. Erwin
Jon H. & Terri M. Evers
Mr. & Mrs. James B. Ewing
Lawrence & Leatrice Faber
Corey & Christy Falink
Jay & Tamie Faw
Marvin Feddes
Faith Chapel
Greg & Dawn Field & Family
Mildred Fieldgrove
Eric & Karen Finstad
First Bank-First Trust Montana
Vain & Harry Fish Foundation
Betty Fjeld
Oren Forthun
Dorothy Fraker
Irene & Otto Framke
Mr. & Mrs. James M. Frankard
Percy & Adrienne Frazier
Hugh Freisman
Roger Allen Fried
Evelene Fulton
Danny Gali
William & Jill Galt
Gene & Fernande Garber
Mr. & Mrs. Gilbert Gardipee
Charles Gaugler
Glenn Gay
Clarence Gebhardt
Marlin D. Geier
Emma L. Genty
Pat & Bev Gibbs
Mary Giesler
Ted Giesler
Gilbert Ranch
Gilman IH Cattle Co.
David O. Gilmore
Gordon & Montana Gipe
The Glennie Ranches

Gary R. Gliko
William S. Goan
Mitch & Wendy Goeddel
Patricia Goedken
Robert F. Goltz
John B. Goodrich
Mary Gordon
William & Mildred Gosden
Mary & Harry Gottwals
Pat Grady
Bob & Helori Graff
Mr. & Mrs. Gary Graveley
David & DeAnna Graves
Robert & Betty Gray
Bennie W. Green
Charles & Beth Green
Kelly & Pat Greenlee
Greenline Dairy, Inc.
Art Greydanus
Richard E. Griffith
Kennth M. Groff
Lorents & Sydney Grosfield
Fred O. & Hazel S. Guider
Don & Maxine Haefer
Hagenbarth Livestock
Paul & Bette Hagenstein
Haglund Ranch, Inc.
Orville & Lois Hakalo
C. Lawrence Haines
Dean W. Hall
Bonnie R. & Leonard A. Hamilton
Helen Hancock
James & Joyce Hannah
Paul Hansen
Mr. & Mrs. Ross Hansen
Ella Quamme Hanson
Vic & Verlie Hanson
Gerald & Alice R. Harbaugh
In Memory: Edward L. Hargis MD
Dr. Grant & Deanna Harrer

Harvest States Coop
Fay K. Harwood
Dave & Janet Hauptman
Terry & Penny Haven
Martha Healy
Jesse, Archie & Jim Henderson
Caroline Pinckney Hennesy
Mr. & Mrs. Donald B. Hepperle
John & Dixie Hertel
Karl & Marion Hertel
Conrad Hess
Mr. & Mrs. Joseph J. Hess
Paul Hesselbacher
Vergil & Lynne Heyer
John Heyneman
Roger & Joyce Hibbs
Flo Hickle
Gary & Kathy Hickle
Sara S. Hinckley
John & Mari Hinman
Dick & Margy Hirschy
Rodney & Carolina Hofeldt
Jean & Reuben Hofferber
The Hoffmans -
    Dale, Jane, Rusty, Annie
Hoiness LaBar Insurance
Les & Ethel Holden
Byron & Opal Holliday
Wally & Carla Holter
Gene & Shirley Homer
Tom Honey
Donna & Duane Horn
Tom & Helen Hougen
John & Barbara Howell
Bill & Dale Hritsco
Charles & Willa Huckins
Harley Hughes
Sena Joslin & Lydia Hundtoft
William & Elizabeth Hupp
James Hurst, Jr.

Rob & Carolyn Hunter
Mr. & Mrs. S. Wesley Hyatt
International Association of Turtles
Thomas & Kathy Irigoin
David J. Iversen
Arnold Iverson
    by Mrs. Lillian Iverson
Mike Iverson
Richard & Connie Iverson
Daisy Bragg Jacobs
Maurice & Jean Burnett Jacobs
Margaret Jager
William H. Jamieson
Janke, Winchell, Ehrlick & Co.
Ronald & Jean Jarrell
Earl & Betty Jensen
Henry E. Jensen
J.C. Jensen, Inc.
Lee & Nancy Jockers
Donald E. Johnson
Sharon Johnson
Victor Johnson
Wally & Jo Johnson
John & Evelyn Johnston
Johnnie & Beverly Johnston
Lucille Johnston
Bill & Anita Jones
Leroy & Kay Jones
Sena Joslin & Lydia Hundtoft
Gertrude Kamps
Karen Kane
George & Kathleen Kahrl
Clifford & Ann Kauffman
Nancy Kaufman
Rev. & Mrs. George Keniston
KG Ranch
Dean Keil
Bruce & Leslie Kesler
Esther Kiamas
Fred & Mary Kindle

Joseph & Elizabeth Kinsella
ElRoy & Ruth Kittleson
Frank & Louise Klingle
Meredith & Patty Klitzke
William Collins Kohler
Matthias & Mabel Koskela
John & Renee Kowalski
Arthur & Alvina Kramlich
Lair Family
Robert D. Lane
Mr. & Mrs. Leo Lapito
Edward & Mildred Larsen
Kleis Larsen
Elmer & Esther Larson
Janice Larson
L. Peter & Donna Larson
Cecelia Carter Lasich
John & Theresa LaVallee
Lawrence Volvo
Leckie Family
Lee Foundation
Andy & Lucille Lee
Leonard & Joanne Leland
Jack & Donna Lenoir
Donald L. Leonhardt
Louise P. Leuthold
Dorothy Marie Lewis
Dorothy Marie Lewis,
    in honor of John Slack
Edward Lewis
Mr. & Mrs. Mike Lewis
Laila Lindberg
Frances Liebig
George Lien
Art & Ethel Lindseth
Ray & Lorna Lindseth
Erna Linton
Gramma (Mary) Lipp
Andre' O. Lippens
Carolyn Lippincott

Bob Little
Bradley & Diane Livingston
William M. Llewellyn
Joel & Andrea Long
Ron & Pat Long
   In Memory of Burton Long
John, Dick & Anne Lower
Irvin Lozier Box R Ranch
Charles M. Lucas
Albert Luce, Jr.
Raymond Luther
Mr. & Mrs. Kip Lybeck
Mabel L. MacDonald
Donald Malmin
Johnny & Roberta Mandros
Sherrie A. Mansfield
Chas & Jody Manuel
Mr. & Mrs. Steve Marks
Morna Marshall
Marilyn Martin
Paul L. Mason
Jennie L. Maston
Leonard & Dolores Matteson
Mike & Joan Matz
Ted Mausshardt
Taylor Mayer
Dorothy G. McCann
McDaniel Family Foundation
Mike & Vicki McGinley
Mr. & Mrs. Joseph McKinley
Marjory A. McKinley
Peggy McLeod
Fred McMurry
Patrick McNulty
Douglas & Kim McRae
Mr. & Mrs. Willard M.
   Mecklenburg
Jack & Elaine Mehlhose
Peter Meike
W. Norman & Ella Menser

Tom & Mary Mercer
Meridian Oil
Sylvia Mick
Bill & Jean Mikkelson
Isabelle A. Miller
Henry & Malea Miller
Lauren P. Miller
Elizabeth Mills
James Moline
Kip Monroe
Mr. & Mrs. Vernon Monroe
Montana Community Foundation
Montana Dakota Utilities Co.
The Montana Power Foundation
Shirley M. Moore
Terry & Tena Moore
Audrey J. Moravec
Frank J. Moravec
Elta M. Moreland
Joe & Brenda Morstein
Gregg, Margaret & Graham Mosley
Hanna Moyer
Aidan Myhre - NEXT LTD
M. W. Myhre
Rebecca Nadler - Curt A. Nadler
Monte & Susan Naff
Joe F. & Roberta Napier
   Foundation
Nance Petroleum Corporation
Roberta H. Napier
Charley Nell
Nelson Familys - Don Nelson
Fred & Joan Nelson
Mark & Sheila Neu
Barbara V. Newman
Jack & Mazie Nicolson
Estelle Noonan
Harold Nordahl
Mabel Nordahl
Mary Nordahl

Norwest Investment
  Management & Trust
June O'Connor
Walter Oedekoven
Mr. & Mrs. Andy O'Hair
Julia Olegar
Martin H. Oleson, Jr.
Ron & Etta Olfert
Mr. & Mrs. Lester A. Olson
A. E. & Virginia Omdahl
Steven & Linda Ough
Mr. & Mrs. Ronnie Pack
Bruce & Winnie Packer
Padlock Ranch
Paintrock Angus Ranch
Ralph Parker
Robert & Ann Pasha
Lynell & Scott Patterson
Ray Patterson
Ronald N. Paul
Dr. Gregory & Mrs. Jana Paulauskis
Geraldine E. Paulus
Wilmer & Nora Pawlowski
Helen Jacoby Payne
Helen Saunders Payne
J. Emery Payne
Clyde & Jeanine Pederson
Scott & Rebecca Pennepacker
Gregg H. Penson
Rose Perttu
Pete Petersen
Barbara Peterson
Clyde & Jeanine Peterson
Dean & Trudi Peterson
Harold & Margie Peterson
Mark & Kate Peterson
Mr. & Mrs. Richard L. Peterson
Russell & Pat Peterson
Pickrell Ranch
Jim Pile

Pioneer Federal Savings & Loan
Hubert & Anna Marie Plymale
Laird Plymale
Charles Pollard Family
In Memory of: Madalyn Jean Porro
Michael H. Power
Mr. & Mrs. David J. Price
Herbert D. & Hazel L. Price
A. L "Les" Qualey
(In Memory Of) Veva Rainey
Mr. & Mrs. Elbert Reed
George Reich & Jack Reich
Bob & Judy Rice
Paul & Dorothy Rice
Alice M. Ridenour
Mr. & Mrs. Clark Ridgeway
Mr. & Mrs. Randal Ridgeway
Wes & Judy Robbie
XZ Ranch - Dave & Diana Roen
Frances W. Rogers
Rosezella Battles Romney
Marion (Mickey) Rosa
Ross 8 Bar 7 Ranch, Inc.
Phil Rostad
Roswell Community Church
Steve Roth
Bernard Rourke
Walter Sales Ranch
Douglas & Mary Salsbury
Wilma D. Santoyo
Mrs. Edward C. Sargent
Floyd & Dagmar Sax
Saylor & Faber Ranch
Herman Scherr-Thoss
Marlea A. Schneider
Schultz Family Ranch
Mr. & Mrs. Sid Schutter
Robert & Betty Scott
Kim Sell
Mr. & Mrs. William Semlek

A Legacy of Caring

Henry Sheffels
Earl D. Shelton
W. L. & Barbara Shryock
Robert & Sandra Sills
Larry & Nancy Simonsen
James Sitz & Robert Sitz
Melva Skaar
Barbara Skelton
George Alfred Slack
John Alvin Slack
Thomas McGregor Slack
Jack Smith
Mr. & Mrs. Jay Smith
Richard & Sharongae Smith
Kenneth Smith
William & Diane Snapp
John J. Sneeringer
Mrs. Island Soape
Jim & Linda Soft
Loren & Janice Soft
Ry & Kathi Sorensen Family
Raymond & Bonnie Soulsby
Bob & Kay Spain
Phillippi & Jodi Sparks
Spring Creek Colony
Sister M. St. Pius
Del & Vera Stamy
Bud & Hennie Starr
State Bank & Trust Co.
Robert & Laura Steele
Steele-Reese Foundation
Richard Sticka
Catherine A. Still-Baxter
Stockman Bank of Montana
Ray & Mabel Stoner
Travis & Nikole Stortz
Walt Story
Maude Strand
Robin & Joyce Street
Jean & Bob Stromswold

Rodney Svenson
Anne Swain
Daryle & Pam Swanson
John & Linda Swanz Family
Edna Swieso
Mark & Sara Taliaferro
Harry Tash of Tash Livestock
Ben Tax
John L. Taylor
Shirley Taylor
Richard H. Thom, Sr.
Clay O. Thomason
Bill & Elaine Thompson
C. Donald & Irene Thompson
Larry Thompson
Virginia K. Thompson
Herman Scherr-Thoss
Tom & Carolyn Tonkinson
Larry Torske
Jerry & Joan Townsend
Bev & Tom Treanor
Jean & Dave True
Tom & Val Tuma
Ann & Tom Urist
Blanche Vavra
Steve VanDyken
Russ & Colleen Vinger
Cornelius A. Visser
Peter Vogel
David & June Voldseth
William & Beulah Voss
Mr. & Mrs. Richard Wachsmith
William Wallace Family
Mr. & Mrs. Paul Walters
Gen & Chuck Walton
Dennis R. Washington Foundation
Winston & Ruth Watt
Waukesha Tool & Stamping, Inc.
Paul Weber
The Webers

Carl & Viola Wetterstrom
Eugene & Ruby Wheatley
Vincent & Martha Wheeler
Dan & Vicki White
Howard White
Mac & Melody White
Miles & Lucille White
Evelyn Wightman
Skeg E. Wiley
Donitza & Paul Williams
Langdon & Joyce Williams
Lora C. & Haydn C. Williams
    Family Trust

Clarice Hardy Williams
Mary E. Williams
Sylvia M. Wittmer
Dr. & Mrs. Ray Woodward
Jerome & Chris Young
Bruce Wright
Walter & Regina Wunsch
Grant & Mary Zerbe
James Joseph Zettel
Ralph W. Zimmer

A BOULDER represents cash or in-kind gifts of thirty thousand dollars or more given during any ten year period

AN ACORN represents cash or in-kind gifts of fifteen thousand dollars or more given during any ten year period

A LEAF represents cash or in-kind gifts of three thousand dollars or more given during any ten year period

Index

Photographs are in italics (e.g. 82f)

A
Abby, *250f*, 250-53
Ackerman, Rubin, 80-83, *80f, 82f, 97f*
Adams, Bud, 312
Adams, Gary, 198, *199f*, 312
Adams, Ken, 112
The Advocate, 17
Alcoholics Anonymous, 82, 122, 251
Alcott, Sammy, *79f*
All-Faith Chapel, 7, 126
Allen, Rex, 145, *145f*
Alliance for Children and Families, 144
Alton, Denver, 25-28, *27f*, 308
Alvina Kramlich Lodge, 225, *225f*
Amanda P., *298f*
American Psychiatric Association, 179
Amy R., *298f*
Anderson, Anne, 232
Anderson, Jim, 44-45, *45f*
Andrea H., *235f, 306f*
Ardock (North Dakota), 16
Area Trustee Program, 222, 240, 242, 247
Aronson, Governor J. Hugo, 35, 36, 62, *63f*
Art Barn, 213
Assessment-Treatment Center, 140, 142, 148-49, 223, 224

B
Babcock, Governor Tim, 145
Baldry, Tammy, 294
Beartooth Nature Center, 285
Bergland, Don and Becky, 289
Bertels, Jenna Kirwin, 184-88, *184-86f, 188f*
Big Ditch, *73f*
Bill and Anita Jones Equestrian Center, 229-30, *229f*, 273
Billings Animal Shelter, 285
Billings Deaconess Hospital, 179
The Billings Gazette, 226-27, 231, 232, 272
Billings Junior Chamber of Commerce, 35
Billings Post Office, 285
Billings Studio Theater, 286
Billings Symphony Orchestra and Chorale, *280f*, 281
Billings Youth Guidance Council, 32
Billy Graham Evangelistic Association, 18
Black, Don, 112
Blankenship, Mrs. M. D., 247

Bliss, Roy, 37
Boehland, Mel, 99
Board of Directors, first 35-36
Boys Industrial School (Miles City, Montana), 25, 26, 46
Boys Industrial School (Worland, Wyoming), 36, 42, 44
Boys Ranch Choir, 127, *128f*
Boys Town, 33, 52
Bradford, John, 59-60
Bradford Roofing (Billings), 59
Brekkeflat, Mary and Sigurd, 224
Brekkeflat Intensive Unit, 276
Brekkeflat North, 224
Brekkeflat South, 224
Britt S., *66f*
Broken Spoke Shop, 230
Brower, Ella, 275-78, *275f, 277-78f*
Brown, Becky *193f*
Brown, George, *58f*
Bryngleson, Jim, 112
Bryson, Tedd, 24
Byrne, Shawn, 288

C
Cal Farley's Boy's Ranch, 33-34, 52
Campbell, Glen, 145
Campus Crusade for Christ's Semipro Athletes in Action, 246
cannery, 218
Carey, Chaplain Tom, 127, 282-83
Carl B. & Florence E. King Foundation, 93, 220, 223
Casper, Alvy and Kathleen, 227
Casper Education Center, 227, *228f*
cattle branding, *184f*, 199
Challenges Ropes Course, *303f*, 304
Champion, Debbie, 234-36, *234f, 235f*, 305-306, *306f*
Chaney, Matt, 115
Christmas celebration, 218-19, 282-83
Clarissa, 262-64
Clemmer, Jason, 49
Clydehurst Christian Ranch, 26
Collins, Jim, 239
Collins, Wendy, 24
Community Based Services
  Community Homes, 290-91
  The LIFE Program, 290
  School Based Mental Health Programs, 288
  Therapeutic Family Living, 288-89
  Therapeutic Foster Care, 289-90
  Youth Case Management, 288

Community Service Program, 283-86
Cooley, Dorothy, *102f*, 106, 108, 313
corporal punishment, 55, 204
Council for Psychiatric Facilities, 149
Council on Accreditation, 202
Crellin, Dr. Paul, *180f*, 181
Crum Forrest, 35, *35f*, *170f*, 172

D
Dabner, Jack, 33, 124, 125
Danny, 192-93
Day Treatment Program, 294
Deaconess Hospital (Billings) 259
Defender of the Faith Ministries, 100
DeHaan, Henry and Mae, 227
DeHaan Administration Building, 212, *212f*, 227
delinquency
    in Billings, 28-*28f*
    boys, 25, 138-39
    calling to help, personal, 25-29, 31
    Denver (Alton), 25-27, *27f*, 308
    girls, 137-42
    homes for boys, 33-34
    juvenile, 26, 27, 31, 32, 149
Demmett, Dallas, 125
Dennis Wear Group Home, 147
dining hall, *See* Donald Nutter Memorial Dining Hall
disabled children/adults, 181, 273
Domestic Violence Fatality Review Commission, 179
Don F., *58f*
Don S., *50f*, *63f*
Donald Nutter Memorial Dining Hall, 8, 125, 145, 158, 212, *213f*, 224
Dorothy's Lodge, 226, *226f*, 232

E
EAGALA (Equine Assisted Growth and Learning Association), 270
Earn While You Learn Work Program, 143-44
East Campus, 140, 221, 223
education. *See also* Yellowstone Academy
    Boys Ranch School District No. 58, 107-108, 264
    Elder Grove School, 72, 105
    Heptner Education Center, 228-29, *228f*
    local schools, 104-105
    on-campus school, 8, 72, 264
    physical education building, 93
Elder Grove School, 72, 105
Eleson, Irwin, 67, 270, *241f*, 247, 313

Emilie A., *298f*
Endowment Fund *See* Yellowstone Boys and Girls Ranch Foundation Endowment Fund
Equine Assisted Psychotherapy Program, *271f*, 272-74
escape stories, 157-63
Evergreen Nursing Home, 285
Experiential Therapy programs, 214
extracurricular activities, 25, 47, 73, 99, 148. *See also* sports

F
Family Services, Inc., 283
Father Flanagan's Boy's Town, 33, 52
Fessler, JoAnne, 185, *185f*, *265f*
"Fine Fittery" clothing room, 144
First National Bank of Whitefish, 36
Flynn, Frank, 36, *36f*
Fort Peck Indian Reservation, 83
Fortin, Phil, 216, 218-19
Fortin Foundation, 223
Fortin Lodge, 116, 205, *217f*, 219
Fortin West Lodge, 163, 165, 219
foster parent model, 32, 105, 172, 276, 278, 289-91
Foundations
    Fortin, 223
    King, Carl B. & Florence E., 93, 220, 223
    Kresge, 126, 223
    Steele-Reese, 223
    Taylor, Ruth and Vernon, 223
    Yellowstone Boys and Girls Ranch, 134, 243, 245, 248-49
Franklin and Merle Robbie Chapel, 7-8, 212
Frazier, Lisa, 151, 153, *153f*, 257, 314
Frey, John, 198
fund-raising
    challenge grant, 229
    chapel building fund, 126
    charitable annuity contracts, 248
    Christmas gifts, annual, 218-19
    by direct mail, 39-40
    donations, livestock, 222
    gift, donor, *91f*
    gifts, memorial, 34, 93-94
    giving, deferred, 246
    giving, planned, 246-48
    gratitude, expressing, 90-93
    Montana Sheriffs and Peace Officers, 106
    partnerships, public-private, 243
    Pierce, Bob, 86-88
    trusts, charitable, 248
    Warsinske, Norm, 36

Yellowstone charitable trust, 247
Yellowstone Foundation Endowment Fund *See* Yellowstone Boys and Girls Ranch Foundation
Fusco, Bob and Alice, 131, *131f*

G
Good Samaritan parable, 292
Good to Great: Why Some Companies Make the Leap...and Others Don't, 239
Gordy, Russell, 231
Grace Bible Church, 286
Grant, Charles, 225
The Great Escape (movie), 158-59
greenhouse, 44, 230-32
Groot, David, 287, 291, *291f*, 315
Groot, Jodi, 181, 200-202, *201f*, 315
group home, 116, 144, 147

H
Habitat for Humanity houses, 284
Hamblin, Stuart, 21
Hamilton, Leonard, 93
Hamilton, Margaret, 225
Hamilton House, 93
Hammer, Mike 176-78, *177f*, 315
Hansen, Dan and Sharon
 career, longtime, 315
 as chaplain, 127, 142, 161-62
 as houseparents, 67, 97-99, 100-101, 142-44
 pictures, *99f, 143f*
Harold A., *63f*
Harr, Dr. Donald, 78, *79f*
Hatcher, Ron, 112, 269, 315
Heather G., *298f*
Help for Homeless Pets, 285
Helsby, Anne, 304
Henson, Ann, 267-69, *267f*, 316
Heptner, Leona and Jeanette, 229
Heptner Education Center, 228-29, *228f*
Hirsch, Wayne, 306-307, *307f*
Hoherd, George, 127
Holiness Methodist School of Theology, 16
Hollatz, Dorothy, 226-27, 316
The Horse Whisperer, 270
Horticulture Center, 232
Horton, Jason, 48
Hospitality House, 17
House, Phil, 181, 196-98, *197f*
Huggard, Mike, 205, *205f*

I
Ideal Bakery, 58
Ismay (Montana), 222

J
J & S Pioneer Service Station, 47
Jamison, Carolyn, 153, 251, 317
Jamison, John
 career, longtime, 317
 as chaplain, 93, 127, 153
 Christmas celebrations, 282-83
 community partnerships, 293
 marriage ceremony, 188
 movie, *The Great Escape*, 158-59, 166
 pictures, *158f, 249f, 250f, 293f, 295f*
 spiritual leadership, 249-52
 Wittman, Fred *131f*, 293-96
Janaya T., *298f*
Jaskot, Mark, 256, 317
Jenkins, Nicki, 150-54, *150-54f*
Jeremiah (prophet), 258, 308
Jessica, 261, *265f*
Jessie Grant Lodge, 224, *224f*, 286
Jim N., *58f*
John H. Uihlein Recreation Center, 151, 214, *215f*
Johnson, Torrey, 18
Johnson, Willard, 126
Johnson boys, *50f*, 51, *63f*
Joint Commission on Accreditation of Healthcare Organizations (JCAHO), 149
Jones, Bill and Anita (Equestrian Center), 229-30, *229f*, 273
Joseph Schlitz Brewing Company, 215
juvenile delinquency. *See* delinquency

K
Keating, Ted, 3, 34, 35, *35f*, 36, 39, *170f*, 172
Keith Chevrolet, 240
Kelly, Sheldon, *3f, 4f, 63f*, 64-65
Ketterling, Jean, 108
Killion, Guy, 19
King Foundation, Carl B. & Florence E., 93, 220, 223
King Group Home, 116
King Lodge, 200, *221f*, 294
Kip, 78-79, 223
Knees Community, 19-20
Knees Community church, *14f*, 19
Koerner, Bob, 125, *125f*
Kootenai Lodge, 224
Kramlich, Alvina, 225
Kramlich Lodge, Alvina, 225, *225f*

Kramlich Vo-Tech Building, 230-32, *230f*
Kramp, Louie, 24, 27, 32
Kresge Foundation, 126, 223

L

Ladies Aid societies, 40
Laundry, Rex, 58
Laura D., *298f*
Lenz, Paul, *197f*
Leuthold, Grace, 36, *36f*, 221-22
Leuthold, John, *170f*, 221-22
Leuthold Lodge, 164, 221-22, *221f*
Lew Chevrolet, 60
Lewis, Dorothy Marie, 227
Lewistown group home, 147
library, 109
"Life's Little Obstacles" exercise, 272
Lipp, Carroll V., 198, 318
Lisa, 140-42, *140f*
Little Boy Lodge, 221
Living Independently Fostering Employment program, 231
Lodge
    Alvina Kramlich, *225, 225f*
    Dorothy's, 226, *226f*, 232
    Fortin, 116, 205, *217f*, 219
    Fortin West, 163, 165, 219
    Jessie Grant, 224-25, *224f*, 286
    King, 220, *221f*, 294
    Kootenai, 224
    Leuthold, 164, 221-22, *221f*
    Little Boy, 221
    Mary Brekkeflat, 223, *223f*, 224, 286
    McVay, *219f*, 220
    Orth memorial, 56, 192
    Paul Stock, 67, 97, 142, 217, *217f*
    Shumaker, 222, *222f*, 235
Logan, Dick, 75
Love, Joe, 81-83
Luckett, Linda, 259
Lundin, Isabel, 206, *208f, 265f*, 318

M

MacKay, Bill, 3, 35, *35f*, 39, *170f*, 172
Marchela F., *298f*
Maring, Maude, 60-61
Martz, Governor Judy, 63
Mary Brekkeflat Lodge, 223, *223f*, 224, 286
Mathews, Leslie, 270-73, *271f*, 273, 277
McCombs, Jim, 46-49, *46f, 48f, 49f*
McFarlane, Bob
    career, longtime, 42-44, 181-82, 231, 240-43, 247
    church, "in and out" approach to, 123
    as houseparent, 55-56
    as Mr. Mac, 49
    pictures, *42f, 49f, 79f, 104f, 241f*
    ranch, planning for, 33-34
    staff recruiting, 52-53, 67
    as superintendent, 3, 41
McFarlane, Doris
    as cook and hostess, 43, 47
    as houseparent, 64, 72, 75
    picture *42f*
McFarlane, Glenn, *42f*, 43, 254-55, *255f*, 318
McFarlane, Gloria, *42f*, 43
McIntyre Motors, 60
McNeal, David 61-62
McNeal, Roy, 61-62
McVay, John, 220
McVay Lodge, *219f*, 220
medical and psychiatric services, 8, 179, 181, 223-24, *223f*
Meghan, 271, *271f, 298f*
mental illness treatment, 191-202
Metzger, Sheryl, 116
Middleton, Merle, 16, *17f*, 19-20. *See also* Robbie, Merle
Montana and Wyoming Youth for Christ, 31
Montana Child Welfare Advisory Committee, 36, 223
Montana lumber mills, 58, 92
Montana Psychiatric Association, 179
Montana Rescue Mission, 284
Montana School District No. 58, 108, 264
Montana Sexual Offender Treatment Association, 196
Montana Sheriffs and Peace Officers, 106
Montana's Foster Parents, 289
Moody Bible Institute, 24
Mountain States Telephone, 39

N

National Association of Homes for Boys, 34, 144
National Association of Homes for Children, 144
Neihart, Doug, 112
Nunberg, Nate, 276-77
Nunberg, Toni, *197f*
Nutter Dining Hall, 145, 212, *213f*

O

off-campus
    group home, for older boys, 147
    group home, for older girls, 147

medical and clinical programs, 181
offices, 147, 287, 291
on-campus school, 8, 72. *See also* Yellowstone Academy
O'Rourke ranch, 38-39
Orth, Carl
    Cal Farley's Boy's Ranch, 34
    career, longtime, 53-57, 66, 85
    as houseparent, 47, 52-53, *54f*, 72
    family picture, *53f*
    Ricky, run-away, 160-61
    vision of, 67
Orth, Dale, *53f*, *182f*, 181-83, 254, 319
Orth Honaker, Betty
    commitment, Christian, 54
    family of, 53, *53f*, 317
    as houseparent, 47, 317
    picture *53f*
Orth Memorial Lodge, 56, 192

P
Pastoral Care Program, 198, 258
Paul Stock Lodge, 67, 97, 142, 217, *217f*
Peale, Norman Vincent, 145
Perrigo, Deb, 115, *131f* 132-33, 319
Pierce, Bob, 86 *86f*, 88
Pioneer Park (Billings), 281
Poetzl Horticultural Center, 230-31, *231f*
Preston, Tracy, 294
Pride, Charley, 145
Pullen, Rick, *197f*

Q
Quillen, Brenda, 289

R
recreation facility, 8, 73, 273, 276, 303
Reed, Jim, *203-205f*, 203-208, *207-208f*
Reilly, Dr. J. Wesley, 180
Residential Assessment-Treatment Center, 140, 142, 148-49, 223
Rich, Joe, *102f*, *179f*, 178-81, *190f*, 254
Riverside Press-Enterprise, 131
Robbie, Franklin
    calling to help delinquent boys, 25-29, 31
    Chapel, 7-8, 212
    as editor and publisher, 17
    fund, parsonage, 19-20
    fund raising, 94-96
    Hospitality House, 17
    as pastor, 1, 19
    pictures, *4f*, *5f*, *17f*, *27f*, *45f*, *95f*, *170f*, *244f*
    World Congress on Evangelism, 22

Youth for Christ movement, 2, 18-22, 24, 27, 31-32
Robbie, Merle (nee Middleton), 16, *17f*, 19-20, *170f*, 245
Robbie, Rudolph, 16
Robbie, Wesley
    career, longtime, 319
    fund raising role, 95, 245
    pictures, *95f*, *244f*
    Yellowstone Foundation, 245
Robert, first graduate, 105, 113, *113f*
Rohrs, Wayne, 125
Ruth and Vernon Taylor Foundation, 223

S
Sawatzky, Harry, 110
Scheetz, Jim, 320
Schwartz, Dr. Harold, 126
Schwartz, Tom, 320
Scott, Tom and Joan, 224
Scott Medical Clinic, 223-24, *223f*
Seabiscuit, 274
Seavy, Lyle, 164-65, *165f*, 305, 320
SED (seriously emotionally disturbed youth), 266, 288
Serrette, William, 110
Shannon, Jeanette, *130-31f*, 130-34, *133f*
Shay, Don, 198, 320
"Shop With A Cop", 66
Shorten, Lois, *260f*
Shryock, Les, 3, 35-36, *36f*, 39, *170f*, 172
Shumaker, Mr. and Mrs. Jake, 222
Shumaker, Joey, *89f*
Shumaker Lodge, 222, *222f*, 235
Simpson, Governor Milward, 36
Slaughter, Larry, 125 *125f*
Slotkowski, Leonard, 206
Smith, Cameron, 115
Soft, Jim, 67, 163, 232, 244-48, *246f*, 252, 270, 287, 321
Soft, Loren, *79f*, *173f-74f*, 208, 240-43, *242f*, 321
Soft, Max, 305
Sorensen, Ry, 252-54, *253f*, 287, 321
Special Education students, 266, 288
Special K Ranch, 231-32
sports
    baseball, 93, 148, 250
    basketball, *167f*
    bicycling, 161
    bowling, 93
    football, 43, 67, *97f*, 99, 148, 276
    hockey, 150f, 152, 153, *162f*
    horseback riding, 131, 271, 273

soccer, 148, 152, 153, 153f, *162f*
softball, 74, *161f*
swimming, 74, 93, 151
team, 73, 98, 148, 211
volleyball, 152
Spotted Bull Treatment Center for Youth, 83
St. John's Lutheran Home, 286
St. Joseph's Catholic Church, 232
Steele-Reese Foundation, 223
Stepanik, Jim, *58f*
Stephens, Tyler, 114-17, *114f, 116f*
Steve, *50f, 63f,* 74-77, *76f*
Stock, Paul, 216-18
"Super Stars" blue ribbons, 151
Svarre, Ingvaard, 147
Svarre Group Home, 144, 147
Swalley, Kevin, 115
Swalley, Peggy, 116, 322
Swenson, Joanna, *190f, 197f*
Symphony in the Park, 281-82

T
Taylor, James, 225
Terry 163
Tetrault, Karen, 277, 322
therapy
chemical dependency treatment, 303
experiential, 214
family, 303-304
horse, *271f,* 272-74
musical, 303
pet, 303
recreational, 151, 303
Todd, Ken, 35, 39, 40
Torres, Tony, *256-57f,* 256-59, *258f*
twenty-fifth anniversary, 142, 148, 171-73, 176, 178

U
Uihlein, John H., 215-16
Uihlein Recreation Center (UC), 151, 214, *215f*
University of Montana-Western, 286

V
Vietnam, 77, 95, 147, 254
vo-ag programs, 111, *111f, 199f,* 200, 202, *257f*
Vo-Tech Building, 230-32, *230f*
Vocational School for Girls, 138

W
Wade, Cactus, 40
Wagner, Vince, 97-101, *97-101f*
Walhowe, Casper, 25-26

Ward, Doris, *110f*
Warsinske, Norm, 36, *36f*
Watson, Rishay, 301-302, *301f,* 323
welding shop, 187, 199, 213, 230
Western, Bob, 112
Western Livestock Reporter, 36
Wheeler, Mona, *260f*
White, Russ, 66-69, *66f, 68f*
Wilson, Ann, *124f,* 127
Wilson, Chaplain Wendell, *125f,* 126-27, 324
Wilson, George, 18, 21
Wilson, Tom, 127
Wittman, Fred, 293-96, *293f, 295f, 296f*
World Congress on Evangelism, 22
The Wrangler
on annual report, 71-72
articles in, 57-58
on Bob McFarlane, 43
on school report, 109
as fund-raising vehicle, 88-90, *89f,* 94
on Lew Chevrolet, 60
on Loren Soft, 243
on over-crowding, 219
on religious training, 119-120
on Sheldon Kelly, 64-65
Wright, Harold, 106

Y
Yellowstone Academy
Casper Education Center, 227, *228f*
doctors, in-house psychiatric, 268
graduates, *114f,* 117, 265, 293-94, *296f*
learning-disabled children, 181
philosophy educational, 108-109
physical education building, 93
pictures, *174f, 212f, 265f, 267f, 269f*
principal, Loren Soft, 173-76
school, on-campus, 8, 72, 264
School Based Mental Health Programs, 288
School District No. 58, 108, 264
Special Education program, 98, 231, 264-69
Special Education students, 266, 288
standards, 111-13
Superintendent, Ed Zabrocki, 269
teaching, Judeo-Christian, 128, 251-52
Yellowstone Boys and Girls Ranch
Articles of Incorporation, 51
board members, first, 35-36
boy, first, 44-45
building and expansion of, 57-62
cannery, 218
cattle branding, *184f,* 199
Challenges Ropes Course, *303f,* 304

chapel programs, *124f*
child care license, 105
child treatment center, 202
Christmas celebration, 218-19, 282-83
church attendance, 122-23
Community Based Services, 288-91
Community Service Award, 286
Community Service Program, 283-86
Day Treatment Program, 294
Earn While You Learn Work Program, 143-44
employees, long-term, 252-53, 312-24
"Fine Fittery" clothing room, 144
fire department, 163-64, *163f*, 250
foster home license, 105
foster-parent model, 32, 105, 172, 276, 278, 289-91
group homes, 147
Individual Treatment Plan, 264
intake workers, 301-302
library, 109
medical assessments, 179, 223-24
motto, 9, 171
naming of, 37
offices, off-campus, 147, 287, 291
open house, annual, 145-46, *146f*
parents, short-term housing for, 214
pastoral counseling, 198, 258
philosophy, educational, 108-109
pictures, *9f, 30f, 50f, 58f, 70f, 73f, 84f, 102f, 104f, 110-11f, 118f, 143f, 146f, 167f, 174f*
ranching and farming, 199-200
renaming of, 137
Residential Assessment-Treatment Center, 140, 142, 148-49, 223
schools, using local, 104-105
security requirements, 195
slogan, 9, 171
Special Education students 266, 288
standards, educational, 111-13
stories, escape, 157-63
therapy, chemical dependency treatment, 303
therapy, experiential, 214
therapy, family, 303-304
therapy horse, *271f*, 272-74
therapy, musical, 303
therapy, pet, 303
therapy, recreational, 151, 303
treatment, emotionally troubled youth, 149
treatment program, individualized, 303
treatment program, mental illness, 191-202
unconditional love, 57, 74, 82, 134, 150, 186

values, Judeo-Christian, 128
vo-ag programs, 111, *111f*, *199f*, 200, 202, *257f*
vocational classes, 111
youth group program, voluntary, 126-27
Yellowstone Boys and Girls Ranch Foundation
    independent non-profit organization, 248
    president, Franklin Robbie, 243
    president, Wes Robbie, 245
    president, Jim Soft, 245-48, *246f*
    sponsor, Symphony in the Park, 281
    Yellowstone charitable trust, 247
Yellowstone Boys and Girls Ranch Foundation Endowment Fund
    Blankenship Trust, 247
    Brekkeflat, Sigurd, 224
    building of, 96, 248-49
    Casper, Alvy, 227
    children of families with financial need, 134
    DeHaan, Henry and Mae, 227
    Grant, Charles, 225
    Heptner, Leona and Jeanette, 229
    Hollatz Dorothy, 227
    King, Carl B. & Florence E., 220
    Leuthold, John and Grace, 221
    Lewis, Dorothy Marie, 227
    McVay, 220
    Stock, Paul, 218
    Svarre, Ingvaard, 147
York, Stacy, 288
Youth for Christ movement, 18-22, *23f*, 24, 27, 31-32, 86, *86f*
Youth Guidance Council, 33

Z
Zabrocki, Ed, 112, 269, *269f*
ZooMontana, 284

For More Information

For information about Yellowstone Boys and Girls Ranch and its admission policies:

Write

Yellowstone Boys and Girls Ranch
1732 S 72nd Street West
Billings, MT 59106

Call

1-800-726-6755

Or visit our website

www.ybgr.org

For information about Yellowstone Boys and Girls Ranch Foundation and its current funding priorities and services:

Write

Yellowstone Boys and Girls Ranch Foundation
PO Box 80807
Billings, MT 59108

Call

1-800-879-0850

Or visit our website

www.yellowstonefoundation.org